St John's School, Leatherhead and the Great War 1914-1919

St John's School, Leatherhead and the Great War 1914-1919

QUAE SURSUM SUNT QUAERITE

Sally Todd and Neil Pudney

St John's School, Leatherhead

Copyright © 2019 Sally Todd and Neil Pudney

The moral rights of the authors have been asserted.

All rights reserved. No part of this book may be reproduced or transmitted in any form or by any means, without prior permission in writing from the publisher.

St John's School
Epsom Road
Leatherhead, Surrey
KT22 8SP

Tel: +44 (0)1372 373 000

Email: school@stjohns.surrey.sch.uk
Web: www.stjohnsleatherhead.co.uk

ISBN 978-1-5272-4228-9

Book design by Alison Wren
Alisongraphics, Sandhurst, Berkshire

Printed and bound by
Short Run Press Ltd, Exeter, Devon

SUBSCRIBERS

With thanks to the following for their donations to support the publication of this book:

Pat Bird, Karen Bloomfield, David Bradney, Paul Casson, The Cluff Family, Paul Deeprose, Richard Devonshire, Thomas Drury, Alexander Duma, Anthony Evans, Martin Fausset, William Foot, Martin Francis, Richard Francis, Richard Freeman, Patrick Gardner, Michael Godwin, The Harris Family, Richard Hartnell, Benedict Hoskyns-Abrahall, Tim Howlett, Cameron Hughes and Cassie Hughes, John Jackman, Richard Jukes, Roger and Gail Partridge, Andrew Peake, The Potter Family, Charlotte Pullen, Julian Spurrell, The Stefanik Family, David Sutch, The Tweddle Family, C J Urwin, Michael Walsh, Jim Warren, Richard Woodman-Bailey, Robert Worthington

St John's School OTC on parade c.1917

Important facts regarding
THE DISTRESS OF THE CLERGY.

ST. JOHN'S FOUNDATION SCHOOL,

FOR THE FREE EDUCATION AND MAINTENANCE OF THE SONS OF THE POORER CLERGY OF THE CHURCH OF ENGLAND.

A very pressing appeal is made to you for a donation of 10s. 6d. towards helping the Distressed Clergy, who are suffering pinching penury, caused by their inability to get in their Tithe or through unlet Glebe Land.

IT IS DEPLORABLE that St. John's Foundation School **SHOULD HAVE MANY VACANT PLACES** at the present time, when numbers of the Distressed Clergy are appealing to have their Sons admitted. **THE REASON IS** that an addition to the funds is required to enable the Committee of Governors to carry out so desirable an object. They have increased the number of boys as far as the present income will permit.

SOCIETY HAS NO CONCEPTION OF THE AMOUNT OF PRIVATION THAT EXISTS IN MANY A CLERGYMAN'S FAMILY, FOR THE REASON ALREADY GIVEN—THEIR SAD CARES NEVER COME TO LIGHT; the self respect of high minded men prevents their making any public exhibition of their need, but it exists, nevertheless, to a frightful extent, chiefly owing to the great agricultural depression.

Under such circumstances **HOW CAN A CLERGYMAN EDUCATE HIS FAMILY?** It is impossible, since in many cases the plainest food and meanest clothing are, with very great difficulty procured.

ST. JOHN'S FOUNDATION SCHOOL MEETS SUCH CASES. Will you enable it to increase its good work, and so relieve the mind of many a hard pressed Clergyman? Your early reply is respectfully asked, to

(REV.) SUTTON PATTERSON, M.A.,
Secretary of St. John's Foundation School,
1, THE SANCTUARY, WESTMINSTER ABBEY, S.W.

[PLEASE TURN OVER.

Appeal for donations, 1887

CONTENTS

Introduction		vii
Chapter 1	The Early Years	1
Chapter 2	Prelude to War	18
Chapter 3	School Life in Wartime	21
Chapter 4	Old Johnians at War	42
Chapter 5	War at Sea	76
Chapter 6	The Missing	79
Chapter 7	War in the Air	86
Chapter 8	Conscription and Conscientious Objectors	92
Chapter 9	Masters serving in the Great War	93
Chapter 10	Brothers in War	96
Chapter 11	Old Johnians in the RAMC	98
Chapter 12	Chaplains to the Forces	101
Chapter 13	Prisoners of War	105
Chapter 14	Armistice 1918	110
Chapter 15	Peace Celebrations 1919	113
Chapter 16	The School after the War	116
Chapter 17	War Memorials and Remembrance	118
Abbreviations		126
Roll of Honour		127
Distinctions awarded		134
Picture credits		138
Bibliography		140
Acknowledgements		143
Index		144

War Memorial, 2017

INTRODUCTION

When war broke out in August 1914, St John's Foundation School had been in existence for just 63 years. The School had grown and changed significantly since its early beginnings in 1851 as a small choir school with just eight pupils at St Mark's, Hamilton Terrace, in the St John's Wood district of north London.

The story told in this book starts with a short history of the School, outlining its development and various locations in London before it settled in Leatherhead in 1872. The rapid expansion of the School and development of buildings on the Leatherhead site in the 1880s and 1890s shaped the environment in which those OJs who served in the Great War spent their formative years. The creation of the School's Officer Training Corps (OTC) in 1912 and the devastating fire which destroyed the main School building in 1913, were key events in the years preceding the outbreak of war.

Our focus then falls on the renewed optimism felt in the early summer of 1914, the reorganisation of the School and the introduction of the House system, followed by the visit of the HRH Duchess of Albany, widow of HRH Prince Leopold, Duke of Albany an early patron of St John's. On Speech Day, Wednesday 1 July 1914, just weeks before war was declared, the Duchess of Albany formally opened the rebuilt school and presented the prizes.

First-hand accounts from OJs who were at school during the war provide a vivid insight into the challenges of daily life of a school in wartime. Food and the lack of it was uppermost in their minds (the boys were perpetually hungry). They describe lessons and punishments, but also recount the excitement of taking part in or watching the various sports and team games. In addition to their accounts, we relate tales of wartime heroes, including the two OJs who won the Victoria Cross, families who lost loved ones, and the young men who gave up the prospect of a university education to serve their country, only to be killed in action just a few months or years later. Edward Kelly was just 17 when he was killed at Ypres on 7 July 1915; more than half the OJs who died in the Great War never reached their 25th birthday.

Nearly 800 members of the St John's community served in the First World War; 769 former pupils along with assistant masters, governors and support staff. Of these, 162 are known to have died. Many of those who served were granted a commission in the British Army with the rank of lieutenant or second lieutenant, often responsible for a platoon of up to fifty men and leading them into action. Some took on non-combatant roles in the Royal Army Medical Corps or as Chaplains to the Forces. Others served with the Royal Navy, the Royal Flying Corps or, from 1 April 1918, the Royal Air Force.

While around 12 per cent of all those who served in the British armed forces between 1914 and 1918 died as a result of the war, 21 per cent of Old Johnians who served died – a figure mirrored by many other public schools. Reflecting on this tragic loss of young life, E M P Williams, a pupil at St John's during the war, wrote in his centenary history of the School, *The Quest Goes On* (Williams 1951, p.20):

> As the years wore slowly on to 1918, the increasing efficiency of the Corps only seemed to accelerate the pace for providing first-class material for the War Office sausage-machine, which in its turn produced Schoolboy Subalterns for the Slaughterhouse of the Western Front and an average expectation of life of some six weeks. If there was this feeling amongst the boys, resilient animals as they are, how much worse was it for the Head and his staff, who saw so much promise come to nought.

Many of the stories told here are enhanced by brief biographies giving further background information and celebrating the wide range of accomplishments and achievements of these Old Johnians.

Finally, as the war draws to its close the emphasis turns to the War Memorial fund and the memorials chosen by the School as a way of honouring and remembering those who died. The story told in this book is one of bravery and service, of tragedy and loss.

The Reverend Anthony Francis Thomson, headmaster 1851-1857

For the Sons of Poor Clergy.

St. John's Foundation School,

IN CONNECTION WITH ST. MARK'S CHURCH,

ST. JOHN'S WOOD, LONDON.

SUPPORTED ENTIRELY BY VOLUNTARY CONTRIBUTIONS.

The object of this School is to afford a first-rate Education with Board and Lodging, free of all charge, to the Sons of Clergymen with small incomes.

The Boys are brought up under the immediate care and direction of the Clergy of St. Mark's, and are associated with them in the celebration of Public Worship.

Boys are eligible on the Foundation between 8 and 10 years of age, and, when on it, are kept till 15 or 16. They are elected by the Subscribers to the School, who have Votes in the proportion of Two Votes for One Guinea.

Communications may be addressed to the Rev. A. B. Haslewood, Incumbent of St. Mark's; Rev. A. F. Thomson, Curate of St. Mark's, and Head Master of the School; or the Churchwardens of St. Mark's, St. John's Wood,—by whom also Annual Subscriptions and Donations will be thankfully received.

Objects of St John's Foundation School card, 1851

CHAPTER 1 THE EARLY YEARS

The School was founded in 1851 by the Reverend Ashby Blair Haslewood, vicar of St Mark's, Hamilton Terrace, in the St John's Wood district of London. Haslewood's purpose in founding the School was to offer free education for the sons of poor clergymen, and to provide a choir for his large church.

Haslewood invited members of his congregation to a meeting to consider this proposal and in November 1851 a committee was formed to establish the rules and raise and administer funds. The Committee drew up a list of suitable candidates for election to the School and those who contributed to the charity were entitled to a number of votes in proportion to the amount of their annual subscription: two votes for each guinea (21 shillings). The rules of the Foundation stated that boys must be between eight and ten on entry to the School and had to leave by their sixteenth birthday.

The first headmaster was the Reverend Anthony Francis Thomson, curate of St Mark's and the first eight boys, known as 'Foundationers', were elected to 'St John's Foundation School, in connection with St Mark's Church', St John's Wood, London in January 1852.

Ashby Haslewood paid Thomson £50 a year per boy for their board and tuition and they were educated alongside his private pupils and day scholars at his house in Upper Hamilton Terrace.

The School was a success, but Thomson's position proved difficult as he was responsible to both the Committee and the vicar of St Mark's. Between 1852 and 1853 there was much discussion about how to end this anomaly and when Haslewood dispensed with Thomson's services as curate, the Committee decided to retain him as headmaster and to separate the School from St Mark's Church. So, in 1854 the School moved outside the parish boundaries of St Mark's to Greville Mount House in Kilburn, just a few minutes' walk away. At the same time, the shortened name 'St John's Foundation School' was adopted, omitting the reference to St Mark's Church. This was the first of three moves before the School moved to Leatherhead in 1872.

St John's Foundation School, Kilburn

St John's School, Leatherhead and the Great War, 1914-1919

A further move to Walthamstow took place in 1857 when the School severed its connection with the Reverend Anthony Thomson and the boys were temporarily transferred to a small private school run by the Reverend Lewis Page Mercier. No images or details of the Walthamstow premises have survived, but in 1859 the School moved to Clapton House. This was a large mansion on a nine-acre site in east London, leased by the Committee from a member of the Baden Powell family. Mercier was appointed headmaster and moved to Clapton House together with his own private pupils. At this time, there were around 43 boys in the School.

By 1861 the number of Foundationers had increased and the School was beginning to prosper, so the Committee agreed to end its connection with Mercier and open the School on an independent footing. They decided to take over the entire management of the School, including the appointment of masters and control of all expenses. The Reverend Mercier retired from his position as headmaster and was appointed Chaplain of the Foundling Hospital.

The Committee advertised for a new headmaster and the Reverend Edwards Comerford Hawkins, Head of Classics at Brighton College, who had been educated at Marlborough and Exeter College, Oxford, was appointed in August 1861 to establish the change of policy. Finally, the School had its own separate identity.

The Reverend Edwards Comerford Hawkins, headmaster 1861-1883

THE MOVE TO LEATHERHEAD

Within a few years there were 65 boys at the School and there was no room to accommodate additional pupils. The Committee wished to expand the School, but Clapton House was only leased. They pleaded with Thomas Baden Powell to sell them the property so that they could develop the site and embark on a building programme, to provide more accommodation for the School, but he refused. Finally accepting that he was unwilling to sell, in 1866 the Committee realised that the School might have to move again and reluctantly started to look for land of about ten acres suitable for building a new school. After much searching, and consideration of sites in Weybridge

Clapton House – watercolour sketch by William Grundy

Construction workers at St John's School, Leatherhead, 1871

and Reigate, a plot of 12 acres of land in Leatherhead came to their attention at a cost of £2,500. This was deemed suitable as the rail links to Leatherhead, which then had two railway stations, would be reasonably convenient for the boys, who in those days travelled considerable distances from home. A ten per cent deposit (£250) for the purchase of the land was paid in August 1867 and a contract signed.

However, there remained the small matter of finding the balance of the purchase price and further funds to design and build the new school. Fortunately, in September 1867, one of the trustees announced that a friend of the School, who wished to remain anonymous, had offered to make a gift of the land to the School and handed over a cheque for the full £2,250 to complete the purchase. Many years later the anonymous donor was revealed to be Henry Dawes of 6 Hyde Park Gardens, London. After his death his family were offered a place on the governing body but they declined. In 2010 the new teaching block was named the 'Henry Dawes Centre' in recognition of his generous donation which enabled the School to move to Leatherhead.

Having purchased the land, the Committee then turned their attention to building a new School House. A building fund was set up and architects Benjamin Ferry and Joseph Henry Good were appointed to draw up plans for the new building. This comprised the H-shaped main building which fronts on to Epsom Road and was designed to provide all necessary accommodation for 100 boys, a headmaster's house, rooms for three further assistant masters, offices and other facilities. Provision was also made for additions to the buildings should future extension become necessary.

In April 1870, Goddard and Son of Farnham quoted £12,490 for the whole of the building works. Work commenced shortly after and the School finally opened in August 1872 with 68 pupils.

Everything took place in the main building – teaching, dining, and sleeping accommodation for both staff and pupils. The west wing of the building was the headmaster's house.

FIRST PUPILS AT LEATHERHEAD

While the School was ready for occupation, the rest of the estate remained open meadow and served as a general playground until all the expenses of the new building had been paid. The ground between the two wings at the back of the School was laid with gravel and here the first pupils played football and cricket and painted their wickets on the wall below the Big School windows. Plans were soon made for landscaping the grounds around the main building and creating a cricket field. By 1875 this work was nearing completion, but there was still no chapel, infirmary, fives courts or dining hall.

The photograph on this page dated 1874 shows some of the first pupils at Leatherhead wearing mortar boards and smartly dressed in the fashionable jackets and waistcoats of the day. The wide collar and lapels are typical of the 1870s.

James Henry Browne spent four years at Clapton House before coming to Leatherhead in 1872. He was Captain of the School, Captain of cricket and football and in 1874, when he was 16 (the age at which he was due to leave under the rules of the Foundation), he became a member of staff and taught the Second Form for one year, finally leaving St John's in December 1875. He was a master at Chigwell Grammar School for a short while, and went on to Emmanuel College, Cambridge, gaining a BA in 1880 and being ordained in the same year. He was appointed Vicar of St Andrew's, Stockwell, in 1892, of Roehampton in 1906, and of St Luke's, Richmond, from 1924 until his retirement in 1931. He was Honorary Canon of Southwark from 1905. Canon Browne was twice elected President of the OJ club and, in 1916, was the first OJ to be elected a member of the School Council. He died on 26 February 1946, aged 88.

St John's School, Leatherhead, 1874

THE EARLY YEARS

Arthur Ernest Buckler left St John's in 1879, trained to be a civil engineer and emigrated to the United States in March 1888. He settled in Utah where he worked for the Utah Power and Light Company. Arthur Buckler died in Salt Lake City, Utah on 24 September 1941, aged 78.

John Timothy Davies left St John's in 1878 for Christ College, Brecon. He was awarded a Scholarship to Wadham College, Oxford where he gained a 1st class honours degree in 1886. Davies was ordained and taught at King William's College, Isle of Man until his appointment as headmaster of The King's School, Chester in 1892. He retired in 1922 and died in 1926, aged 63.

Edward Charles Blackmore, son of the Reverend M Blackmore of Finchley died in 1875, the same year that this photograph was taken. He was just twelve years old.

James Henry Browne, September 1875

Canon Browne's son was also a pupil at St John's from 1903-1908. Richard Maddison Browne played for the 2nd XI football and cricket teams and on leaving School found employment with the Bank of England. He served as 2nd Lieutenant with the Liverpool Regiment in the Great War and was wounded at Ypres in 1915.

Charles Haslewood Shannon, Arthur Ernest Buckler, John Timothy Davies and Edward Charles Blackmore were all Foundationers who joined St John's in 1873, aged 10. They were photographed together in 1875 by Richard Huck, a Leatherhead photographer.

Charles Shannon played cricket and rugby for the School and left in 1881 for Lambeth School of Art. He was renowned for his portraits, lithographs and engravings which were exhibited world-wide in galleries and public collections of art. Shannon became a member of the Royal Academy in 1911 and was elected Royal Academician in 1920. While at art school he met his lifelong friend and partner, Charles Ricketts. Shannon died in 1937 after a long illness.

C H Shannon; A E Buckler; J T Davies; E C Blackmore, 1875

St John's School, Leatherhead and the Great War, 1914-1919

St John's Foundation School, 1880

CHAPEL AND INFIRMARY

The foundations of the Chapel were laid in 1876 and the completed building was dedicated on 7 July 1877 by the Right Reverend Harold Browne, Bishop of Winchester. This freed up a large dormitory previously used for daily worship and allowed the Committee to increase the number of Foundationers to over 100. The newly built Chapel was designed to hold 200 but within twenty years the School was nearly 300 strong and chapel services had to be duplicated.

By 1881 a separate infirmary was needed to care for boys suffering from infections and epidemics of measles, mumps, scarlet fever and tonsillitis, which were a regular occurrence. A two-storey building, (now Haslewood House) was constructed and the infirmary remained there until the 1970s when it was renamed the 'Sanatorium' and moved to the west wing of the main building.

CURRICULUM AND EXAMINATIONS

The curriculum in the 1860s and 1870s was chiefly classical, comprising English, mathematics, divinity, Greek, Latin and history. Music and drawing classes were optional extras and had to be paid for by parents. Annual internal examinations were held, but boys could only move up to a higher class if they reached the required standard. As pupils had to leave before they reached the age of 16 there was no Sixth Form provision, so the brightest pupils competed for scholarships at established public schools.

ST JOHN'S BECOMES A PUBLIC SCHOOL

Edwards Hawkins resigned as headmaster in 1883 on his appointment as vicar of St Bride's, Fleet Street.

The Infirmary, 1881

THE EARLY YEARS

The Rev. ARTHUR FOSTER RUTTY, M.A.,
Headmaster of St. John's School, Leatherhead,
1883 - 1909.

Ever yours A. F. Rutty

He was succeeded by the Reverend Arthur Rutty, who set out to widen the intake of the School. Rutty introduced the 'Supplementary Foundation' whereby parents paid partial fees of 30 guineas per year for their sons' board and tuition. 'Non-Foundationers', whose parents paid full fees were also admitted to the School. The introduction of the Supplementary Foundationer enabled Arthur Rutty to establish a Sixth Form so that boys could be prepared for university entrance. Parents of the more able Foundationers and Supplementary Foundationers could apply for bursaries to provide a further two years of education at St John's. Prior to 1883, bright pupils such as William Grundy who became headmaster of Malvern, Thomas Layng, headmaster of Abingdon School and later chaplain of Clifton College and Anthony Hope Hawkins (son of headmaster E C Hawkins) who found fame as the novelist Sir Anthony Hope, all left St John's before they were 16 to continue their education at other schools and gain a place at university. In 1899 a commercial class was introduced at St John's; boys in that class were expected to go into business, while the classical Sixth Form prepared boys for university entrance examinations.

ALBANY SCHOLARSHIPS

HRH Prince Leopold, Duke of Albany, youngest son of Queen Victoria and Prince Albert became a patron of St John's School in 1883 and took a great interest in the School. He chaired the annual anniversary dinner that year but died just one year later, following an accident in France in July 1884 when he slipped on a staircase. Prince Leopold had haemophilia and suffered from epilepsy from an early age. The accident brought on an epileptic fit and a brain haemorrhage, from which he died. The Committee recorded its sorrow on hearing of his death, saying that they:

Could not refrain from expressing their grief at the early and lamented death of HRH the Duke of Albany, the Chairman at the Dinner in 1883, whose genial presence and kind words so materially aided the School.

In his memory, the first two Albany Scholarships were established in 1885. A further six Albany Scholarships were funded over the following years and these were awarded annually to the boy who obtained the highest place in a competitive examination. The aim was to attract bright boys to the School as well as deserving candidates who were sons of the poorest clergy and was designed to help raise the reputation and profile of the School.

Rutty's wish to see the School take its place alongside other leading schools in the country was realised when he became a member of the Headmasters' Conference (HMC) in 1890 and from 1892 St John's was listed in the Public Schools Yearbook.

The expansion of the School continued and in 1889 the main School Room and Dining Hall in the original

Duke and Duchess of Albany with their daughter Princess Alice, Countess of Athlone, 1883

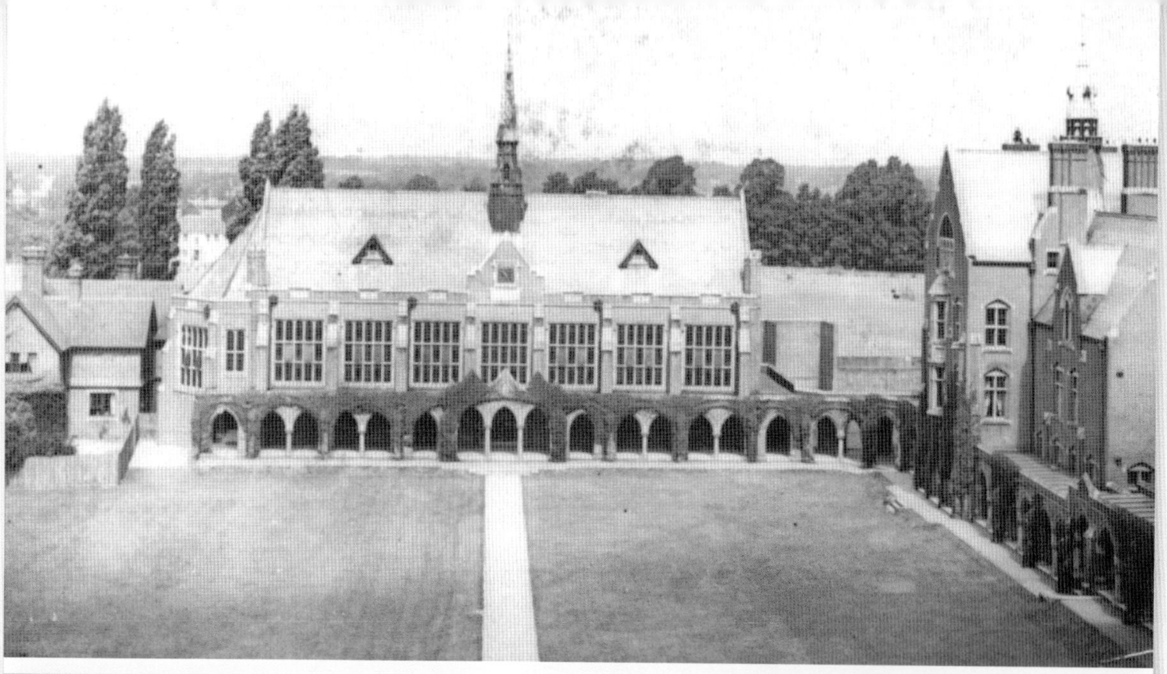

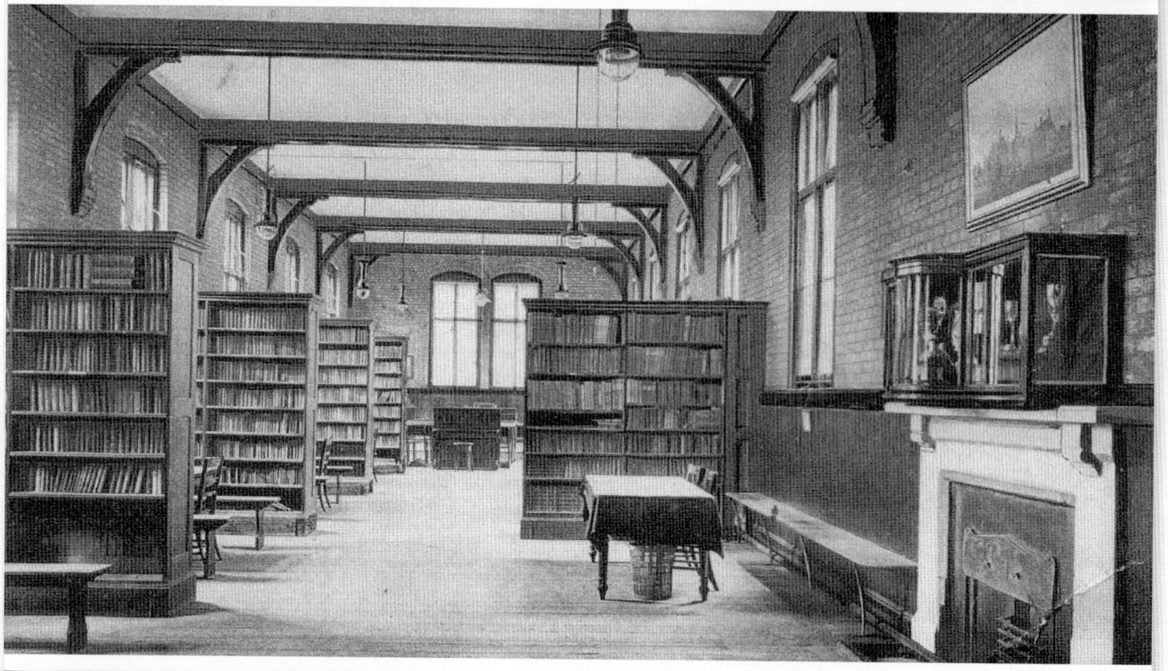

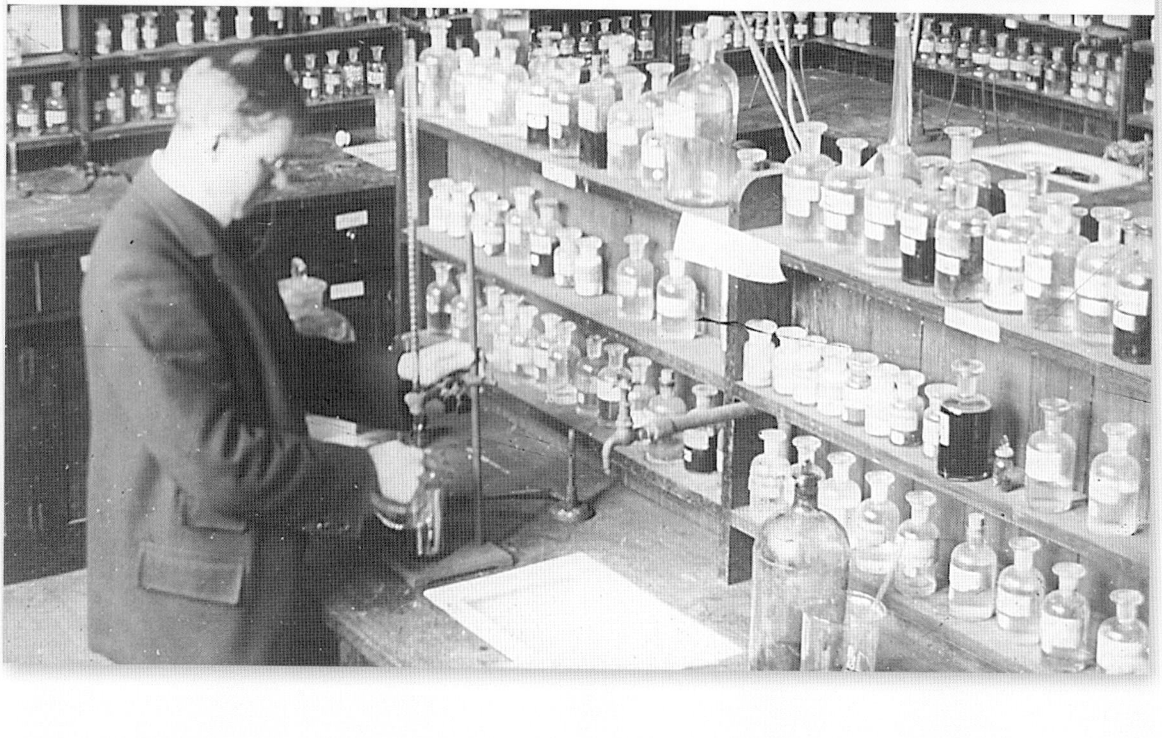

building were extended to accommodate the growing numbers. Two further buildings were added in 1891 and 1894. These were boarding houses known as Block A and Block B and their construction freed up much needed space in the main building. A grand Dining Hall was added in 1898 thus forming the shape and extent of the buildings which a boy, born around 1900, entering St John's in 1912 and destined to spend the war years at school in Leatherhead would have known. By now there were 271 pupils and 18 assistant masters living at the School.

The opening of the Dining Hall freed up further space in the main building and in 1903 the old dining hall was turned into a library and reading room with sufficient bookcases to house 10,000 books. In the same year, the old kitchens were converted into a chemistry laboratory and classroom.

DEVELOPMENT OF SPORT

Sport played an important part in the life of the School in the years before the war. On arrival in Leatherhead in 1872, the School set up competitive rugby and cricket teams but, before the introduction of a Sixth Form, teams were limited in the number of games they could play against other schools. So, for local games, teams were regularly supplemented by young athletic teachers such as the Reverend William Henry Murray Ragg and William Hargreaves, shown here in this masters' group photograph of 1885.

By 1890, St John's teams were playing regular fixtures against other leading public schools including Christ's Hospital, Cranleigh, Epsom, Hurstpierpoint, King's College School (Wimbledon), and Whitgift. Such fixtures significantly raised the profile of the School. The School appointed its first cricket professional in 1890 and the earliest known photograph of a St John's team is the 1st XI cricket team of 1891.

With only three members of the previous year's 1st XI still at the School, the 1891 side suffered a number of defeats. Bowling was their strong point, but the batting was described as disappointing. Only Cyril Warton Perkins and Gilbert Stephen Forder Rutty (the headmaster's eldest son) distinguished themselves with their fielding. The 1st XI cricket team of 1891 were all Foundationers or Supplementary Foundationers who went on to have varying careers which included the Church, teaching, banking, farming, engineering and law. Three served in the South African (Boer) War; Perkins who had also worked as a mining engineer in Johannesburg died of meningitis in Accra in 1902. Five members of the team served in the Great War, those who were ordained remained in charge of their parish and others worked in reserved occupations or in service of the government at home.

Above: Masters' Group 1885. L-R: A F Fraser-Smith; O O Brooksbank; Reverend W H M Ragg; A A Sykes; Reverend R D Eves; R Bulmer; W Hargreaves
Top left: Quad and Dining Hall c.1912; Middle left: Library c.1910; Bottom left: Chemistry Laboratory c.1910

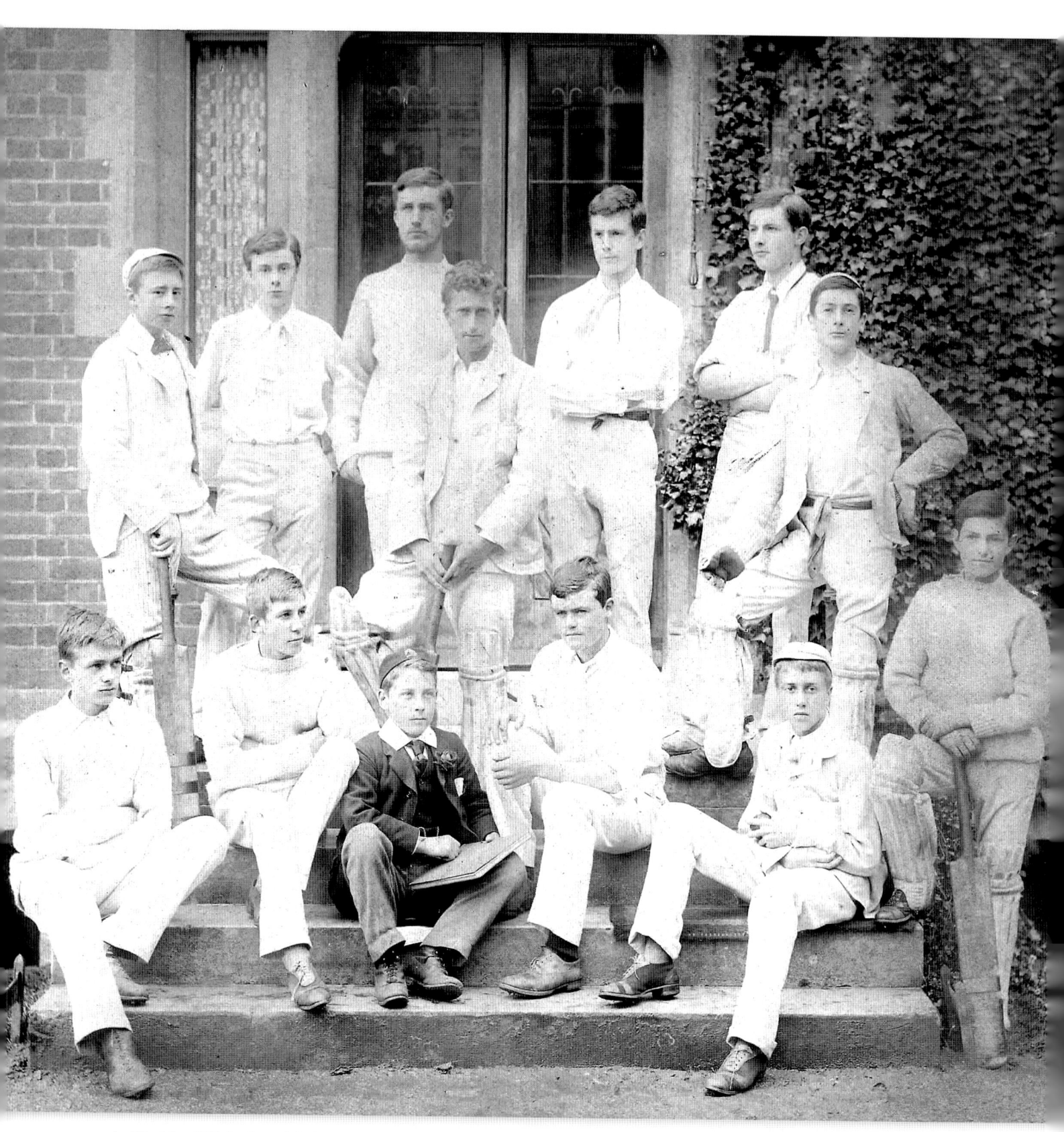

St John's School, Leatherhead and the Great War, 1914-1919

1st XI cricket 1891. Back row L-R: J A Frances; B Hall; G S F Rutty; G E Wollen. Middle row L-R: A E Bonsoy; E Cleave (Captain); E G Williams. Front row L-R: F J Yonge; C Muckleston; A C Brown; C W Perkins; A H Hodson; R M Rees

THE EARLY YEARS

NEW HEADMASTER

Arthur Forster Rutty retired in 1909 aged 62 and became Rector of Lyminge near Folkstone. His successor, the Reverend Edmund Audley Downes, a much younger man, had spent the previous seven years teaching at Wellington College. Aged just 31, Downes brought renewed enthusiasm and energy to the School, yet within a few short years he had to contend with the aftermath of the disastrous fire which destroyed the main building in 1913 and the challenges of leading the School through the difficult years of the Great War.

LEVELLING THE PLAYING FIELDS

Discovering that there were plans to build houses on land next to the cricket pitch in 1912, the Committee decided to purchase and enclose this piece of ground with iron railings, to safeguard the School field. However, the ground was not fit for playing sport as it was rough and uneven and required levelling. John Harold Burnside, an assistant master, was given the task of making it an integral part of the existing field. Burnside had the ground surveyed and engaged a gang of half-a-dozen men to begin the work of improvement under the direction of Amos, the School groundsman. He then bought 300 yards of light rails and four skips to match, and accepted help from senior boys and masters to fill the skips. As soon as they were filled, smaller boys, who had been impatiently waiting, seized the trucks and ran them along the rails to the part of the field which was to receive the excavated soil. A bank was made, all along the new railings, up to the level which the whole field was planned to reach on the completion of the work. On the bank, hundreds of trees and flowering shrubs were planted. A new cricket square was prepared, and drains laid across the football pitch. The work began in the winter of 1912 and was completed in 1914, the new part being sown in the first month of the war. Several years elapsed before the ground could be used and it was not until the summer of 1917 that the first game of cricket was played on the new square.

Levelling the playing fields, 1912

ST JOHN'S SCHOOL OTC

In 1912, the Committee announced its approval of the formation of an Officer Training Corps, saying that it:

> Felt strongly that the St John's boys should not be debarred from taking part in a movement which enables the boys of other public schools to express their love for their country by learning to be ready to defend it in case of need, or from the excellent education which such a corps affords in patriotic sentiment and in habits of discipline and obedience to the call of duty.

Officer Training Corps had been established nationally in 1908 as part of the Haldane reforms to develop and encourage military skills in public schools and universities, with a view to providing candidates for commissions. University OTCs formed the Senior Division while those in the Public Schools formed the Junior Division; both were part of the Territorial Force which was the volunteer reserve section of the Army.

Although couched in terms of a desire to emulate other public schools and focusing on the educational and patriotic benefits of the OTC, the decision to form a Corps at St John's in 1912 was made easier when former pupil Lancelot Townshend Driffield, a captain in the Special Reserve, returned to the School as an assistant master. His military experience gained at Cambridge, at Derby School and St Edmund's, Canterbury, enabled the headmaster to obtain the consent of the Army Council to set up an OTC contingent. The cost of establishing the Corps was a further consideration – the initial cost, in addition to a grant from the War Office, was met by donations collected by members of the Committee. The funding of the Corps was clearly seen as a potential liability that could have an impact on the School's general funds, which relied heavily on charitable donations for income, so an appeal was made to friends of the School to contribute to a special OTC fund in future years.

THE EARLY YEARS

Two members of staff, Albert Evelyn Alderson and the Reverend Clarence White Ingram, assisted Lancelot Driffield in his role of Commanding Officer. Service in the OTC was compulsory for all boys over the age of fourteen unless forbidden by doctor's orders. The Corps consisted of 100 boys who formed A Company and the others were placed in B Company. The B Company boys received the military training designed for new recruits and were drafted, according to their efficiency, into A Company as vacancies occurred.

The newly formed OTC had an eventful first year; the weather was poor, there were epidemics of mumps and measles and all kit was lost in the fire of June 1913. This extract from *The Johnian*, October 1913, describes their misfortunes:

The Corps has now been in existence for a year and, having survived such a year it ought to be capable of surviving anything. Misfortune has patiently dogged its footsteps. The weather began it, of course – last Christmas term; measles devastated the Company in the Easter term; mumps followed in the summer, and the great fire added the finishing touch. The fire destroyed almost everything except the arms and ammunition – and the mumps! When all other defects had been remedied and every preparation made for camp, that miserable disease out-lasted the term and – well, we hope to go to camp next year.

The first Annual Inspection was made on 23 July 1913 by Captain F H Moore, General Staff, and his report was encouraging:

Considering the fact that the contingent has had to contend with great difficulties during the first year of its existence, I consider that the result is very creditable. Captain Driffield appears to take a great interest in the Corps and is helped in every way by the Headmaster and the Governors of the School.

The Corps also possessed three challenge cups for shooting: the House Cup, the Sangar Cup, and the Davy Cup. Teams selected from each house competed for the House Cup, while the other two cups were awarded for individual shooting. In July 1913 the School Captain, William Haldane Round, won the Davy Cup and Edmund Trevennin Gray (School Captain in 1914) won the Sangar Cup. Both enlisted in 1914 and both were subsequently killed in action.

Top left: Lancelot Driffield; Middle left: OTC badge; Middle right: Davy Cup; Bottom: OTC on parade c.1917

Fire, 1913

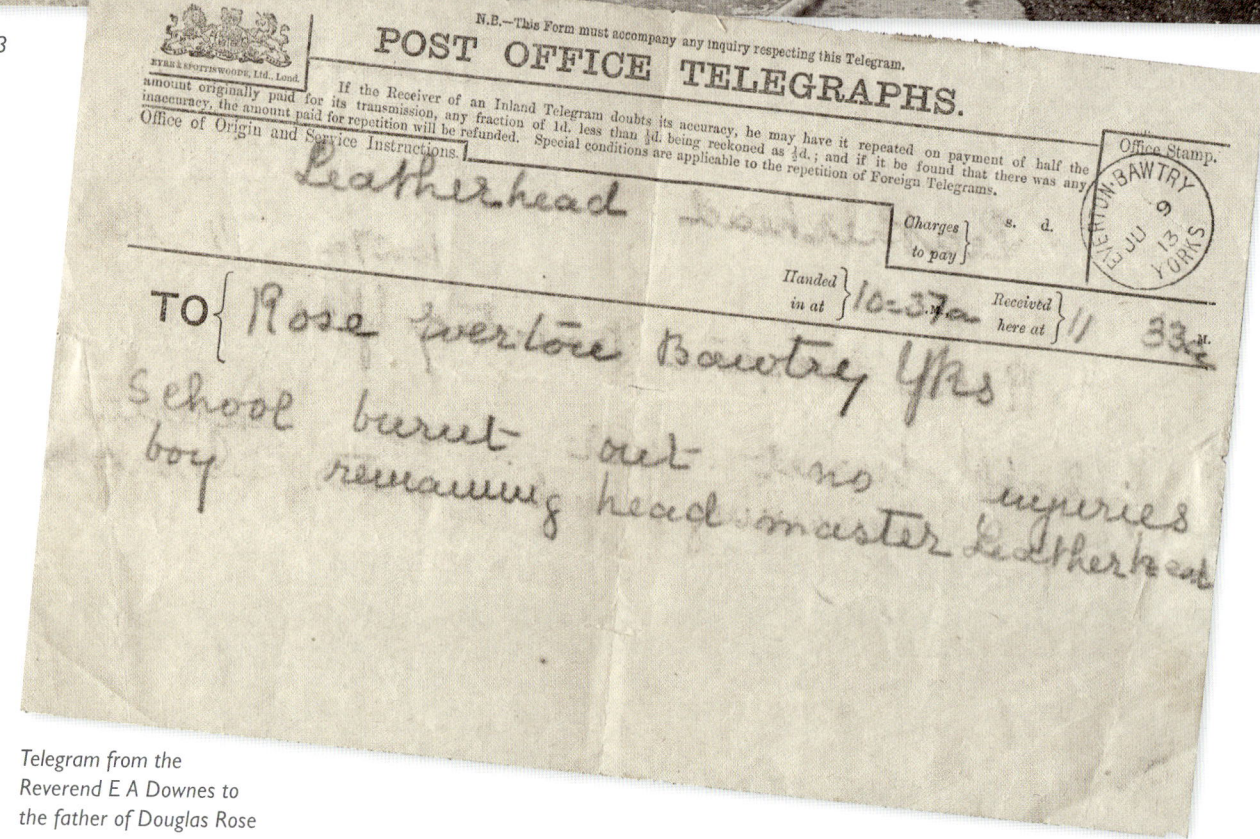

Telegram from the Reverend E A Downes to the father of Douglas Rose

THE EARLY YEARS

School Library destroyed by the fire

THE SCHOOL FIRE

On 9 June 1913, a serious fire destroyed the main building. The fire was discovered at about 2.30am and the alarm was raised. Fire engines from Leatherhead arrived within ten minutes, while the headmaster telephoned the fire stations at Epsom, Dorking and Guildford, and they were soon on the scene as well.

The fire spread rapidly and dormitories, classrooms, assistant masters' rooms, the headmaster's house, the matron's room, the Big School Room and the library were completely destroyed. Roofs and ceilings fell in and the wooden floors were burned beyond recognition. School furniture, beds and bedding were lost together with the personal effects of many boys and masters. The uniforms and equipment belonging to the newly established OTC and Band were destroyed as were all the books in the library. Just one set of *The Johnian* magazine was saved and the School's trophies including the Sangar Cup, the Davy Cup and the House Shield were also rescued.

Thanks to regular fire drills no lives were lost and some of the boys escaped from the upper floors down the canvas fire chutes. At first the cause of the fire was a mystery, but it soon transpired that it was due to a midnight escapade by pupils who, entering a master's sitting room while he was in the infirmary, accidentally set it alight.

The headmaster sent telegrams to 300 parents with the words: *'School burnt out no injuries'*. Two hundred boys were sent home on 10 and 11 June and about 80 of the older boys stayed at the School and lodged in the detached buildings to which the fire had not spread. Most of these boys were preparing for exams. The Committee rented three empty houses near the School and by 3 July 150 boys had returned for the rest of the term, while 50 of the youngest boys remained at home. The whole School reassembled after an extended holiday on 17 September 1913.

Fortunately, the School was insured and compensation of about £15,000 was received from the insurance company (London Assurance Corporation) which covered most of the cost of rebuilding the School. A further £5,000 was raised from donations, special collections and a grant from the School's general fund to cover individual personal losses and to replace furniture, books and library fittings. An extensive building programme was put in place and the Committee saw this as an opportunity to enlarge

Fire drill, boys escaping down fire chute

St John's School, Leatherhead and the Great War, 1914-1919

View of the Quad after the fire

THE EARLY YEARS

Front of the School after the fire

and improve the facilities. The front of the building was extended forward by two feet so that the main corridor could be widened, internal staircases fitted, and the outside walls of the new building raised.

Early in 1914, in addition to the re-construction of the main building, the boys were looking forward to improved sports facilities as the levelling of the new playing fields was completed. A Natural History Society and a Photographic Society were started, in addition to the existing Literary, Dramatic and Debating Societies. But, there was also a lot of sickness in the School with mumps and measles epidemics affecting the boys. Sadly, in March 1914, Henry Walton Boldero, who was just twelve years old, died in the School infirmary. He had been ill for some days with scarlet fever and seemed to be recovering, when he developed meningitis and died. The boys in his form, his four cousins who were also pupils at St John's and many of the teachers, sent flowers for the funeral which took place in his home village of Dymchurch in Kent. A memorial service was subsequently held at the School at which Henry was described as having a bright and happy disposition as well as showing unusual promise – the previous year on Speech Day he had been awarded the Fourth Form prize and a prize for French.

Henry Boldero's grave, St Peter and St Paul's Church, Dymchurch, Kent

CHAPTER 2 PRELUDE TO WAR

On 27 June 1914, the St John's 1st XI cricket team played Cranleigh. It was, by all accounts, an excellent match. *The Johnian* magazine reported that the School had won '*thanks chiefly to some fine batting by Du Pre, followed by some good bowling by Roberts*'. For the 1st XI it was an emphatic win at the end of a successful season, and the School was looking forward to Speech Day, the end of term and the long summer holidays.

The following morning, 28 June 1914 at just before 11.00 o'clock, the heir to the Austro-Hungarian throne, Archduke Franz Ferdinand and his wife Sophie were assassinated in the Bosnian capital Sarajevo by a nineteen-year-old Serbian, Gabril Princip. The next morning the assassination was headline news across the world, but in the days that followed, the story disappeared from the front pages. Tension in the Balkans was not unusual and the Balkan crisis had been a topic of discussion by the School debating society in the latter part of 1912 when they met to discuss the motion (carried by a narrow margin of one vote):

That this House is in sympathy with the Balkan States in their offensive league against Turkey.

SPEECH DAY 1 JULY 1914

A few days later, the Duchess of Albany came to Leatherhead to re-open the restored main building and to give away the prizes. It was the hottest day of the year as – according to the School magazine – one or two members of the Guard of Honour found to their cost. The two most prestigious awards – the

1st XI, 1914. Edmund Gray (Captain) seated centre

PRELUDE TO WAR

Speech day c.1914

Governors' Prizes as they were known – went to Lionel Henry Shuckforth Grigson and Victor Leopold Stevens Bedwell. This was not surprising as Grigson had recently been awarded a prestigious scholarship by the Dean and Chapter of Truro Cathedral and Bedwell had been awarded a top Classics scholarship at Oxford. Edmund Trevennin Gray received the Downes Prize for giving the best example and having the best influence. Again, this was little surprise, earlier in the year Gray had been awarded an Exhibition worth £40 per annum to go up to St Catharine's College, Cambridge. He was also School Captain and Captain of the 1st XI. The Upper Sixth Form which left St John's in the summer of 1914 were by all accounts, talented and able, full of optimism and ambition.

Little did any of those assembled on 1 July know that this would be the last formal Speech Day for nine years as the ceremony was discontinued for the duration of the war and was not resumed until 1923. As the School broke up for the long summer holiday, there still was no hint that the assassination in Sarajevo would trigger decisions and a series of events – through July and August – which would change the course of history and the lives of so many.

OTC – TIDWORTH CAMP 1914

St John's OTC attended their first summer camp at the end of July 1914 when a contingent of three officers and 53 cadets went to Tidworth, in Wiltshire, for eight days' training. Frank Cecil Allan, one of the cadets, described their experiences in an article for

The Johnian, saying that for weeks beforehand they practised pitching tents, wrestling with guy ropes and tent poles. On Monday 27 July, the corps marched in uniform to Leatherhead station, attracting the curious stares of local children. They regretted that they had no band to accompany them, having lost all their bugles and drums in the fire of 1913, and vowed to rectify that the following year. Joining around 3,000 boys from 40 schools divided into battalions of around 800, by the next evening they felt themselves to be seasoned veterans and, as Frank Allan describes in his article, they were:

Strolling casually round the camp with swagger sticks and saluting sundry sergeants under the impression that they were officers.

St John's was in No 2 Battalion, along with contingents from Bedford Modern School, Dover College, Guildford Grammar School, Haileybury, King's School Canterbury and Reigate Grammar School. Inspections and night operations followed and the Commander of their battalion commended St John's cadets several times for smartness when marching back from manoeuvres. Another feature of camp life was the daily 'sing song'; the cadets also played football matches against other school contingents, a St John's team losing a game to Cranleigh on the Sunday evening. The cadets were due to be in camp until 6 August, but on the Bank Holiday Monday, 3 August, with the declaration of war imminent, the order was given to strike camp early. Frank Allan wrote:

The war caused considerable excitement and evolved much patriotism. In the end it was also the root reason for our departure two days before the arranged date.

Few had foreseen the catastrophe which had been just around the corner; Archduke Franz Ferdinand's assassination at the end of June prompted a chain of events and when Germany invaded Belgium on 4 August 1914, Britain declared war on Germany. All 21 boys who left St John's at the end of the Summer Term 1914 enlisted in the armed forces. Nearly half were, in due course, killed in action, including five of the successful 1st XI who played their last game against Cranleigh at the end of June 1914 and prize winners Grigson, Bedwell and Gray.

St John's OTC swagger stick

CHAPTER 3 SCHOOL LIFE IN WARTIME

As pupils and masters returned to Leatherhead for the start of the Autumn term in 1914 the impact of the war on the School could already be felt. Writing his monthly report for the Committee on Friday 18 September 1914, the headmaster explained that had it not been for the war, numbers in the School would have increased to 290, but five boys who were due to return had received commissions in Kitchener's New Army so the actual number on the School roll was 285. In addition to those five boys, there were a further two who had also applied and were awaiting a reply from the War Office.

Rising food prices and an increase in taxation made an impact on the School over the course of the war. The cost of provisions for nearly 300 boys, masters and support staff in 1915 was £800 higher than in the previous year. In the early 1900s milk cost 1d a pint, but by the end of the war the cost had risen to 6d and in January 1918 the Government introduced food rationing.

Receipts from donations, annual subscriptions and church collections were down by £1,262 in 1915 and concern about lack of funds was a constant source of anxiety for the Committee. Consequently, further economies were put in place and the Quad was dug up to grow vegetables. Expenditure on the repair of buildings and renewal and repairs of furniture was curtailed and, while the School sports took place as usual in March, for the first time no prizes were awarded. The Committee decided that *'all further improvements not absolutely necessary should be put off till happier times'*. They stopped purchasing books and the library was left half stocked. Money which had been earmarked for a much-needed swimming pool was to be used for general purposes and the number of boys admitted to the School each year was reduced. The grand occasion of the annual Speech Day with invited guests was suspended for the duration of the war and the School prizes were distributed without ceremony at the end of each Summer Term. Book prizes – traditionally heavy leather-bound tomes, embossed with the School crest – were abandoned on grounds of economy and, in their place, war prize certificates were issued. An exception was made for a few special prizes funded by legacies or donations such as the Gatehouse Divinity prize.

Gatehouse Divinity Prize

As the war years went by, the School found it increasingly difficult to balance the books and, in 1917, the Committee decided to reduce the number of boys in the School to save money. They raised the age of entry to 11 and closed the junior boarding house. But there was another reason behind this – medical officers had said that according to modern ideas on sanitation the number of pupils was too large and buildings over-crowded. By not taking in boys under 11 there was more space for the other pupils and some of the rooms could be used for recreation in the winter or in bad weather.

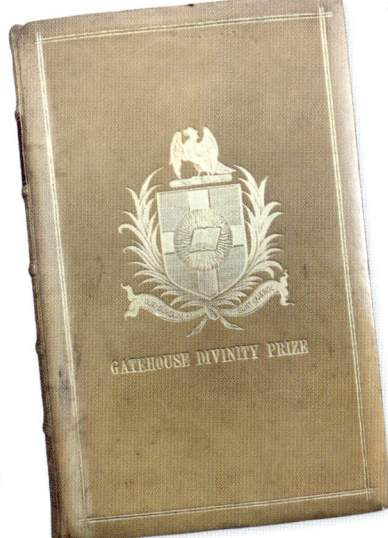

SCHOOL FOOD

Mealtimes were formal occasions, and masters sat at the end of each table to ensure good table manners; but the food was poor and there was little choice. Breakfast was porridge, skimmed milk or bread and margarine, lunch was meat and stodgy pudding with boiled fish on Fridays. Afternoon tea was

Boys in the Dining Hall

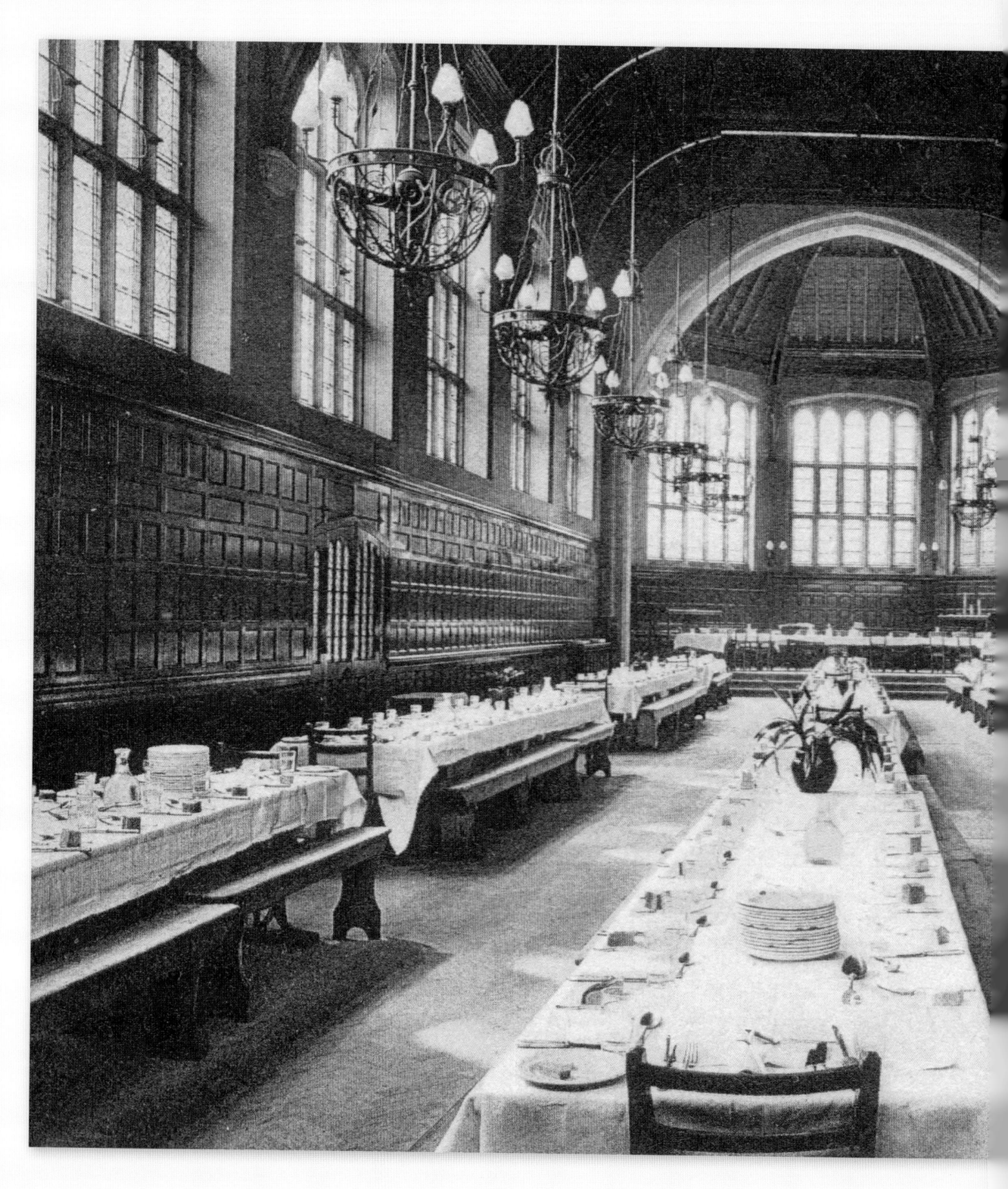

St John's School, Leatherhead and the Great War, 1914-1919

SCHOOL LIFE IN WARTIME

Interior of the Dining Hall, c.1910

bread and margarine and supper was a biscuit. Penry Whitefoord, writing in 1988 said *'The food was badly cooked and unpalatable and we were perpetually hungry'*.

Billy Rivers, who joined the School in 1912 aged nine and a half, described the food as *'awful'* and wrote in *The Johnian* in 1965:

So it was that I wrote home on my third day to say I was starving, and I threatened to run away. My poor father was terribly worried and came dashing down to Leatherhead where he arranged for me to have special 'extras' for breakfast. These consisted of a sausage, a piece of bacon, or an egg, which had a good selling value if I was broke or did not fancy them.

In July 1917, the Committee agreed that a *'war levy'* should be imposed to cover the increased cost of provisions. Parents were asked to pay an extra £1 per term for each pupil. As a result, there was an improvement in meal times from September 1917. Up to this point, there had been a long period in the School day between 2pm and 6.20pm without food, which the boys found hard especially as they played football in between these times. The change introduced a preliminary tea (cocoa and bread and jam or butter) from 4.20pm to 4.30pm, followed by afternoon lessons and then tea proper at 6.45pm which also consisted of tea, bread and butter and jam.

Left: Billy Rivers in choir robes, 1916
Right: Billy Rivers, St John's School Bursar, July 1940

POCKET MONEY

Parents (including those of Foundationers who were entitled to free board and tuition) were required to send 14 shillings to the School each term to cover the weekly allowance, games and School stationery. The weekly allowance was 3d and was given out on Wednesdays by the 'master in charge of pocket money' and was supposed to pay for postage stamps and Chapel collections. This allowance was supplemented by what cash the pupils brought back with them at the beginning of the term and which they could bank with one of the masters and spend at the tuck shop. But few could afford to eat as much as they wanted or needed.

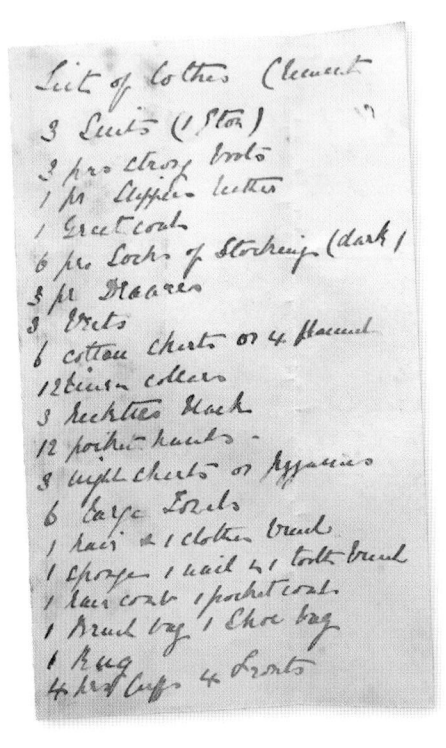

TUCK SHOP

Young Billy Rivers was luckier than some as his father not only paid for him to have 'extras' for breakfast, but also decided to send him a shilling a week so that he had something to spend at the School tuck shop. This was opened immediately after lunch each day and here boys could buy buns, sweets and square cakes called 'stodgers'. It was a grave offence to buy food or sweets anywhere else as the profits from the tuck shop were a valuable source of income for the School's Games Club.

SCHOOL UNIFORM

A handwritten uniform list discovered among papers belonging to Clement Barrington Furmston, who was killed in action in France in 1917, shows that boys were required to bring the following items to School each term: three suits (one Eton suit); three pairs of strong boots; one pair of slippers (leather); one greatcoat; six pairs of socks or stockings (dark); three pairs of drawers; three vests; six cotton shirts or four flannel; 12 collars; three neckties (black); 12 pocket handkerchiefs; three nightshirts or pyjamas; six large towels; one hair and one clothes brush; one sponge, one nail and one tooth brush; one hair comb, one pocket comb; one muck bag, one shoe bag; one rug; four pairs cuffs and four fronts.

The accompanying typewritten notice to parents stipulates that:

Every item must be sent to School clean and in good repair. Socks etc properly darned.

HOUSE NUMBERS

Each item had to be marked with the owner's surname and house number (issued when a pupil was first registered). For boots and shoes there had to be small brass nails on the waist of the boot or shoe showing the house number only. For brushes and combs the house number had to be burnt in, while on socks, rugs and all flannels it had to be stitched in silk or cotton. All other clothes could be marked with marking ink or tape in the lining.

SCHOOL CAPS

School caps were supplied by the School (price one shilling and eleven pence) and according to the notice were to be worn on all occasions. No felt hats were to be brought to school!

COST OF UNIFORM

Many pupils came from very poor clergy families, some of whom must have struggled to provide all the clothing items listed. John Leonard Wilson, who was at St John's from 1908-1915 and later became Bishop of Birmingham, was one such pupil. In Roy McKay's biography of Wilson (McKay,1973 p.52), Richard Millard, one of his contemporaries at St John's is quoted as saying '*We were all poor, but I think Wilson was exceptionally so*'. McKay goes on to say that '*He [Wilson] went back to school with nightshirts, as the family purse could not afford to buy pyjamas and wearing the leather boots of his village home.*' He was teased mercilessly by the other boys for wearing nightshirts rather than pyjamas.

LESSONS

Lessons took place in classrooms which were situated on the ground floor below the dormitories. We know what the classrooms looked like as we have a collection of glass lantern slides taken by one of the masters, Eustace Coddington. Mr Coddington was a chemistry teacher at St John's from 1902-1938, Housemaster of North House from 1914-1938 and, for a short while, acting headmaster. He was also a keen mountaineer and athlete and gave regular lantern slide lectures to the School on climbing in the Alps. He followed these lectures by showing his collection of informal scenes of school life to the great amusement of all.

The main classroom was situated in a large room known as 'Big School'. The curriculum was limited compared with today – mainly mathematics,

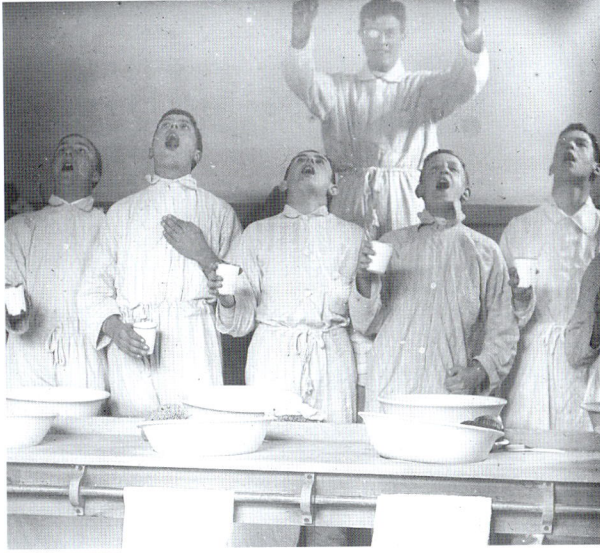

Top: Boys in school uniform; Middle: Boys in pyjamas; Bottom: The Big School Room c.1910

Eustace Coddington

literature and classics, with some history, French and German. Science became an integral part of the curriculum from 1899 when the School obtained its first laboratory.

TEMPORARY TEACHERS

In some senses, life at St John's carried on much the same during the war. Boys continued with their lessons, though one of the consequences of the war was that older temporary teachers were brought in to replace those younger ones who had gone off to fight.

Such was the shortage of available teachers that women were appointed as temporary teachers for the very first time. By 1918 there were three women on the staff teaching science, drawing and languages.

Miss Rasmussen, who joined the School in the summer of 1918, with a BSc from London University, taught science and was form mistress of the Special Form (the form in which boys were prepared for the Navy, Army, and Civil Service Examinations and for Entrance Examinations to the Universities) until she left in 1919. Miss Rasmussen appears to have played a full part in school life, contributing books and papers to the library and on one occasion played a violin solo in a school concert.

Grace Margaret Wanklyn was employed to teach drawing at St John's in 1917. Drawing lessons were an '*extra*' subject for which parents were billed separately. Grace and her sister Edith had a long connection with St John's. Daughters of the late Reverend Hibbert Wanklyn, Vicar of Deopham, Norfolk, Edith was born in 1860 and Grace in 1862. After their father died in 1895, they moved to Leatherhead and attended the Parish Church of St Mary and St Nicholas. The two sisters played the hand bells in a St John's School concert on 21 November 1896.

Grace Wanklyn continued to teach drawing at St John's after the war and *The Johnian* recorded the School's '*great regret*' when she resigned in 1925.

Ethel Mary Congreve was appointed form mistress for the Upper Third in 1918 and taught French. Ethel had studied at Cambridge University before the war but although women could sit the undergraduate examinations at Cambridge and have their results recorded from 1882 onwards, they were not awarded a 'Batchelor of Arts' degree. From 1921 women were awarded diplomas, but it was not until 1948 that they were admitted as full members of the University and could finally enjoy the same status as men. Ethel stayed on at St John's after the war. Her temporary post was made permanent in March 1919 and the headmaster wrote in his monthly report to the Committee:

Miss Congreve has proved herself a most valuable colleague and a first rate teacher and disciplinarian.

A classroom c.1914

SCHOOL LIFE IN WARTIME

Mr and Mrs Millbourn, 1922

She is a very good French scholar and has made herself especially useful in her work among the younger boys.

Ethel took over the running of the Field Club, helped to establish a school museum and in March 1920 gave an illustrated talk on the 'Development of Modern Painting' to members of the Literary and Debating Society. In September that year, aged 42, she married Arthur Russell Millbourn, a fellow teacher and Housemaster of East House, who was aged 28. Arthur Millbourn joined the staff at St John's in 1915 to teach modern history and geography. He was also a Lay Reader, president of the Literary and Debating Societies and master in charge of photography.

After their marriage, Ethel Congreve continued to teach, which was most unusual in those days. Had she worked in a school run by the Board of Education, Ethel would probably have had to give up her post under the terms of the 'marriage bar', which restricted the employment of married women in certain occupations, particularly in teaching and the civil service.

Ethel and Arthur left St John's in 1922 when Arthur Millbourn was appointed headmaster of Colston's School, Bristol. In 1929 Arthur was ordained and in 1939 was made Canon of Bristol Cathedral. Ethel died in December 1960 in Bristol, they had been married for 40 years.

DISCIPLINE AND DETENTIONS

Discipline both before and during the war was strict. The usual form of punishment awarded by all masters was detention. Penry Whitefoord remembers that:

Every Monday morning, the headmaster, a towering clerical figure in black with a mortarboard and rustling gown, swept into the classroom to inspect the week's marks and threaten to give impositions or detention to those of us reported to be idle.

Impositions or lines, had to be written on special green paper, presumably to stop the culprit writing during prep which took place every evening, except Saturdays and Sundays, in the Big School Room and was supervised by prefects.

Canings were another form of punishment, and each week boys in the lower forms who came bottom in the class tests were summoned to the headmaster's office and beaten. They were then automatically put into two hours detention drill on the following Saturday afternoon. This meant parading with the School Sergeant in the gymnasium and walking round and round the inside of the gym for periods of half an hour to two hours, which the boys found extremely boring.

John Leonard Wilson not only suffered relentless teasing by other boys but according to his biographer Roy McKay (McKay 1973, p.52) was also the '*butt of several masters*' and his school work in his first term at St John's was reported to be distinctly unsatisfactory. He was caned '*once for lateness*' and '*once for dissembling*'. During the Second World War, while serving as the Bishop of Singapore, Wilson was interned and tortured by the Japanese. Bishop Wilson died on 18 August 1970, aged 72 and his obituary in *The Old Johnian* 1971 notes that:

Buggy Wilson as he was known to his contemporaries, was, at School, unorthodox and slightly rebellious. He was heard to say, in later life, that anything he suffered at the hands of the Japanese in the Second World War was child's play in comparison to what he endured in his first term at St John's.

The Gymnasium c.1910

SCHOOL REPORTS

These were very brief compared to the detailed reports children receive today. Written on one side of a single sheet of paper, one line or even single word comments were acceptable in those days. In the final report for Sixth Form pupil Douglas Rose, his subject teachers described his work as '*fair, weak, fair to moderate and lacks thoroughness*' yet his tutor's report says '*excellent*' followed by the headmaster's closing remark of '*Excellent I wish him all success*'. One wonders if they had taken the trouble to read the preceding comments!

Few academic prizes came his way but in 1915 Douglas won a choir prize and a prize for mathematics. His father, a vicar in Bournemouth, had paid around £36 per year for his board and tuition as a Supplementary Foundationer. Douglas had hoped to go up to Cambridge University in September 1915 for one term before enlisting, but the headmaster was under pressure from the War Office to get boys who were leaving the School to apply for the Special Reserve at once and not to wait. Accordingly, Downes wrote to Douglas Rose's father to say that he had advised Douglas to apply for a Commission in the Officers Special Reserve as soon as possible and said that in his opinion going to Cambridge for one term would be a waste of time.

Douglas obtained a commission in the 9th Northumberland Fusiliers and went to France in January 1916. He was wounded and spent some time recovering at Osborne House on the Isle of Wight which was used as an officer's convalescent home during the war. Rejoining the 3rd Northumberland Fusiliers, he remained with them in England and France until April 1919.

After the war, Douglas went to Worcester College, Oxford where he gained a teaching diploma. In 1923 he was an assistant master at Giggleswick School, then taught at the King's School Chester and the Liverpool Institute before being appointed headmaster of Banbury County School in 1935. The Reverend Downes' confidence in his former pupil seems to have been justified.

School report for Douglas Rose, 1915

School fees receipt, 1914

SCHOOL LIFE IN WARTIME

Above: Letter from the headmaster, E Audley Downes to Mr Rose, 21 July, 1915

Below: Letter from Douglas to his father which reads:

Dear Pater

I enclose the Board Papers. Only 2 more to come. I feel I have done well & so hope for good results. Coming home on Monday. Busy packing – it's a business of 2 into 1 won't go – so don't expect any news.

Love Douglas

Left: Board result card from the headmaster to Douglas Rose, congratulating him on his examination board results, which reads:

You passed in Latin, Greek, Maths, Divinity, & English Essay – & have been awarded a certificate with exemptions from Responsions and Parts I and II of the Previous. You have also gained the 2nd Math. set prize. Congratulations on an excellent result.

One of the Big Dormitories c.1910

Chapel interior c.1910

DORMITORIES

Boys slept in dormitories of about twenty beds, with wash bowls down the centre and a prefect in charge.

Despite the staff shortages in wartime, the boys had no domestic duties of any kind and were waited on hand and foot. Each House had its own Matron and maids looked after their clothes and made the beds each day. While we have no official records of the names and numbers of school 'servants' during the war, the 1911 census shows that there were forty domestic staff at that time – eight male staff, porters, gardeners etc; twenty-seven housemaids and kitchen maids and five matrons for a school of 253 pupils and 14 school masters.

School life in winter was often cold and cheerless, with no fires and only lukewarm pipes. Further improvements were made to the bathroom and changing rooms of the main building during the summer of 1914: the four original changing rooms were completely renovated with new basins and taps, the floors were re-laid in cement, electric light was installed and hot water laid on. In addition, two more changing rooms were added in the basement, each supplied with two shower baths and hot water system and fitted with new wash basins. In the bathroom, the old baths were replaced by twelve more up-to-date ones. A hot bath was a weekly event and boys were sent off to the basement in groups during evening prep sessions, rapidly re-dressing afterwards and returning to the Big School Room.

SCHOOL CHOIR

The School choir has always played a significant part in the life of St John's and in September 1914 Dr Leslie Henry Brett Reed, a young organ scholar from Cambridge University, joined the School as organist and choir master. Known to all as Doc Reed, he was renowned for his sense of humour and credited with the high standard consistently maintained by the choir. He enlisted with the Artists' Rifles in 1916, gained a commission in the Royal Field Artillery (RFA), was wounded in 1918 and then returned to St John's where he remained for the next thirty-two years.

During the war the Chapel was open on one evening in the week, and, in common with many other churches, the practice of singing the National Anthem before morning service was adopted.

Choir boys, c.1916

SCHOOL LIFE IN WARTIME

There is no doubt that school life was tough, especially for the younger boys during the war – far from their families, with only the weekly letters from home and the hope of extra pocket money for the tuck shop to sustain them.

HOUSE SYSTEM AT ST JOHN'S

At the start of the Autumn Term 1914, a new tutorial system was set up with a house tutor in charge of each of the four Houses. A House system had been established as early as 1892 for sporting competitions. At that time boys were allocated to the House named after the region from which they had come from; e.g. Wales; West of England; London and District; Home Counties; East Anglian and so forth. But the system of having nine houses was unwieldy and, in 1896, the House system was simplified into four Houses: North, South, East and West.

From 1914 onwards, every boy was to be a member of a House, not just those who played sport for a House team. There were still no physical buildings for Houses, but corridors were designated for the Houses in the main building. Also introduced in 1914 were House Captains, one of whose jobs was to hand out House colours and manage the House Prefects who had to ensure good order in the Dining Hall where boys ate at House tables.

SPORTS, GAMES AND PASTIMES

Before the war there were several clubs and societies in the School which boys could join. A photographic society, natural history society, hare and hounds club, debating society and a literary and dramatic society were all organised by the boys under the guidance of a member of staff. These dwindled in number during the war years until there were just two remaining: a natural history society called the 'Field Club' and the 'Literary and Debating Society' formed by the amalgamation of the Literary and Dramatic Society and the Debating Society. The latter was restricted to older pupils, School and House prefects and the Sixth Form. The boys held debates and presented

West House Juniors, 1915

papers or readings on literary and scientific subjects under the presidency of Mr Ingram, meeting weekly on Saturday evenings in the library.

What kept the younger ones going was their passionate interest in games – not especially the games they played themselves, but those of the older boys, the Senior and Junior House matches and School matches, all of which they watched with keen interest.

The new House system proved its worth in 1915 as many matches against other schools and teams had to be abandoned. As a result, there was more interest than usual in the House ties. Established in 1892, the House Challenge Shield was awarded for inter-house competitions including football, fives, gymnastics, cricket and athletic sports.

A further challenge shield, the Downes Shield, was introduced in 1915. Presented in memory of Dr Downes, the headmaster's father, who had taken a great interest in the School, this shield recognised academic achievement and was awarded to the House which gained the most points for School Prizes.

ATHLETIC SPORTS

The annual sports day took place on a Saturday towards the end of the Spring Term, between the end of the football season and the beginning of the cricket season. Events included the high jump, hurdles and long jump as well as a series of distance races. An inter-house tug of war and inter-house relay races also provided an opportunity for individual houses to win points towards the House Shield competition. In 1918, one boy was particularly successful:

The feature of the week was W St G Hombersley's hundred, 1/5 second behind the record time. Hombersley also secured the quarter, shared the first place with Evans in the high jump, ran first in the mile, and secured second place in the open hurdles, the cross-country and the long jump. For these performances he got the Victor Ludorum Cup with 52 points.

Inset top: House Challenge Shield
Inset middle: Downes Shield
Bottom left: Hurdles 1918
Bottom right: High jump 1918

CRICKET

Cricket was played in the Summer Term and the 1st XI sides played other public schools, as well as matches with visiting teams, who included the Anzacs and the Canadians from Woodcote Park in Epsom, the Royal Engineers and Irish Guards, the King's Royal Rifle Corps Wimbledon and the Inns of Court OTC.

FOOTBALL

The main winter game was Association Football. Rugby had been played until 1885 when the headmaster, the Reverend Arthur Rutty, decided that St John's should be a soccer school rather than a rugby one. One reason for the change might have been that one of Rutty's boys had been seriously injured in an accident on the rugby field soon after he arrived in Leatherhead.

Fixtures were arranged with schools such as Cranleigh, Horsham Grammar School, Forest School, Brighton College and the City of London School as well as with the men of the University and Public Schools (UPS) Battalion of the Royal Fusiliers.

Formed in September 1914, the 18th, 19th, 20th and 21st Battalions of the Royal Fusiliers were part of Kitchener's New Army and carried the name 'University and Public Schools' as the vast majority of recruits were from those institutions. Over 30 OJs signed up, including Cecil Roberts, who left School in the summer of 1914. Once enough men had been attested to make up four battalions, the search began for an initial training area. With the decision taken to move to Epsom Downs, the boys from St John's were back on familiar territory, especially those in the 20th Battalion as half that unit was billeted in Leatherhead itself.

Top: 1st XI cricket, 1913
Inset: Cecil Roberts, football captain, 1914

St John's School, Leatherhead and the Great War, 1914-1919

Royal Fusiliers marching through Ashtead park

Sketch of the UPS at Ashtead

SCHOOL LIFE IN WARTIME

On 24 October 1914, Cecil was back on the football pitch at St John's, representing D Company of the 20th Battalion in a winning match against the School 1st XI. St John's had a poor start to the season, losing their first four games, but in January 1915 they defeated a scratch XI from the UPS Battalion, captained by Cecil and including at least one other OJ, Eric Young (1902-07). The match report in *The Johnian* declared:

In spite of this being their first game this term, the School showed dash and vigour on a snow-covered and treacherous ground. They had easily the best of the game and won by 5 goals to 3.

FIVES

Fives was a popular game, particularly with the masters, and boys would crowd round to watch. Individual and house matches were arranged and competition for cups and points which counted towards the House Shield was fierce.

FOOTBALL SEASON, 1914—15.

1914	Opponents	Goals for	against	Result
Oct. 11	Merton F.C.	1	8	Lost
,, 24	U.P.S. 3rd Batt., D Co.	0	2	Lost
,, 30	Manchester Batt., R.F.	1	3	Lost
Nov. 4	Brighton College	2	4	Lost
,, 7	Forest School	1	1	Drawn
,, 18	University College F.C.	9	0	Won
,, 28	U.P.S. 4th Batt. A Co.	0	5	Lost
Dec. 2	Cranleigh School	4	5	Lost
,, 5	Brighton College (return)	4	6	Lost
,, 9	City of London School	4	8	Lost
1915				
Jan. 30	C. L. N. Roberts' XI.	5	3	Won

Results of Matches. Won 2. Lost 8. Drawn 1. Goals for 31, against 45.

Top right: Football fixtures 1914-1915; Inset: Fives court; Bottom: Fives match in progress

35

AUTOGRAPHS

Collecting autographs was a hobby enjoyed by many pupils. These pictures are taken from an autograph book in the School archives. It is the only example we have, and we don't know who it belonged to, but the entries date from 1916-1919. It is a typical autograph book of its day containing poems, quotations in English, Latin and Greek, jokes, drawings, and signatures from classmates and teachers. There are some light-hearted sketches and only a few written references to the war, but these two drawings show that the boys were very aware of the continuing hostilities. The illustration of the car is by Philip Farrer Shenton (East House 1912-1919) and dated 18 March 1916. His older brother, Captain Austin Kirk Shenton MC, died of wounds in France on 26 July 1918, aged 22. Henry Edward Walton (East House 1914-1918) contributed a topical drawing, dated 19 May 1917, of a tank going into action on the battlefield. British tanks were first used during the Battle of Flers-Courcelette (part of the Battle of the Somme) on 15 September 1916.

Top: Tank drawing by Henry Walton, 1917
Bottom: Army vehicle drawing by Philip Shenton, 1916

SCHOOL LIFE IN WARTIME

EPIDEMICS, DEATH AND DISEASES

In mid-February 1916 the temperature plummeted, and heavy snow fell. At first, the boys welcomed the break in their dull routine and began snowballing and indulging in snow fights. Later, some began tobogganing and the Sixth Form were allowed to go down Box Hill. Just at this point, the School community fell victim to an influenza epidemic. Starting with twelve, the total rapidly increased until, a week later, 170 boys were suffering from the flu. Both the blocks and part of the main building became temporary infirmaries, work became a thing of the past and no games were played. Eventually, those suffering from the flu were sent home and the annual athletics competition was postponed until the Summer Term.

Worse was to come just a year later, in March 1917, when pupils and staff alike were devastated by the death of six boys in a measles epidemic which, incidentally, affected many other public schools. Fifty-five boys were initially taken ill, and most of those were mild cases giving little cause for concern. Then, over the course of a week in February, twelve of the more seriously ill pupils were admitted to the infirmary. Within a short time, they all developed pneumonia and became dangerously ill. Eight additional trained nurses were brought from London and Sir Dyce Duckworth, the Honorary Consulting Physician to the School, visited the boys as did Dr Stansfeld who was a physician on the staff of St Bartholomew's Hospital. On their advice, the headmaster decided to send all the boys home immediately and to delay the start of the Summer Term so that the School could be thoroughly disinfected and repainted.

Tragically, despite all the efforts of the School and medical staff, six of the boys who developed pneumonia died at the School. The youngest, Robert Lewis Fitzackerley Freeman, was just twelve years old. There is a brass plaque in memory of these pupils in the School Chapel.

Penry Whitefoord recalled that these deaths affected the boys at the School even more deeply than the reports they received of the carnage on the Western Front. He was friendly with Sam Thursby, another of those who died, and kept a photograph of Sam together with the name label over his bed which read 'Thursby 100' (his school number). Sam was a popular boy and another of his friends, Henry Walton, had a photograph album in which he pasted photos of himself and Sam taken on the School playing fields. Four of the boys were buried in their home town, but Sam Thursby and Arthur Rix were buried in the churchyard of Leatherhead parish church. These two funeral services were taken by the headmaster, with many of their school friends and teachers present. Describing this sad event, *The Johnian* magazine said:

> We deeply lament the loss of these young lives, and the sympathy of the whole School is felt for the parents who have suffered such a bitter sorrow.

Top: Brass memorial plaque
Bottom: Henry Walton (left) and Sam Thursby (right)

St John's School, Leatherhead and the Great War, 1914-1919

Hugh Penry Whitefoord

Hugh Penry Whitefoord, OTC record of service

PARADES AND ROUTE MARCHES

The OTC began to play a more important part in the life of the School in 1916. The work of the Corps suffered in the early part of the year, first from the weather and then from the influenza epidemic. Both the officers succumbed to the disease and most of the cadets followed suit. But the older boys found themselves giving up still more of their time to military study and practice. The War Office had requested that the OTC officers, Captain LT Driffield and Lieutenant C W Ingram, undertake the preliminary training of pupils who attested under Lord Derby's scheme. These recruits also received instruction from Sergeant Lindsell in the gymnasium three or four evenings a week. Penry Whitefoord remembers that the OTC affected their lives profoundly. He wrote: *'There were at least two parades every week, sometimes in uniform but generally not.'*

Route marches were invariably in uniform and Whitefoord recalls that:

As soon as the 'March at Ease' was ordered the cadets broke into song, singing the usual marching songs such as 'Keep the Home Fires Burning' and 'There's a Long, Long Trail A-Winding' and occasional rude ditties. We carried rifles and felt very military.

A drum and fife band was re-established in 1916 for the first time since the OTC lost all their original equipment in the School fire of 1913. Two drums and eight fifes were purchased initially and, with tuition from assistant music master Mr Hailes, the band developed both in number and quality and was much valued on OTC route marches.

Some boys took their uniforms home and wore them on the journey. They also got themselves photographed in the town with a special pass signed by the headmaster. The miniature range at the end of the Junior Field was well used and boys prized the little red symbol which they put on the sleeve of their uniform jackets denoting 'first class shots'.

Many of the older boys, knowing that they had to be in uniform sooner or later took the examination set by a visiting officer for 400 marks to be credited in their Regular Army exams. They crammed for these exams, studied old exam papers, took copious notes and worked very hard. Those approaching military call-up had themselves inoculated and proudly sported the red ribbons on their punctured arms.

Captain Lancelot Driffield, St John's highly respected OTC Commanding Officer, gave lectures in the Big School classroom to a squad of the Royal Fusiliers officers and non-commissioned officers (NCOs) on the theory and practice of rifle fire. Their presence was clearly felt by the School and was noted in *The Johnian*, December 1914:

Khaki pervades the atmosphere. The UPS battalion of the Royal Fusiliers billeted in the village is using the Big School for lectures, the rifle-range for musketry instruction and the Junior Field for football on Saturday afternoons.

HELPING THE WAR EFFORT

Writing in *The Johnian* in 1936, Arthur Norman Evans, who was School Captain in 1919, remembered his years at St John's throughout the war:

The war will always remain a shadowy period for me, I think because we were kept so busy... We did strange things besides. We cleared a field of potatoes for a hospital. We collected vast quantities of conkers for munitions.

COLLECTING CONKERS

An article appeared in *The Times* for 26 July 1917 headed '*Horse Chestnuts: Nuts required for munitions making*' and, in the autumn of 1917, a notice from the Ministry of Munitions appeared on the walls of classrooms and scout huts across Britain:

Groups of scholars and boy scouts are being organised to collect conkers... This collection is invaluable war work and is very urgent. Please encourage it.

With plenty of horse chestnut trees in the area and in the School grounds, St John's pupils would have had no trouble collecting conkers as they fell. However, there was some secrecy about this activity and at the time boys were not told exactly what they were to be used for.

The conkers were in fact sent by train to secret factories in Dorset and Norfolk, where the plan was to use them as a source of starch for fermentation to produce acetone. Acetone was used as a solvent in the production of cordite, a smokeless propellant used in the manufacture of shells and bullets. It was not a great success as conkers are a poor source of acetone and eventually piles of unused conkers were left to rot at railway stations around the country.

AGRICULTURAL CAMP

To help with the shortage of labour on farms during harvest time, the National Service Department set up special camps in rural areas for boys and masters from public schools. On 14 August 1918, a party of St John's boys and one master went off to an agricultural camp, near Cambridge, for three weeks. While the boys found the work interesting, they grumbled about the shortage of rations in an article for *The Johnian* in October 1918:

The work was varied and not too hard, and very interesting to those who had never done harvest work before. The farmers gave us a warm welcome, and even went so far as to say they were sorry we were going! Had everything been as pleasant at the camp as it was at the farms, the camp would have been in all respects a great success: it was a success from the work point of view but, like many of the other public school camps we were on very short rations, and only the fact that we were in a village where there was a plentiful supply of bread, saved us from having rather an unpleasant time.

BELGIAN REFUGEES

Around 250,000 refugees from Belgium are estimated to have arrived in Britain during the Great War. Some formed communities in purpose-built villages where they had their own shops, schools and churches, prisons and police, all run by the Belgian government. Others were accommodated by local residents and, across the country, local committees were set up to provide funds, clothing, hospitality and accommodation. In Leatherhead, St John's headmaster, the Reverend E A Downes, became Chairman of the local Belgian Refugee Committee. Writing in the Leatherhead Parish Magazine in February 1915 he said:

The Committee feel sure that those who have supported them by their gifts or personal services will be both interested and pleased to learn that their efforts have enabled our town to take its proper share in affording help to the Belgian people to whom every Englishman and Englishwoman owes so much.

Grace Wanklyn, who later taught drawing at St John's (see page 26), was a member of the Belgian Refugee Committee and helped to co-ordinate donations of furniture, linen, carpets, china, cutlery and kitchen utensils to furnish one of the three houses loaned rent free to the refugees. On Saturday 8 December 1916, an afternoon concert given in the School library in aid of the Leatherhead Belgian Refugees' Fund was described as *'a most successful effort both musically and financially'*. The School Oratorio Choir sang Coleridge-Taylor's 'Hiawatha's Wedding Feast' but could not produce a tenor capable of taking the 'Onaway' solo, and this was sung by Mr Samuel Masters, who had previously performed with the New Queen's Hall Orchestra at a Promenade Concert conducted by Henry Wood in 1901.

Around 25,000 wounded Belgian soldiers also came to Britain to convalesce and the Red House Hospital in Leatherhead run by the Red Cross opened in October 1914, initially with 20 beds for wounded soldiers. Some of these men came to watch football matches on the School playing fields and St John's pupils attempted to converse with them using their schoolboy French, with limited success as *The Johnian* magazine for December 1914 describes:

Wounded Belgian soldiers who have recently been watching our football matches, have gone away with the impression that even if the rest of England is not starving, at least the School is. The only conversational French (direct method) with which our modern language scholars could greet them was; Avez-vous du pain? – or was it de la?

SCHOOL LIBRARY

The School library was opened on wet afternoons during the war. Here boys eagerly read the newspapers and popular magazines of the day such as *The Illustrated Sporting News, Punch, Tatler, The Field* and *The Daily Graphic*.

The shelves of the library were filled with books on classical history and literature: Euripides, Livy; Tacitus; Virgil; and Homer, while fiction authors writing tales of heroism, adventure, and valiant deeds in times of trouble were popular with the boys. Books by Thomas Hardy, R M Ballantyne, Rider Haggard; James Fenimore Cooper, H G Wells, Alexandre Dumas and G A Henty were widely read in the years before and during the war.

Copies of *The Johnian* were also available in the School library. The magazine included poems and articles written by pupils, as well as poems, articles and letters from the front, contributed by OJs on active service. The style of writing is heavily influenced by their classical education, and the romantic and heightened language they encountered in the pages of popular fiction.

NEWS FROM THE FRONT

News of old boys on active service was reported in the School magazine and in local papers. However, news of the progress of the war was heavily censored. The Defence of the Realm Act (DORA) passed just four days after the start of hostilities, imposed censorship on the press and on letters sent home from the front. Journalists could not report precise troop movements or any other information which might be of use to the enemy. Within weeks of the start of the war, Lord Kitchener, Secretary of State for War clamped down even more heavily on the press and in the first year of the war, no journalists were allowed to accompany troops to the front line. The newly created Press Bureau censored all reports from the front and the War Propaganda Bureau produced posters, leaflets and booklets to promote the Government's view of the war situation and boost morale.

In November 1914, the *Dorking Advertiser* reported

that 241 OJs were serving in the armed forces, together with a request from the headmaster for information on any others known to have signed up.

The Johnian was published five or six times a year and, throughout the war, featured a Roll of Honour section where details of those killed or wounded on active service were recorded. Copies were kept in the School library, together with daily newspapers, where pupils could read the exploits of OJs in the armed forces and see the growing list of casualties. We don't know if the names of those who died were read out in Chapel by the headmaster, as happened in many schools, but can imagine the shock felt by pupils on learning that recent leavers, whom they remembered so well, had been killed in action.

Copies of *The Johnian* were also sent out to servicemen abroad who were keen to receive news from home and from their old school.

The October 1914 issue of *The Johnian* opens with a poem written by former pupil Kenneth Gill, dated September 1914. Clearly a response to the outbreak of war and a pastiche of the 1890 poem Tommy by Rudyard Kipling with a similar rhyme and metre, Gill calls his poem 'The Grousing Tommy Atkins'.

THE GROUSING TOMMY ATKINS.

There's the tramping, tramping, tramping, all the blessed broiling day,
The slogging, slogging, slogging, all along the dusty way,
There's the grousing, grumbling Tommy that it don't seem right or fair,
'E should 'ave to march fer choking miles without 'is pint o' beer !

There's the distant boom of ' summat ' agrowling on ahead,
The rolling roar of cannons as they hurl their ton o' lead,
There's the grousing, grumbling Tommy—" It's enough to make yer swear—
Another blinking twenty miles, afore yer even near ! "

There's the ' mind-yerself-I'm-snarling ' of the big artillery guns,
The rumble, rumble, rumble right along the line it runs,
There's the grousing, grumbling Tommy, that, tho' it's better now,
'E 'adn't slogged, or bust 'is boots, just to 'ear this bloomin' row !

There's the crackle, crackle, crackle of the rifles on the go,
The crashing, shrieking, shrapnel, just to liven up the show !
There's the grousing, grumbling Tommy aswearin' mighty 'ard,
'Cause 'is shoulder's full o' bullets, and 'is ugly face is scarred.

There's the pinging, pinging, pinging of the little bits o' lead,
There's the wounded, and the dying, all amingled with the dead ;
There's the grousing, grumbling Tommy still afirin' deadly straight,
But 'e's grousing, cursing, swearing, 'cause they've been an' shot 'is mate.

CHAPTER 4
OLD JOHNIANS AT WAR

THE FIRST OLD JOHNIAN CASUALTY

Although Britain officially declared war on 4 August 1914, the Royal Navy had mobilised and sent its ships to sea several days earlier, on 29 July. By the time the Army, in the shape of the British Expeditionary Force (BEF), began its move to France on 9 August the School had already suffered its first loss. Staff Paymaster Joseph Gedge went down with his ship, HMS Amphion, after she struck a mine off the Thames Estuary early on the morning of 6 August. He was the first British officer to die in the war.

On land the BEF was soon in action, first at Mons and then at Le Cateau, as the Allies fell back before the invading German Army. That advance was eventually halted, first at the Battle of the Marne then at the Aisne. As the two opposing armies tried to outflank each other, the fighting moved back north until, between 19 October and 22 November 1914, the BEF found itself in action around the Belgian town of Ypres in the First Battle of Ypres.

Away from what was now being called the Western Front, fighting had also begun in Mesopotamia and in East Africa. A number of OJs, regular soldiers in the Indian Army, were taking part in these engagements.

By the end of the year, a further seven OJs had lost their lives, four in the army and three in the Royal Navy. Two of these, Basil St Merryn Cardew and Bernard Paul Mainprice, were just 19 and had only recently left school.

BOY SOLDIERS

When the war broke out, large numbers of men and boys were keen to sign up. The official age of enlistment in the armed forces was 18, but men had to be 19 to serve abroad. An exception to this was the Territorial Army which accepted recruits from 17 for home service. Recruitment offices across the country had to process thousands of applications in a short space of time and many underage or 'boy' soldiers passed the height and fitness tests and joined up, claiming to meet the minimum age limit which went unchallenged by overworked recruiting officers.

Victor Silvester in uniform, 1914, aged 14yrs 9 months

At least two OJs lied about their age in order to join the Army. Richard Millard, one of the class of 1914, enlisted as soon as war broke out even though he had not yet had his 17th birthday. Wounded at Gallipoli and on the first day of the Battle of the Somme, Richard Millard's story is told in subsequent sections of this book.

Victor Silvester, who in later years found fame as a dance band leader with the BBC, also lied about his age in order to join up. Born in 1900, Victor had been a pupil at St John's for just two years when, in 1913, he ran away (he had run away from his previous school, Ardingly College, after just a few months). His father, the Reverend John Silvester, Vicar of Wembley, promptly sent Victor to the John Lyon School, Harrow, where he stayed for a year, before running away for a third time.

Declaring that he wished to join the army, Victor enlisted in the London Scottish, a battalion of the London Regiment, in November 1914 at just 14 years and nine months by adding four years to his age. Recruitment officers turned a blind eye to his youth and no doubt his father, who elected to serve as an army chaplain in 1914, felt that army discipline would benefit his son.

Richard Millard, August 1914

Staff Paymaster
Joseph Theodore Gedge
HMS Amphion, Royal Navy
Killed in Action 6 August 1914, aged 36
St John's School, 1888-1895

Joseph played football for North House and for the 2nd XI. He excelled in classics and history and, on leaving School in 1895, he immediately joined the Royal Navy as an assistant clerk. He was an exemplary officer and while serving on HMS Brilliant, his commanding officer, Captain Woollcombe, singled Joseph out for particular praise for carrying out his duties with '*zeal, tact and efficiency*'.

On 28 December 1912, Joseph was appointed to HMS Amphion, a new ship undergoing sea trials. Amphion (an Active-class Scout Cruiser) was commissioned on 13 March 1913 and immediately assigned as leader of the 3rd Destroyer Flotilla, operating out of Harwich, defending the eastern approaches to the English Channel. On 29 July 1914, HMS Amphion was ordered to sea. Before they sailed, Joseph wrote a letter to his Uncle Alfred which began:

The news is very serious, and we are going to sea tonight. It may be war. If so there is of course the chance of my being killed.

Joseph enclosed a second letter addressed to his parents and he asked his uncle to pass it on in the event of his death. Despite his obvious concern, Joseph finished his letter with a more positive post script:

I think everything will be settled in a day or two and this will blow over as so many many scares have in the past few years. God grant that it may.

On 5 August, the day after war was declared, Amphion was in action after her flotilla was tipped off by a trawler skipper that another vessel was acting suspiciously. This was the Königin Luise, a former German North Sea ferry converted for mine laying. With Amphion in the lead, the 3rd Destroyer Flotilla set off in pursuit and caught and sank the German ship. Some of the 46 survivors of the 100 crew were picked up by Amphion, who continued with her patrol into the early hours of the next day, 6 August, before turning to head back to Harwich.

At around 6.30 in the morning, Amphion struck a mine. The resulting explosion killed many of her crew instantly and within 15 minutes HMS Amphion had sunk.

This was the Royal Navy's first loss of the war. Around 150 members of her crew were lost. Joseph was the only officer killed and is now recognised as being the first officer casualty of the First World War. For the Gedge family worse was to come as two of Joseph's brothers were also killed during the war.

In his memory, the Royal Navy instigated a 'Gedge Medal' to be awarded to the highest marked Paymaster Sub Lieutenant in each year's exams. At St John's, one of the physics laboratories in the classroom block which opened in 1936 was named 'The Gedge Laboratory' with the full approval of the Royal Navy – indeed they encouraged donations to a fund to help finance the building of the laboratory.

Shortly after the war, Victor went with a cousin to a tea-dance at Harrods. His natural flair on the dance-floor was noticed and he was offered a job partnering ladies at tea-dances. In return he would receive training and a small wage. He accepted the offer and became World Ballroom Dancing Champion in 1922, with his partner Phyllis Clarke, just three years after beginning his dance career. He went on to open a dance academy in London and in 1935 formed his own orchestra.

Victor Silvester wrote highly successful books on ballroom dancing and was responsible for bringing dancing into the mainstream media, initially through hosting the BBC radio show, *Dancing Club* in 1941. Then, in 1948, he moved into television with *Television Dancing Club* which ran for 17 years and was the forerunner of *Come Dancing* and ultimately *Strictly Come Dancing*.

Victor died in 1978, but his orchestra continued under the direction of his son, Victor Silvester Junior, until the 1990s.

Victor Silvester with his first exhibition partner, Vera Clarke (sister of Phyllis)

I desire to claim my son Victor Marlborough Silvester 3717. Although he is such a big powerful fellow, as the birth certificate will reveal, he is not 16 years of age until the 25th next.

He went on to request that Victor be '*transferred to the 104th Battalion for home service or any other capacity in which he can best serve his country*'. Two days later the Reverend Silvester received a reply from the Officer in charge of the Territorial Force Records, to say that the discharge of his son had been put in hand. Victor was formally discharged on 26 February 1916 in consequence of, '*Having made a misstatement as to age on enlistment*'.

Frustrated by the lack of real action and keen to distance himself from the protective arm of his father, Victor then applied to join the Argyll and Sutherland Highlanders. He attested in London on 4 September 1916 and joined them at Stirling Castle on 6 September. Victor was sixteen and a half years old, still too young to serve abroad, but this time he gave his age as 20, presumably thinking that this would allow him to be sent to the front.

Silvester's subsequent war service is unclear as official records indicate that he was discharged

With the popular view held that the war would be 'over by Christmas', and the general agreement that recruits would not be sent to the front line before they were 19, it must have seemed to John Silvester that his son was in little danger.

Victor was posted to Dorking and spent the next two years mainly on training manoeuvres on the North Downs. By 1916 John Silvester clearly had concerns that his son was at risk of being sent overseas and, on 12 February 1916, he wrote to Lieutenant Colonel Dunmore at Sutton Veny, Wiltshire, where the London Scottish were then based. He enclosed a copy of Victor's birth certificate and wrote:

from the Argyll and Sutherland Highlanders on 12 September and British Red Cross personnel records show that he served as an orderly with the Red Cross from 30 September 1916 until 30 June 1919. The Medal Roll Index listing individuals entitled to the Victory Medal and/or British War Medal records his qualifying period of service on the Western Front (France and Belgium) as 1 October 1916 to 30 June 1917.

Despite the conflicting evidence, Victor claims in his autobiography *Dancing is my Life* (Silvester 1958), that his plan worked and that after seven months' intensive training with the Argylls, he was finally drafted to France in 1917. He recalls that he went with his platoon up into the front line near Arras and, as they were moving along the communication trenches, a shell burst in front of them and one his colleagues was killed:

He was the first man I ever saw killed, with both his legs blown off and the whole of his face and body peppered with shrapnel. The sight turned my stomach. I was sick and terrified, but even more frightened of showing it.

Victor writes that his time in France was short-lived as word got out that he was under-age. He was sent back to Etaples on the coast near Boulogne and given a series of mundane duties. After two weeks he was transferred to the 1st British Ambulance Unit in Italy. Here, Victor experienced further traumatic events, but his courage was recognised by the Italian Government and in 1917 he was awarded the Italian Bronze Medal for Military Valour. While on home leave in February 1918, after being wounded in the leg by flying shrapnel, Victor reached his 18th birthday. He saw this as an opportunity to re-join the Argyll and Sutherland Highlanders; this time he did not have to lie about his age. He was sent with the third battalion to Kinsale in southern Ireland where there was some unrest after the Easter Rebellion.

LETTERS HOME

During the war, letter writing was the main form of communication between servicemen and their families. Many letters received from OJs fighting overseas or describing life in the trenches and at sea were published in *The Johnian*. They provide a fascinating source of information about life on the front line despite the censorship which limited what they could say.

Edward Kelly found himself censoring letters shortly after he arrived in France in 1915 and wrote that they were '*far better than books for insight into human nature. Here humour and pathos, comedy and tragedy mixed.*'

The sense of service, duty and obligation to set a good example to 'their men' instilled into young officers through their schooling and early training in the OTC is apparent in many of these letters. Just occasionally we perceive how horrifying their experiences must have been, as seen in this extract from a letter written by Edward Kelly five days before he was killed in 1915:

I had my platoon-serjeant killed on Tuesday morning; it was my first case and I can't say I felt very cheery about it. The sight of death is all right, but it was the hour between the time he was hit and the time he died that was rather trying.

James Newton Soden, who played 1st XI football with Edward Kelly in 1914, left St John's at the end of the Easter Term, 1915 and joined the Indian Army. The following September he wrote to his old school from the Cadet College, Quetta, India, describing his newly acquired skill in riding:

We are doing a most interesting course of riding, now that we have got over the first few preliminary lessons in the school. We usually go for cross-country rides which, owing to the roughness of the country are pretty exciting. All the way there are nullahs and streams and hills which prevent it from becoming monotonous, and when we come to a fairly flat stretch of ground we generally have a cavalry charge when we go as fast as we can, only just holding our horses in enough to keep them under control.

1st XI football, 1914 with James Soden standing far left

James also commented on the difficulties of playing football in Quetta which is over 5,000 feet above sea level compared with Leatherhead which is just 134 feet above sea level:

> I used to think a match at St John's was one of the most tiring things possible, but I had only to play one game out here to find out my mistake. I thanked my stars I was playing back because before the end of the game you get absolutely tired out. Owing to the air being rarer here it is much more difficult to keep your wind, and you have to add to that a temperature of 80 degrees. If only we could play at night it would be all right because it is jolly cold then, but it gets dark after 8 o'clock, so we have to start about 6.30. At the end of the game you feel like drinking up a river.

Other more personal letters to family and loved ones were not published in *The Johnian* but were kept and treasured by the families concerned. Just over two months before he died, Arthur Starr Jukes wrote to his wife, Annie, and their three children, to say that he had had enough of the war and wished he was at home with them all:

> 29 December 1916
> My darling ones
> I have been all day censoring letters again & I have just been warned to go to the front in the desert in the morning leaving here at 8am, so that I shall not be able to write tomorrow. I expect to arrive about breakfast the following day. It is somewhere near Suez I think. I am enclosing some views of Alex. I don't know if they will get through, but I have censored them myself so I ought to be lucky. I shall be glad to be settled. I wish I was at home with you all. I have had quite enough of this. I don't seem to keep well somehow. Well darling, I send you all my love and kisses. Kiss the children from me & tell Dick to kiss Mum each night & morning for Dad. God bless & keep you all in the loving prayers of
>
> Your loving husband & Dad
> Arthur
>
> A S Jukes. 2Lt.1/10 Lon Reg, Expeditionary Force, Egypt

Arthur Starr Jukes with wife Annie and their three children, Richard (Dick), Olive and Muriel

The Reverend Arthur Starr Jukes
2nd Lieutenant, 10th Battalion, London Regiment
Died 6 March 1917, aged 46
St John's School, 1881-1883

Arthur Starr Jukes, the son of the Reverend Richard Starr Jukes and Mary Bate, was born 18 December 1871 and baptised on 24 March 1875 together with his brothers Harry and Harold and sister Ada at All Saints Church in Dewsbury, Yorkshire.

Little is known of the two years spent at St John's but it seems that his school days were not entirely happy. The register shows he entered the School on 21 December 1880 and left on 23 February 1883 and the original handwritten register notes that he: '*Ran away from School (third time)*'.

Arthur enlisted with the King's Own Scottish Borderers on 27 May 1892 and was transferred to the 8th Hussars as a Private on 11 July 1892. He transferred again on 1 February 1893 to the Royal Fusiliers and was appointed Lance Corporal in March that year. In 1898, he was discharged at his own request on payment of £18 and returned from India to train as a missionary at the Church Missionary Society Training College in Islington.

On 17 June 1900, Arthur (aged 28) married Annie Florence Norris (aged 25) in Gravesend. After being ordained by the Bishop of London for service in the Colonies in 1901, he spent time as a missionary in India from 1901 to 1904. He also served in Ontario and Fife, Scotland and visited Puerto Rico.

When war broke out in 1914, Arthur and his family were living in Northampton where he was Curate of St Giles Church. Arthur immediately volunteered and was gazetted Temporary Chaplain to the Forces (4th Class) on 29 September 1914. However, a year later, on 19 November 1915 he joined the London Regiment as 2nd lieutenant. It is not clear why he made this change, but by the end of 1915, the War Office was struggling to recruit volunteers for active service and it may be that with his previous experience and training he was persuaded to take a more active part in the war.

Arthur died of enteric fever at the Government Hospital in Suez on 6 March 1917 aged 46 and is buried at Suez War Memorial Cemetery, Egypt.

Above: Original grave marker
Left: CWGC memorial headstone

St John's School, Leatherhead and the Great War, 1914-1919

J C R Godwin in Royal Naval Volunteer Reserve uniform, while serving as a Marconi Radio Officer on Merchant Navy ships, 1909-1911

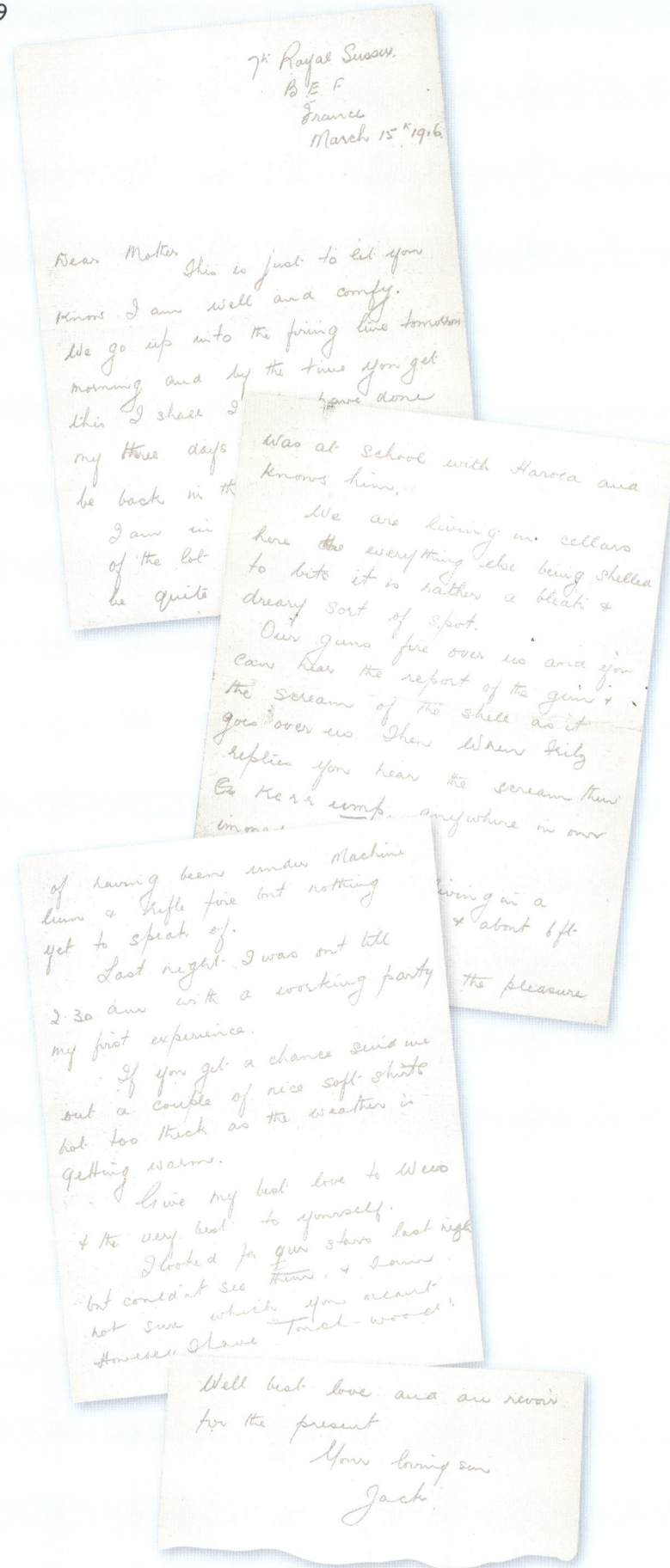

Godwin's letter to his mother, March 1916

John Charles Raymond Godwin (known as Jack to his family and friends) wrote a reassuring letter to his mother from France in March 1916, saying '*This is just to let you know I am well and comfy*' and continued:

We go up into the firing line tomorrow morning and by the time you get this I shall I hope have done my three days in the fire line and be back in the support trenches. I am in the best company and will I hope be quite happy.

But on the next page he reveals some of the hardship they are experiencing:

We are living in cellars here everything else being shelled to bits, it is rather a bleak and dreary sort of spot… Four of us are living in a cellar about 10 by 5 and about 6ft in the middle.

He goes on to describe how they can hear gunfire – the report of their guns and the scream of the shell as it goes over them:

Then when Fritz replies you hear the scream then kerrump anywhere in our immediate vicinity

The letter ends on a more domestic note with a request for shirts;

If you get a chance send me a couple of nice soft white shirts not too thick as the weather is getting warm…

*Well best love and au revoir for the present
Your loving son Jack*

Godwin later sent three field postcards to his mother in April 1916, but this was the last handwritten letter Mrs Godwin received from her son before he was declared missing (and later presumed dead) during the Battle of the Somme on 7 July 1916.

FIELD POSTCARDS AND HONOUR ENVELOPES

Letters from serving soldiers were vital in boosting morale during the war, but everything they wrote was subject to censorship, to prevent the enemy from discovering crucial information and to stop bad news about the progress of the war from reaching home.

The Army introduced various alternative methods of censorship. One of these was the field postcard. These pre-printed cards listed multiple choice options which could be crossed out if not relevant. No messages could be written on them, but they did provide a means of sending basic information to those at home or as confirmation of receipt of letters, telegrams or parcels.

Pictured above is one of the field postcards which 'Jack' Godwin sent home to his mother.

The honour envelope put the onus on the sender to sign a declaration to say that the contents referred to nothing but private and family matters. The letters could be checked by postal workers at home but would not need to be read by senior officers. The letter in the green honour envelope shown below was sent by Clement Barrington Furmston to his mother in 1916.

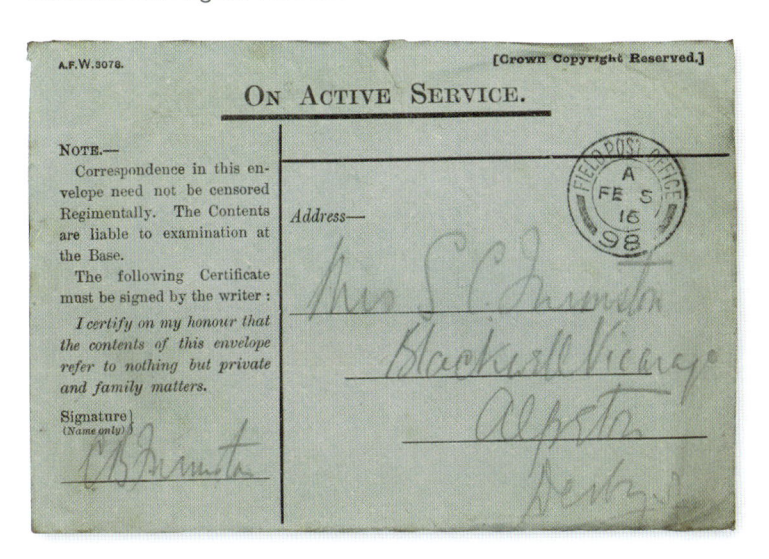

FOR CONSPICUOUS BRAVERY – VCS OF THE FIRST WORLD WAR

Early in 1915 came news of the first VC awarded to an OJ, Geoffrey Harold Woolley, a second lieutenant in the Queen Victoria's Rifles. He was also the first Territorial Army officer to receive the Victoria Cross.

Hill 60, a strategic location about three miles south of Ypres, is not a natural hill but one of several spoil heaps in the area formed when the nearby railway cutting was built. The higher ground gave an unimpeded view over the surrounding countryside and was the scene of almost continual fighting during the course of the war.

On 17 April 1915, mines were detonated under the German lines on the Hill and the resulting craters occupied by British troops who held their ground over the next few days in the face of numerous German counter attacks and artillery barrages; it was for his part in this defence that Woolley won his VC.

His citation published in the *London Gazette* on 22 May 1915, reads:

For most conspicuous bravery on 'Hill 60' during the night of 20–21 April 1915. Although the only officer on the hill at the time, and with very few men, he successfully resisted all attacks to his trench and continued throwing bombs and encouraging his men till relieved. His trench during all the time was being heavily shelled and bombed and was subjected to heavy machine-gun fire by the enemy.

Woolley was affected by gas on 21 April 1915 and was sent to the No 2 Red Cross Hospital at Rouen before being evacuated to Osborne House on the Isle of Wight. He was appointed Acting Captain on 27 April and during his convalescence Woolley helped train the Cambridge University OTC.

In June 1915, while still on home leave, Woolley visited St John's and the boys were granted a half day holiday in honour of his VC. An account of his action, and a comment by Woolley himself, was published in the June issue of *The Johnian*:

Woolley, who was at St John's from 1902 to 1911, is the first Johnian and the first Territorial officer to win this honour. The Queen Victoria's Rifles reached Havre on November 5th and soon after they were at the front near Ypres, where they have been ever since, engaged chiefly in trench work. On the first day that Woolley went into the trenches he picked up a hand-grenade that was thrown in, and before the fuse had burned to the charge, threw it out and so saved not only his own life but that of six or seven men besides.

Woolley writes:

By the way I nearly did lose my head on '60'. A hand grenade fell on my head and the concussion persuaded it to explode. By some miracle it exploded upwards and tore out the top of my cap without touching my head. I picked up my cap and felt my head to see if it was there, found it was, so had perforce to stay too!

Woolley returned to St John's the following year, 1916, and on Thursday 1 June went out with the Corps and worked out an Outpost scheme with them. That evening Captain Woolley gave a talk to the cadets on the second Battle of Ypres, in which he won his VC. Aged just 23, Woolley's visits made a deep and lasting impression on the boys – many of whom would have been juniors during his final years at the School.

Woolley's VC citation in The Johnian, June 1915

2nd Lieutenant
Geoffrey Harold Woolley
1/9 (County of London) Battalion, London Regiment (Queen Victoria's Rifles)
St John's School, 1901-1911

Victoria Cross 1915

Born in Bethnal Green on 14th May 1892, Geoffrey Harold Woolley was one of eleven children of the Reverend George Herbert Woolley, the curate of St Matthew's, Upper Clapton, in London, and his wife Sarah. His older brother, the archaeologist Sir Charles Leonard Woolley attended St John's from 1891-1899.

A member of East House, Woolley played fives, was a member of the cross-country team, and was awarded School colours for 2nd XI cricket in 1910. He gained an exhibition to Queen's College, Oxford and was there studying theology, with a view to becoming ordained, when war broke out in 1914. He promptly obtained a commission in the Queen Victoria's Rifles and arrived on the Western Front in 1915. Woolley was awarded the VC for his actions at Hill 60 and subsequently promoted to Acting Captain. In 1916, he returned to the Western Front and served on the staff of Third Army headquarters. Twice mentioned in dispatches, Woolley was awarded a Military Cross in the King's Birthday Honours of 1919.

After the war, Harold Woolley resumed his studies at Oxford and was ordained in 1920. He taught at Rugby for three years, was vicar of Monk Sherborne from 1923 to 1927 and from 1927 until the outbreak of the Second World War was School Chaplain at Harrow.

Woolley served as a chaplain to the Forces in the Second World War and later held the livings of Harrow and West Grinstead, Sussex. When he retired, he went to live in West Chiltington, Sussex in the parish of another OJ, the Reverend R M Jones (1917-1924) who wrote:

Hal Woolley was an 'Old Boy' of my own school, St John's, Leatherhead. When I arrived there as a ten year-old New Boy, he had just recently been awarded the Victoria Cross for extreme gallantry, and one of the first things that I learnt was the story of his amazing courage on that lethal mound known as Hill 60.

He naturally became the object of our boyhood hero-worship. Also, like the rest of us, he was a parson's son, and parsons' children have a mysterious bond of fellowship and pride in each other's achievements.

To us, Hal Woolley was the latest of our long line of heroes, in the tradition of the great Admiral Lord Nelson.

Geoffrey Harold Woolley died in 1969, aged 76 and is buried in St Mary's churchyard, West Chiltington, Sussex.

Later in 1915, the School celebrated the award of a second VC to an OJ when the news of Eric Gascoigne Robinson's decoration was received.

The action for which he was granted a VC had taken place in February 1915, two months before Woolley's heroic defence of Hill 60. However, it was not cited in the *London Gazette* until 16 August 1915. Robinson was awarded the Victoria Cross in recognition of his services in the Dardanelles and the citation reads:

Admiralty, 16 August 1915.
The following awards have been made in recognition of services during the operations in the vicinity of the Dardanelles prior to 25-26 April:

The KING has been graciously pleased to approve of the grant of the Victoria Cross to Lieutenant-Commander (now Commander) Eric Gascoigne Robinson, R.N., for the conspicuous act of bravery specified below.

Lieutenant Commander Robinson on 26 February advanced alone, under heavy fire, into an enemy's gun position, which might well have been occupied and destroying a four-inch gun, returned to his party for another charge with which the second gun was destroyed. Lieutenant Commander Robinson would not allow members of his demolition party to accompany him as their white uniforms rendered them very conspicuous. Lieutenant Commander Robinson took part in four attacks on the minefields – always under heavy fire.

Lieutenant Commander Eric Gascoigne Robinson
Royal Navy
St John's School, 1894-1896

Victoria Cross 1915

Eric Gascoigne Robinson was born in 1882 at Greenwich, the son of the Reverend John Lovell Robinson and Louisa Aveline Gascoigne. John was chaplain of the Royal Naval College at Greenwich.

Robinson left St John's in 1896 and went to the Limes, Greenwich. In 1897 at the age of 15 he joined HMS Britannia, the Royal Navy's officer training ship. He took part in the Boxer Rebellion in China between 1899 and 1901 and in 1910 was promoted to Lieutenant Commander. When war broke out in 1914 he was sent to the Mediterranean on board the battleship HMS Vengeance.

In 1915, Robinson led a commando force of sailors and Royal Marines tasked with destroying the Turkish gun battery at Orkanieh in the Dardanelles. On the morning of 26 February, his force destroyed two small artillery pieces but were cut off by Turkish snipers while on their way to the main battery. Taking the decision to protect his men who, with their white naval uniforms, were an easy target for snipers, Robinson climbed up to the main battery alone and laid fuses which destroyed the large main gun.

Robinson was immediately recommended for a VC by Admiral de Robeck who had observed his actions from HMS Queen Elizabeth just offshore.

Two months later, Robinson was promoted to Commander for his part in another dangerous mission and his citation in the *London Gazette* for 23 April 1915 reads:

OLD JOHNIANS AT WAR

Lieutenant-Commander Eric Gascoigne Robinson has been specially promoted to the rank of Commander in His Majesty's Fleet in recognition of the distinguished service rendered by him on the night of the 18 April 1915, as Commanding Officer of the force which torpedoed and rendered useless Submarine E15, thus preventing that vessel from falling into the enemy's hands in a serviceable condition.

Dated 20 April 1915.

Robinson retired as a Rear Admiral in 1933 but re-entered the service in 1939 and commanded convoys across the Atlantic before retiring again in 1942.

During his long career he received many other awards, was twice mentioned in dispatches and was given an OBE in 1919.

Eric Robinson married Edith Gladys Cordeaux in 1913 and they had three children, two sons and one daughter. His wife died in 1938 and both his sons were killed in the Second World War.

Robinson died at Haslar Naval Hospital, Gosport, Hampshire on 20 August 1965 and was buried in St John's churchyard, Langrish in an unmarked grave.

Thirty-three years later, the grave was traced and, on 20 August 1998 a ceremony was held at St John's church to dedicate a memorial grave stone.

Eric Gascoigne Robinson in RN Commander uniform

St John's School, Leatherhead and the Great War, 1914-1919

GOING OVER THE TOP

Allied troops (British, French, Australian and New Zealand) landed on the Gallipoli Peninsular on 25 April 1915. Initial planning had called for land forces to be used only in support of a naval breakthrough of the Dardanelles Straits but the Royal Navy's attempt to bombard the Turkish guns and forts along the coast and force their way through the heavily mined waters had failed and there was now a requirement on the infantry to disable the guns from the land.

Twenty-eight OJs are known to have served at Gallipoli and of these eight were killed in action. A further 13 were wounded, three of whom later died as a result of their injuries. Others were killed in subsequent battles and only 12 survived the Great War. Lieutenant Stanley Squire took part in the landings at Suvla Bay, and was killed in action on 9 August 1915, at Chunuk Bair, while in charge of the machine gun section. He was 22 years old.

Oswald Whaley, 1915

The following day, Tuesday 10 August 1915, Second Lieutenant Oswald Whaley, aged 25, was killed while serving with the Hampshire Regiment. His battalion suffered heavy casualties at Chunuk Bair when their positions were overrun by the Turkish defenders. It proved impossible to recover the bodies of the vast majority of those killed. Today, Oswald is remembered on the Helles Memorial, alongside Stanley Squire and the names of some 21,000 other men lost in the Gallipoli campaign who have no known grave.

Lieutenant Stanley Charles Squire
7th Battalion, Gloucestershire Regiment
Killed in Action 9 August 1915, aged 22
St John's School, 1903-1912

Born 26 June 1893 at Langrove Vicarage, near Ross, Hereford, Stanley Charles Squire was the son of the Reverend Charles Edward Squire, Rector of Southrop, Gloucestershire.

Stanley played football and cricket for the School and was awarded colours for both sports. He was made a prefect in 1911 and left St John's in 1912 with an Open Natural Science Scholarship at Corpus Christi College, Oxford. At Oxford he studied chemistry, mechanics, and physics and was Secretary of his College Association Football Club.

Stanley was commissioned as a 2nd Lieutenant into the Gloucestershire Regiment on 26 August 1914 and posted to the 7th Battalion.

Promoted to Lieutenant on 27 January 1915, he sailed on 19 June for Gallipoli, landing at Cape Helles on 11 July. The battalion remained here until the end of the month then returned to the British base on the island of Lemnos. On 3 August they landed back on Gallipoli, at Anzac Cove, to support the proposed August offensive. Stanley was killed in action on 9 August 1915, at Chunuk Bair, while in charge of a machine gun section.

He has no known grave and is commemorated on the Helles Memorial.

Richard Millard was wounded at Gallipoli. He was just 17 when he obtained his commission with the Border Regiment in September 1914 and shortly after Christmas heard that he was to go abroad. He got his final orders in April 1915 and in May he sent a telegram to his brother, Spencer Millard, at St John's:

To Millard Senior
St John's Leatherhead Surrey

Am ordered to the Dardanelles
I am going on Friday
Goodbye to you and Johns.

Give my love to the Head
Dick

One of the letters Richard wrote home from Gallipoli, dated 29 May 1915, was published in *The Johnian* and here he recounts the events of his first week:

At present we are in the reserve trenches and expect to go up to the fire-trenches any day, or rather any night. I am in command of a platoon and have been made reserve machine gun officer, so with the two jobs I get plenty of work to do. My platoon is an excellent lot and nearly all regulars, and my platoon-serjeant has won the DCM.

I have a top-hole little dug-out. We start with platoon-drill every morning at 5.30 and the rest of the day is spent in making roads and communication trenches and in burying the dead. We have shells flying over us all day, but the casualties are very few. The first day I was ducking every minute, but now I am more used to them.

In 1984, Richard Millard spoke about his experiences in Gallipoli in an interview for the Imperial War Museum Oral History Project 'Voices of the First World War'. He said that he had felt excited to be going to the Dardanelles, but the terrain meant that they were in constant danger from Turkish snipers:

It was a perpetual battle going on all the time. It was rifles, they were mostly snipers, it wasn't a set battle like all the guns and all the airplanes and the bombs and this and that going off like, say, the Battle of the Somme. It was quite a different thing altogether. And the Turks were well placed on Achi Baba and they were in a commanding position. Here we were. And they sniped us all night, you never knew quite where they were getting, they crept round and that was the sort of thing.

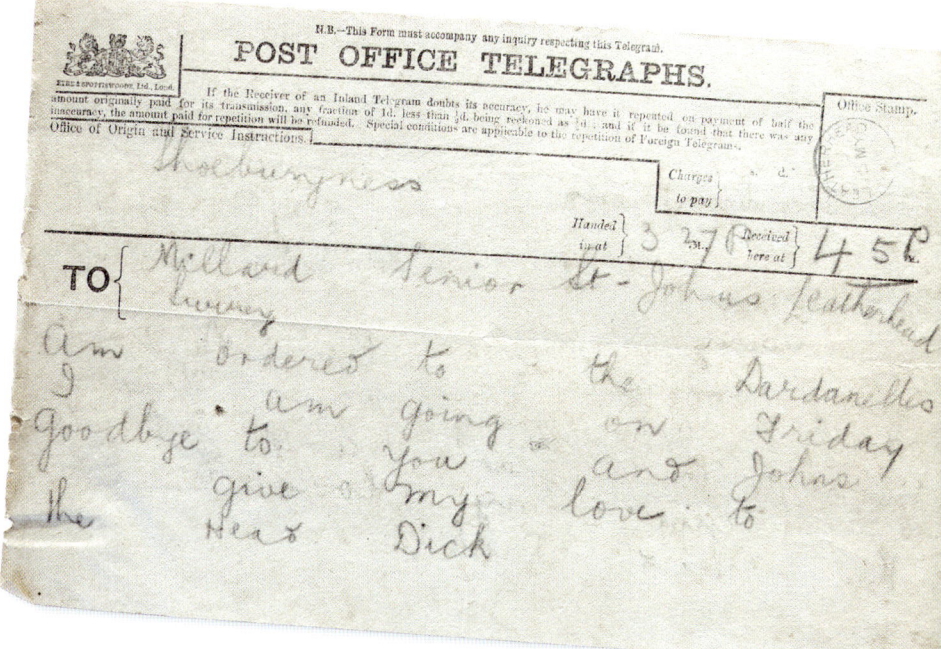

Richard Millard's time at Gallipoli was cut short when he was badly wounded by sniper fire. He described how it happened:

I got into a hole… a bit of a trench… and they were sniping at us. Like a silly cuckoo I thought I'd better see where they were. So, I got up with my glasses and before I knew where I was, I had a shot through the shoulder.

Richard was taken to hospital, first in Alexandria and then to The Blue Sisters Hospital in Malta where he discovered that he had had a lucky escape:

I was told afterwards in hospital that the bullet went clean through my shoulder. It went under the collar bone and over the lung, which I am told is a very remarkable thing because if it had touched the lung, I should probably have bled to death immediately.

Richard Frederick Millard
Captain, Border Regiment
attached Royal Air Force
St John's School, 1911-1914

R F Millard, Nottingham, 1935

Born on 11 August 1897, Richard Millard was the eldest of three sons of the Reverend Frederick Luke Holland Millard, vicar of St Aiden's Church, Carlisle and his wife, Marjorie Josephine Millard. Richard and his youngest brother, Patrick Ferguson Millard came to St John's in September 1911, joining Spencer Harold Millard, who had been admitted as a Foundationer in January that year. Richard and Patrick were Supplementary Foundationers, and all three boys were members of North House.

Richard and Spencer played football for North House and the 2nd XI team during their time at the School and both boys were awarded Senior House colours and 2nd XI football colours. Spencer also won an engraved tankard for athletics in 1911, coming 2nd in the 220 yards handicap race.

Leaving at the end of the Summer Term, 1914, Richard immediately signed up. He had training at Hythe, Chatham and Shoeburyness, where he was placed in charge of the machine gun section. Richard was commissioned as a 2nd Lieutenant in the Border Regiment in September 1914, with effect from 15 August 1914, making him among the first batch of men to be commissioned into the Special Reserve of Officers after war was declared. Ordered to the Dardanelles in May 1915 with the 1st Battalion, Border Regiment, and still only seventeen years old, he was the youngest officer in the regiment.

In a letter to his family, written shortly before he was wounded in Gallipoli on 25 June, 1915, during the attempt to take Achi Baba, Richard expressed his thanks for several letters and newspapers which he had just received by post, saying: *'You have no idea how much a mail bucks one up out here'* and adding:

Please when you send anything out here, send something in the way of edibles. Shortbread is excellent stuff in the heat.

Wounded for a second time on 1 July 1916 (see page 58), Richard was sent back to England to recuperate. During 1917 he served in Salonika, was seconded to the RFC on 26 September 1917 and, on 1 April 1918, was given a temporary commission in the newly formed RAF, where he served as an observer.

After the war Richard had hoped to resume his education and take up a place at university, but his father was unable to afford it. With no qualifications to his name, he was fortunate to be offered employment with a firm of brokers on the Liverpool Cotton Market. In the 1920s, he started working with boys' clubs, including Shrewsbury House, a boys' club in one of the worst slum districts of Liverpool. By 1930 he was secretary of the National Association of Boys' Clubs and was offered the challenging post of warden of the Dakeyne Street Boys' Club in Nottingham, an educational and institutional centre for boys.

Richard was a successful fund raiser and, during the Second World War, was involved in charity work with organisations such as the Aid to Russia Fund and the Air Raid Distress Fund. He also served with a Home Guard unit in South London.

Spencer Millard left St John's in 1916 and was killed in a flying accident in October 1918 (see pages 86-87). Patrick Millard excelled at art and, after leaving school in 1917, studied painting at the Royal Academy, winning a Royal Academy Gold Medal and Travelling Scholarship for painting in 1924, which enabled him to travel all over Europe. Back in England, he taught painting and drawing before becoming joint principal of the St John's Wood Art School in 1933. Later, he became art master at Oundle and was Head of Painting at Goldsmith's college until his retirement in 1967. Patrick died in 1972.

Richard Millard always regretted his lack of further education and qualifications and was determined that his own son and daughter should receive an excellent education and be encouraged to go on to university, recognising the importance of education for girls as well as boys, at a time when relatively few girls went to university. He died in 1987 just days before his 90th birthday.

Temporary Commission issued to R F Millard for service with Royal Air Force, 1918

R F Millard medals
L-R: 1914-15 Star
British War Medal, 1914-20;
Victory Medal, 1914-1918;
Defence Medal, 1939-45

L-R: S H Millard; F L H Millard; P F Millard; M J Millard

THE BLACKEST DAY

On 1 July 1916, six OJs died fighting for their country. The Battle of the Somme, which began that day, was a joint British and French operation that continued through to November 1916. It is chiefly remembered for the heavy casualties suffered by the British Army on the first day of fighting. With more than 57,000 casualties, of which just over 19,000 were killed, it was the worst single day for the British Army in the entire war. It was also the blackest day for the School and, as the fighting continued into November, another seventeen OJs fell on the Somme battlefields.

The initial British attack was launched along a fifteen-mile front, from Montauban in the south to Serre in the north, with a further attack a mile or so further north, at Gommecourt. Old Johnians fought, died or were wounded along the whole length of the front. Richard Millard, having returned to the Border Regiment after recovering from his wounds at Gallipoli, was now in France with the 2nd Battalion, who received their operational orders on 26 June 1916.

The Border's task on 1 July 1916 was to attack and capture the village of Mametz and in this they were successful but, having led his Company over the top, Richard was wounded once again. Undaunted, as the Battalion war diary for 1 July 1916 records, he continued to direct his men:

Lieutenant Millard, who though badly wounded in the arm, continued his duties and gave his orders clearly and coolly.

Richard wrote a hurried note home to his family to let them know that he was safe:

1.7.16
My Dearest People

You will be interested to hear that I am slightly wounded. A piece of German shell cut my left arm just above the elbow. It is only flesh. I am fast on the way home. You will be glad to hear that I was in command of a company and took it over the top, absolutely victoriously to its objective – Am very tired.

Don't worry
Richd FM

A telegram was sent by the War Office Secretary to his father, the Reverend F L H Millard at St Aiden's Vicarage, Carlisle, which read:

Beg to inform you Lt R F Millard Border Regt admitted 2 Red Cross Hospital Rouen 2 July suffering gunshot wound arm slight further news sent when received.

Two of Richard Millard's contemporaries at St John's were not so lucky. Second Lieutenant Charles Fouracres Greenlees was a couple of years older than Richard and a School Prefect when he left St John's in the summer of 1914. He was attached to the 1st Battalion of the Royal Dublin Fusiliers who, on 1 July 1916, were part of the second wave of an attack towards the village of Beaumont Hamel. Hampered by the failure of the first wave to make much, if any, headway they suffered heavy casualties and Charles was one of those killed in action. A letter to Charles' father from the Brigade commander said:

We lost very heavily in our attack on the 1st July, and many fine officers fell; of these I miss your boy more than any. He was so quick, straightforward and intelligent that I had him marked down for advancement at the first opportunity.

He died leading his men in an attack on what proved to be an impregnable position; he exposed himself absolutely recklessly, as officers have to, and died a splendid death.

Richard Millard would also have known William Haldane Round (known as Hal to his family and friends), who was School Captain and Captain of North House, to which Richard belonged. William left in 1913 and went up to Downing College, Cambridge but gave up his studies on the outbreak of war and received a commission into the 7th (Robin Hood) Battalion, Sherwood Foresters (Nottinghamshire and Derbyshire Regiment).

On 1 July 1916, William, by now a temporary Captain, led his company into action as part of the attack on Gommecourt, but had barely stepped on to the parapet before he was killed by a shell. The Battalion history ('The Robin Hoods' 1921, p.204) notes:

Another very serious loss was sustained by the Battalion… No Officer in the Robin Hoods was more loved than he, and those who had the honour of serving under him… will remember with gratitude, the kindly interest he took in each member of the Company, their happiness and welfare being ever in his thoughts.

Over the next few months, other OJs who were at School with Richard Millard were killed on the Somme including two members of the 2nd XI cricket team in which he played: Charles Lewarne Teape and Cyril Vincent Noel Puckridge.

Richard's son, John Millard, recalled in 2014 that his father was deeply affected by his experiences during the Battle of the Somme. He never spoke of it to his family but always remembered the anniversary of that first day, 1 July 1916.

2nd XI 1914.
Back row: L-R, C F Mermagen; J N Soden; S B Good; H R Lachlan; A N Evans; J L Fairclough.
Middle row: L-R, C L Teape; C V N Puckridge; J W Hampton;
Sitting on ground: L-R, R F Millard; A W Whitehead.

OLD JOHNIANS KILLED IN ACTION ON THE FIRST DAY OF THE BATTLE OF THE SOMME, 1 JULY 1916

Private Arthur Frederick Clarke
12th Battalion, York and Lancaster Regiment
Killed in Action 1 July 1916, aged 21
St John's School, 1905-1911

Arthur was studying at Sheffield University when war broke out and along with many of his fellow students, he joined the Sheffield City Battalion: the 12th (Service) Battalion York & Lancaster Regiment.

On 1 July 1916, the battalion was part of an unsuccessful attack on the village of Serre. At 7.30am, Zero Hour, the British bombardment lifted from the German front line; this was the signal to the men laying out in no man's land to rise to their feet and move steadily forward. They did so into a hail of machine gun and rifle fire and immediately began to suffer casualties.

Confusion surrounds the fate of many from this point on and Arthur is no exception. He may have been one of those killed in the first few minutes of the assault, he may have been one of the few who made it as far as the German wire, only to find that it was mostly intact, or he may have died from wounds in no man's land – one source (de Ruvigny) states that he was reported as *'wounded and missing'* implying that he was seen to be hit. His body was never identified and today his name is engraved on the walls of the Thiepval Memorial.

2nd Lieutenant Charles Fouracres Greenlees
9th Battalion, The Queen's (Royal West Surrey Regiment) attached 1st Battalion, Royal Dublin Fusiliers
Killed in Action 1 July 1916, aged 21
St John's School, 1904-1914

Charles Fouracres Greenlees was a School Prefect, secretary of the Protestant Club (the School debating society), a member of the Literary Society and a member of the OTC. He took up a place at University College, Oxford in September 1914, but by November he had deferred his studies and obtained a commission in the infantry, training at first with the 9th Queens (Royal West Surrey) Regiment.

Eventually posted to the 1st Battalion of the Royal Dublin Fusiliers, Charles arrived on the Somme front in March 1916 (via Gallipoli and Egypt). On 1 July they were in the second wave of the attack towards Beaumont Hamel but, hampered by the failure of the first wave to make much, if any, headway they suffered heavy casualties and Charles was one of four officers killed. He lies today in Auchonvillers Military Cemetery.

Lieutenant Henry Stewart Jackson

8th Battalion, King's Own Yorkshire Light Infantry
Killed in Action 1 July 1916, aged 20
St John's School, 1905-1907

Henry Jackson came to St John's shortly after his tenth birthday and spent two years at the School before moving on to Whitgift Grammar School in Croydon and then, in 1913, to the London Hospital Medical College. Originally volunteering to work with the Red Cross in France at the start of the war, Henry later gained a commission in the King's Own Yorkshire Light Infantry (KOYLI), joining the 8th Battalion just a few days before the Somme offensive was launched. On 1 July, the Battalion's objectives were the German trenches north of the village of Ovillers. They failed to hold any ground taken and suffered devastating losses, with every combatant officer becoming a casualty. Henry was one of those killed, but his body was never identified and today he is named on the Thiepval Memorial.

Corporal Frederick Thomas Croydon Payton

5th Battalion, (Special Brigade), Royal Engineers
Killed in Action 1 July 1916, aged 20
St John's School, 1906-1912

Frederick Payton joined North House in 1906. After leaving St John's at Easter 1912, he moved to Ellesmere College in Shropshire for four terms.

When war broke out he was an apprentice analytical chemist, but volunteered for military service, initially joining the 12th (Service) Battalion of the Royal Fusiliers. He soon moved on to a new branch of the Royal Engineers responsible for the delivery of chemical and other 'specialist' weapons (Smoke, gas and flame projectors). On 1 July, Frederick was part of a Stokes Mortar team delivering a smoke barrage near Carnoy at the southern end of the British front when he was killed in action. Today he is buried in the military cemetery in Carnoy.

OLD JOHNIANS KILLED IN ACTION ON THE FIRST DAY OF THE BATTLE OF THE SOMME, 1 JULY 1916

Captain William Haldane Round
7th Battalion Sherwood Foresters
(Notts and Derby Regiment.)
Killed in Action 1 July 1916, aged 23
St John's School, 1903-1913

William Haldane Round (known to family and friends as Hal) left a deep and indelible mark on the School community, excelling both academically and in sport. He was Captain of the School (for two years), Captain of North House, Secretary of both the Protestant Club and the Literary Society and a member of the choir and orchestra and the OTC. He played 1st XI cricket for three years and captained the side in 1913.

During the great fire that destroyed so much of the main school building in 1913 and in the hours and days that followed, Hal proved himself to be a real leader of others causing *The Johnian* to remark that:

The School has every reason to be grateful to him for his coolness and sense of responsibility.

William went up to Downing College, Cambridge but gave up his studies on the outbreak of war and received a commission into the 7th (Robin Hood) Battalion, Sherwood Foresters (Nottinghamshire and Derbyshire Regiment). William, by now a temporary Captain, led his company into action on 1 July 1916 as part of the attack on Gommecourt and was killed. He lies today in the military cemetery at Foncquevillers.

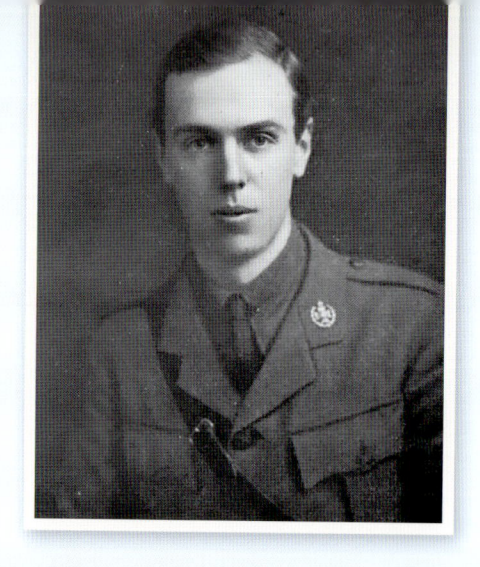

A fellow officer, Geoffrey Vickers, who went to Oundle and Merton College, Oxford and won a VC in 1915, served in the Sherwood Foresters with William Round. Vickers wrote to Round's father to express his own personal sense of loss of a companion and friend:

South Somercotes, Lincs, July 9th, 1916.
Dear Mr Round,
I don't know how to write to you about Hal, but I hope you won't mind my trying. I saw such a lot of him out there, first when we were subalterns together, then when we both got our companies, and finally when I served under him at the Hohenzollern, and there are so many nights and days we spent together that I shall never forget. He was always so cheery and cool and so absolutely sound. However, I don't need to tell you what he was. I only want to tell you of another, among very many, who wants to sympathise with you all as far as ever he can, and who has lost a pal whom he will never forget. Please forgive my intruding on your sorrow, and believe me,

Yours sincerely,
G GEOFFREY VICKERS

School Captain W H Round with prefects, 1912

OLD JOHNIANS AT WAR

Captain John Bedell Rutledge
7th Battalion, East Yorkshire Regiment
Killed in Action 1 July 1916, aged 33
St John's School, 1892-1897

John Rutledge was a pupil at the School for five years before returning home to Ireland where, in 1900, he was commissioned into a local Militia unit, the Donegal Artillery. Having been promoted to Lieutenant and seconded to the Royal Garrison Artillery, he resigned his commission in January 1903.

John moved to South America and by 1914 he had married and was a rancher in Argentina. Following the outbreak of war, he and his wife Theodora returned to Britain. Arriving in early 1915, John gained a commission as a temporary Captain in the 7th Battalion of the East Yorkshire Regiment. On the first day of the Battle of the Somme, the battalion took part in a phased attack on the village of Fricourt, but casualties were high, and John was killed as he led his company into action. He lies today in Fricourt New Military Cemetery.

Foncquevillers Military Cemetery, France

John Rutledge grave, Fricourt New Military Cemetery, France

ON FLANDERS FIELDS

The following year, 1917, was to prove to be as costly as 1916 in terms of casualties. In April 1917, an Anglo-French offensive, named after the French Commander-in-Chief Robert Nivelle, ended in failure. The same month, the Americans joined the war on the side of Britain and France, but it would be some time before their troops would be ready to cross the Atlantic. But the British commander, Sir Douglas Haig, believed that the morale of the German army was cracking. It was time for the British to break out of the Ypres Salient. What was to follow was a series of battles, the first of which on 7 June was, for the British, to be a relative success; nineteen huge mines exploded beneath Messines Ridge, the infantry attacked and the ridge was captured – a large number of Germans were taken prisoner. But then the battle got bogged down – in this case literally so. For above all else, the Battle of Passchendaele will be remembered for the mud.

The rain in August was unseasonably heavy, five inches was double the average and it turned the battlefield into a quagmire. In October, during the two battles for the village of Passchendaele, it rained and rained – and then it rained some more. The battlefield turned into a muddy swamp – a desolate landscape. Men who fell off the sodden duckboards sank into the mud where they drowned in their thousands. Stretcher-bearers struggled to reach the wounded. Those who sought shelter in shell holes found them to be full of water and many of them drowned also. The appalling conditions in mid-October led to a number of British generals suggesting that the offensive should be called off – but Field Marshall Haig insisted it must carry on – Passchendaele must be captured. In November 1917, the village and ridge were finally captured but at the cost of half a million British and German casualties. Ironically, the following year, a German offensive recaptured all of the land lost in a matter of days.

Neville Vernon Evans and Robert Percy Hoult were both killed on 16 August 1917, the first day of the Battle of Langemarck. This was one of a number of battles that made up the 3rd Battle of Ypres (which we know better today as Passchendaele). They were nineteen years old and, though serving with different regiments, had been at St John's together between 1911 and 1913.

Second Lieutenant Neville Vernon Evans was posted to the 2nd Battalion South Wales Borderers. He arrived in France on 28 May 1917 and joined his unit at Candas, south-west of Arras, on 11 June 1917. His arrival coincided with a period of intense training, and a move north to the Ypres Salient in Belgium. When the battle opened, on 31 July 1917, Neville's Battalion was in reserve, but supplying working parties to assist the assault near Boesinghe to the north of Ypres. Their time soon came however, and on 16 August 1917, while attacking German positions at Langemarck, Neville was hit and killed by machine gun fire. Unlike so many on the Passchendaele battlefields, his body was recovered and initially buried close to where he fell. After the war his grave was moved and he now lies in Artillery Wood Cemetery, near Boesinghe.

His Chaplain wrote:

There are many, officers and men, who will remember his cheery manner, his encouraging smile, to the end of their days. In order to find and bring in his body, his men worked continuously under great difficulties for nearly nine hours – a tribute of affection more significant than any words could ever be.

Handwritten illuminated War Memorial, 1918

OLD JOHNIANS AT WAR

Robert Percy Hoult

Neville's former school friend, Second Lieutenant Robert Percy Hoult, was serving with the 2nd West Yorkshire Regiment when it took part in the Battle of Langemarck. On 16 August 1917, the battalion attacked Westhoek Ridge, near Ypres, with early success. However, before the day was out they lost all the ground that had been taken. Robert was one of nine officers who were killed and there were many other casualties. His body was never identified, and Robert is commemorated on the Tyne Cot memorial to the missing. His Commanding Officer, Major E E Baker, wrote:

I had not been very long with the Battalion, but Lieut. Hoult was the first officer I got to know. I was very much struck by his frank and friendly attitude – which seems to have appealed as well to his brother officers and also to his men, who knew him as a friend as well as a good leader. He was much liked by all who greatly feel his loss and join me in offering heart-felt sympathy.

By the end of September 1917, Captain Cecil Llewellyn Norton Roberts, 2nd Battalion, Royal Warwickshire Regiment, had been at the front for almost two years with just a fortnight's home leave. In all that time he had come through the Battles of the Somme and Arras totally unscathed. Now, with the 3rd Battle of Ypres entering its final stages, his luck was about to run out.

By the early hours of 9 October, just to the south-east of Polygon Wood, the attacking troops were formed up and were waiting for zero hour. At 5.20am the attack began, and Cecil led his company into action. Their objective, code named the Red Line, was barely 500 yards from their start point. All along the front, German machine guns slowed down the advance and inflicted further casualties and it was well into the evening before confirmation reached Brigade Headquarters that all objectives had been taken. The cost of success however was high; over 80 men were killed, including six officers, one of whom was Cecil Roberts. The war diary notes that news of his death reached Battalion HQ at 9am. Writing to his parents, his Commanding Officer gave some indication as to the circumstances of his death:

Your son, Captain Roberts, was beloved by the men of his company, who were following his leadership on the 9th inst. when he fell mortally wounded by an enemy bullet. His loss is keenly felt by his brother officers with whom he was highly popular and by all ranks of the battalion.

Even though all objectives were taken, the appalling ground conditions, withering machine gun fire and devastating artillery barrages meant that the majority of those from the regiment who died on 9 October, including Cecil, have no known grave. Today he is remembered on the walls of the memorial at Tyne Cot along with almost 35,000 other men.

Captain Cecil Llewellyn Norton Roberts

2nd Battalion, Royal Warwickshire Regiment
Killed in Action 9 October 1917, aged 23
St John's School, 1905-1914

Cecil Roberts came to St John's in September 1905 as a Foundationer and joined West House. By the time he left the School, in the summer of 1914, Cecil was 2nd Prefect, Head of West House and one of the editorial team that produced *The Johnian* magazine. However, it was as a quite exceptional sportsman that Cecil made his name.

He was just fourteen when he made his first appearance for the 1st XI football team in 1909, receiving his half-colours at the end of that year. In 1910, he was awarded full colours and the critique for the 1st XI said:

C L N ROBERTS (left half): Though somewhat diffident and undeveloped as yet, he has come on splendidly in the course of the season. Feeds his wing well but tackles somewhat undecidedly. Has the makings of a sound half in time.

In time, Cecil made more than just a 'sound half'. He captained the School XI in the 1911-12, 1912-13 and 1913-14 seasons and in January 1913 was called up to the Welsh Amateur International squad ahead of a fixture against England.

His prowess at football was more than matched in the summer months by his ability with bat and ball. Making his first appearance for the school 1st XI in 1910, by the end of the 1912 season he was topping the batting averages. The following season he was appointed secretary of the Cricket Club, vice-captain of the team and headed the bowling averages. In the 1914 season, his last at the school, he took 40 wickets and scored 329 runs.

A place at Keeble College, Oxford awaited him as he left St John's in July 1914, but war already loomed on the horizon and, when it came, like thousands of other young men, Cecil decided it was his duty to serve his country.

The 3rd Battle of Ypres lasted just over three months and, in October 1917, Army Chaplain the Reverend Wilfrid John Harding and Lieutenant Richard Dacre Turton were both killed in action. The battle officially ended on 10 November 1917 but there was a further attack on the village of Passchendaele on 2 December 1917 during which OJ Basil Walker Griffin, aged 22, was killed. His death was reported in the *Retford Times* on 21 December 1917 and included a tribute from his colonel:

He was one of my most promising officers, and one I felt I could fall back on to replace more senior officers if required. He always behaved in a most gallant manner, and died a most gallant death leading his company, of which he was in command at the time of the attack.

Griffin's name is commemorated on the Tyne Cot memorial to the missing of Flanders and the Ypres Salient.

Tyne Cot Memorial, Belgium

TRENCH LIFE

Trench warfare developed early in the Great War, offering protection to soldiers of both sides against enemy fire. As the war progressed so the complexity of the trench systems increased, with front or firing lines, support and reserve trenches, all linked by an extensive network of communication trenches. Conditions within the trenches, especially in the winter months, could be atrocious. To prevent collapses, the sides were reinforced with timber or corrugated iron or built up with sandbags while wooden duckboards were laid across rudimentary drains in an attempt to keep the trenches passable in the wettest conditions. Trenches were often given familiar names from home by the occupying troops, such as Harley Street, Wimpole Street and Kingsway.

The 'fatigue' or working parties that were used to construct and maintain the trenches, and dig tunnels and mines, came under the control of the Royal Engineers (RE). An article dated February 1916 with the title 'Cambrin' and signed 'Fatigue Party', was published in *The Johnian* in July 1916. The report describes some of the dangerous work they carried out:

RE fatigues are 'anathema' to the infantryman; he does not call it that, but it means much the same; they are invariably wearisome, often dangerous, and always at inconvenient hours. Try carrying a twelve-foot trench board up two miles of trenches after three or four hours rain, or four six-foot sheets of corrugated iron over a brick path smeared with mud.

The writer goes on to describe his own experience of a fatigue party:

We entered the trenches, lit pipes and made our way up by Wimpole Street, Wilson's Way, Robertson's Alley, Arthur's Keep and Boyau 19 to the firing line. We knew the way blindfold, as we had been up at all hours of the day and night. We knew exactly where the gaps in the trench boards came, the corner of Kingsway where a shell caught one of our working parties two days before, and where the sentry in the Keep stood as pointsman to direct parties how to find places he did not know himself. At last we got there and found our reward a mining fatigue.

Picture a hole under the parapet something like a cellar door under the stairs. We step down and proceed along the mineshaft bent nearly double. It is a long tunnel, fairly dry, shored up all the way by baulks of timber, the labour of previous luckless fatigue parties, and lit every six feet or so by a candle stuck in the wall in a sort of clay sconce. The tunnel gradually dips and makes its way nearly straight out under no man's land towards, or rather under, the Hun lines – its big neighbour on the right is reputed to go under their third line. On the right side runs a long, wired rubber snake, the air-pump, which was not working to-night.

'Sapping' involved digging short trenches or 'saps' towards the enemy trenches to enable soldiers to move forward without coming under enemy fire:

We spread out in a chain from the Minehead where the engineers were sapping, down as far towards the mouth as we could, about ten yards each, and passed sandbags, the products of the sapping, from one to the other.

Now a sandbag of wet clay weighs, at a moderate estimate, seventy pounds, and bent double passing these as quickly as you can is exhausting work; it makes a cold man sweat in well under five minutes, and we dropped exhausted, where we stood, or rather stooped, every few minutes, and lay panting.

Moving to the front line in 1915, young Edward Rowley Kelly described some of the drawbacks of trench life; evil-smelling waterlogged communication trenches and lack of sleep:

We set off by companies at about 9 o'clock and moved straight up along a road in which shell-holes were fairly plentiful. Along here bullets were quite frequent and every time the enemy put up a star shell I thought that my end had come and began to meditate on what a promising officer the country was losing and hoping that they wouldn't put me in with a dead horse.

However, I was awakened from this dream by my platoon-serjeant saying,

'This 'ere communication-trench is full of water, sir; shall we go along the top?'

A lightning mental comparison made me choose the ills of snipers, which I knew, rather than the evil-smelling, water-logged communication trench that I knew not of. The chief drawbacks to the trench system are the lack of sleep (one is lucky to get three or four hours at a stretch, and I hate sleeping on and off) and the lack of washing accommodation. I got two washes and one shave in four days and was the envy of the company for getting so much…

2nd Lieutenant Edward Rowley Kelly

3rd Battalion, Border Regiment
Killed in Action 7 July 1915, aged 17
St John's School, 1911-1914

Edward Kelly gained a reputation as an excellent debater within the Protestants' (Debating) Club. He was a member of the Literary and Dramatic Society and an editor of *The Johnian*.

On the playing field, Edward was the 1st XI goalkeeper in his final two years at St John's. He left school in December 1914, by which time he was a School Prefect, Captain of South House and had been awarded an Exhibition to study Classical History at Merton College, Oxford the following autumn.

The reason for his unexpected and rather premature departure soon became clear; despite being only 17 years old Edward was granted a commission with the Border Regiment at the end of January 1915. He joined the 3rd (Reserve) Battalion at Shoeburyness for training before being sent overseas.

Posted to the 2nd Battalion of the Lancashire Fusiliers near Ypres, Edward soon found himself in the trenches on the front line. He was killed by a shell during 3 days of heavy fighting to repel a German counter-attack at Pilkem, three miles north of Ypres, on 7th July 1915, a few months before his 18th birthday.

His Commanding Officer Major W Bowes later wrote of Kelly, highlighting the fact that he was so young:

I have made inquiries from the NCOs. and men of his platoon and from what I can gather he was killed by a shell and was buried in the hole made by the shell which struck him. The place where he fell is called Pilken [sic], about three miles north of Ypres.

In the three days, July 7th to July 9th, we lost ten officers killed and eight wounded, and about 350 men killed and wounded... He was such a cheery youth and we all liked him immensely, and he got on very well with his men.

He was very young and boyish – too young in fact for this work, but he was very plucky and did his work well.

Although the letter gives the impression that Edward was buried by his men, if his grave was originally marked it was subsequently lost. Today he is named on the walls of the Menin Gate in Ypres, one of over 54,000 men commemorated there who were killed during the fighting in the Ypres Salient and who have no known grave. Edward Kelly is also remembered on the Hitchin Grammar School memorial, on the Carshalton War Memorial website and at Merton College, Oxford.

ROUTE MARCHES

To reach the front-line trenches, soldiers often marched long distances carrying their kit and equipment. Frank Cecil Allan was posted to France in September 1916 with the Durham Light Infantry. He writes eloquently of his Brigade's route march to the front line, though he could not reveal their exact destination:

We started at 11.30am, marched ten miles to entrain, travelled from 4.30pm to 1.30am in a cattle-truck; not bad going, but naturally only a little sleep. On getting out we had to march about twelve miles here – all this on two sandwiches. I am told it was the most gruelling march, or rather move, the Brigade has ever had. It was rather a sweat, with a ponderous pack. The men were done to a turn. The funny thing is that about half-way they groused hard, but towards the end, being too tired to grouse, they marched finely. None of my platoon fell out. We are much under strength but are going once more into action – you can guess where – so I am in for the worst of it all at once.

EQUIPMENT

An unsigned article in *The Johnian* for December 1916 gives a detailed account of the equipment soldiers carried on their backs in packs or haversacks during route marches:

The battalion paraded at 4.00pm in fighting order; fighting order on this occasion meant wearing the haversack on the back in place of the pack. In the haversack, amongst other things, were carried the unexpired portion of the day's ration and the iron ration. Fastened on his belt at the back each man carried a rolled waterproof sheet containing one sandbag and his reserve ration. Round his water bottle was entwined another sandbag, and each man, in addition to his usual 120 rounds of ammunition, wore two bandoliers of 50 rounds each and two bombs. In addition to this, one unfortunate platoon per company had to carry one tool per man, slung over the shoulder by a torn strip of sandbag. Two more sand-bags were tucked away in the entrenching-tool carrier. Of course everyone had the usual supply of anti-gas helmets and so on.

BILLETS

During respite leave or at the end of a day's march, officers and their men sought shelter for the night in villages, farms, cellars and fields. Officers were usually allocated the best accommodation but frequently found there was none to be had. Charles Edward Vernon Kingsbury Peberdy, 4th Battalion, West Yorkshire Regiment, found himself sleeping in a pig sty in December 1914:

Our billet is a none too comfortable barn a mile and a half from this village. We came to it on December 6th for about three days' supposed respite. The last place we were at was a village which was untenable for inhabitants, because it was periodically shelled. We were just the other side of it, so all shells passed over us. I was with six others in a pig-sty for three days. We were not allowed to leave the farmyard in the day time, because it was to be seen from the German lines. At night we made dug-outs in the earth with good solid roofs in case the farm was shelled.

A few months later in March 1915, Kenneth Carlyle Gill, serving with the Cambridgeshire Regiment wrote a letter home from his billet in a cellar near St Eloi, a small village south of Ypres:

I'm sorry you have not heard from me for a bit, but I think I may say I am pretty lucky to be alive now to write. We have had a taste of the worst and from all accounts I don't think there is anything to complain about in our regiment; we have fought, lost officers and men, have had tremendous tests of our marching powers, have come through it all, and are now resting for six days!… Well, we did arrive and in the early hours of Sunday morning shook down in the ruined houses of this desolate village. What a place it was! Not a house standing whole, the church smashed in, and ruins and debris everywhere. The officers' H.Q. was a cellar and there we six dossed down as we were and slept as best we could on the cellar floor.

And in September 1916, Frank Allan wrote:

On arriving here, we discovered that no billets had been procured for officers, but only a field which had been rather freely used as a latrine. However, we didn't fancy a night there as rain seemed imminent, so found an estaminet, where we sleep in the bar among beer-barrels and bottles, etc.

NIGHT WORK

Frank's letter goes on to describe the work they did at night, taking bombs, food and water up to the trenches:

We are attached to another Brigade and do all the dirty work: we are hewers of wood, drawers of water – and grousers above all. Every night from about 7.30 to 2.30 I am on carrying work; I take parties varying from 30 to 70 up to the trenches with bombs, bully,

Frank Allan's letter from the trenches

water, etc. As we are advancing so quickly there are no communication trenches dug, and one goes over the open up to the front line. As a matter of fact, it would be no use going up trenches if they were there, as the mud is so deep. Last night my party did the impossible: all got up to the front line, none fell out, and all got their bombs up.

Later he writes of his concern for the men in his platoon:

You get sniped at and shelled, but a little astuteness enables you to dodge 'em. I am getting used to grovelling on my belly in the mud, hoping that the shell will miss everybody. You get beastly anxious that nothing shall hit your men. If a man gets hit, however badly, you must patch him up and leave him till the stretcher-bearers come, and they may never come. The men stick at it like heroes; grouse of course but hang on till death.

2nd Lieutenant Frank Cecil Allan
21st Battalion attached 13th Battalion, Durham Light Infantry
Killed in Action 29 September 1916, aged 20
St John's School, 1906-1915

Frank Cecil Allan joined North House in 1906. By the time he left Leatherhead in the summer of 1915 he had been Captain of the School, Captain of cricket, football, fives and running (winning the Victor Ludorum in his final year) and choir prefect. Frank left St John's with three scholarship awards: £40 from the School, £30 from the county and a £60 classical scholarship from Jesus College, Oxford. However, like so many others he decided not to take up his place at university and chose instead to join the army.

On 25 September 1915, Frank was gazetted as a second lieutenant into the Durham Light Infantry. Initially he joined the 21st Battalion, a home-based reserve battalion, for training where he became an instructor in bombing (grenades were usually known as bombs at that time). Eventually he was posted overseas, joining the 13th Battalion in France on 7 September 1916.

Three days after his arrival Frank, along with the rest of the battalion, found himself heading south, to the battlefields of the Somme. The Battalion war diary records that at 11.35pm on 25 September the enemy shelled the Battalion HQ. Three men were killed and several others wounded, including Frank.

Correspondence shows that he was wounded in both the hand and the thigh; injuries serious enough to evacuate him back to the 2nd Red Cross hospital at Rouen, one of several medical base establishments to be found in and around the French coastal town. Despite the best efforts of the hospital staff, the wound in his thigh became infected and he succumbed to gas gangrene at Rouen on 29 September.

Writing to Frank's father his colonel said:

He was one of my most promising officers and one of the finest characters I have ever met. Always cheery, and with the true Public School spirit, he always played for the game. I am quite sure that he died as he lived, putting his whole soul into his work. It makes one sad to think of the wastage, but it surely must be that he has passed into a fuller service.

Frank was buried at St Sever cemetery, south of Rouen, and now lies in the company of over 11,000 other servicemen, the majority of whom died of wounds.

ON OTHER FRONTS

The majority of OJs killed in the Great War died on the Western Front in France or Belgium. The war however was fought on many fronts and a number of OJs served in Africa and the Middle East. Two former pupils who left St John's in 1907 and 1912 had very different experiences of the conflict in the Middle East.

Captain James Wilfrid Haynes Park graduated from Keble College, Oxford in 1911. He had been a member of the University OTC and, in March 1912, joined the Indian Army and served in the 22nd Cavalry (Sam Browne's). When war broke out he went to Mesopotamia with the 33rd Cavalry. There he was wounded, contracted typhoid and was sent back to India for some months. On his recovery he went back to Mesopotamia. Shortly after, he was reported missing and, on 14 January 1917, reported killed in action. He was killed about three weeks after returning to the front.

Above: J W H Park at Keble College, Oxford

Right: J W H Park in uniform

Captain James Wilfrid Haynes Park
22nd Cavalry (Sam Browne's)
Killed in Action 14 January 1917, aged 28
St John's School, 1901-1907

James Wilfrid Haynes Park left St John's with the reputation for being one of the best athletes and sportsmen the school has ever had.

A tribute published in *The Johnian*, February 1917 said:

He played football for the school for three seasons and was captain in 1906-1907; he was in the 1st XI cricket during his last two years. In sports he won the mile in 1905, the mile, quarter and hurdles in 1906, and was Victor Ludorum and the mile and quarter in 1907. He represented St John's at the Public Schools meeting at Stamford Bridge, and won the mile in 1906 and the steeplechase the year after.

A personal reminiscence from one of his teachers:

Park first came under my notice as a boy of fifteen, when he was hauled by the headmaster out of a long line of starters for the school mile. He had only been dismissed from the infirmary the day before. The next occasion was the time that he cut chapel and lunch on a Saint's Day to go birds-nesting. Five hundred Greek lines with accents was the result of that little adventure; but in after years he told me that it was quite worth it, especially if one took into consideration the number of times he wasn't caught. Later on he used to sit just in front of me in chapel, and to save my eardrums I had him removed to the choir.

It was on the school games, however, that he left his mark. As captain of football he worked as no captain has worked before or since, and the successful years that followed his departure were due almost solely to his efforts. Cutting games was no light offence in his eyes.

I think his character is very well shown by a quotation from a letter he wrote me when he was back in India from Mesopotamia, wounded and recovering from malaria:

I have just purchased a dog-cart, rather rickety, and am driving tandem. I don't know much about it yet, but it is very fast and pre-eminently unsafe, so what more could you want?

Of all men to have by me in a tight corner I should have chosen Captain J W H Park, Sam Browne's Cavalry, and late of St John's School.

W T Wrigley memorial, St Andrew's Church, Hartburn, Northumberland

The Colonel commanding the 22nd Cavalry in Mesopotamia wrote to Captain Park's father to say that he had recommended his son for a posthumous VC. The recommendation was not approved but the Army Commander recognised the great gallantry shown by Park and stated that he would give Captain Park a mention in dispatches as a record of his fine work. The Colonel ends his letter with the words:

His loss has been deeply felt by all his brother officers as well as by the rank and file, particularly those of his squadron, who were full of praise for his great bravery. His general disposition made him beloved by all. I never heard him say a nasty thing of anyone, and he was a really fine hard-working soldier. He met the fate that most of us would prefer when our time comes, and we are proud to have owned him as a member of the Regiment.

Just four years younger than James Park, Willoughby Thornton Wrigley also joined the University OTC at Keble College, Oxford and, in September 1914, enlisted with the 5th Battalion Wiltshire Regiment. There is something of a mystery about Wrigley's time at Keble. On his attestation papers he gives his education as St John's School, Leatherhead, Bristol University and Keble College, Oxford. Wrigley's name does not appear on the Bristol University Roll of Honour nor is he listed in the Keble College Register or on the Roll of Honour outside the College Chapel. It is possible that he had applied for admission to the College, but as the outbreak of war coincided with the term he would have gone up, he decided not to accept the offer.

Wrigley served in Gallipoli and was promoted to lieutenant and later acting captain. He went with his regiment to Mesopotamia and took part in the operations at Kut and later in the fighting for Baghdad and the region beyond, for which he received the Military Cross.

In April 1918, Wrigley was appointed an Assistant Political Officer and Administrator at Bagubah, Deltawn, and Deli Abbas, in what is now Iraq. He went home on leave in July 1919 and returned to Mesopotamia the following November. In mid-1920 Captain Wrigley was posted to Shahraban, nearly 50 miles north east of Baghdad, to take charge while the officer there was on leave.

Wrigley was shot dead by local tribesmen during an uprising at Shahraban on Sunday 15 August 1920. An obituary which appeared in *The Times* newspaper on 25 August 1920 reported that Wrigley was killed *'after three days gallant defence against local rebels.'* He was laid to rest in the North Gate Cemetery, Baghdad.

REPORTING DEATH

TELEGRAMS, NOTIFICATIONS AND CASUALTY LISTS

Families of those on active service came to dread the loud knock at the door which heralded the delivery of a telegram from the War Office. With its distinctive pink envelope, it almost invariably brought bad news.

Clement Barrington Furmston serving with the Machine Gun Corps (154 Company) was wounded on 5 March 1917 and in the space of six weeks his mother received three telegrams. The first, from the War Office, was sent at 8.00am on 9 March 1917 and read:

Regret to inform you Sec Lt C B Furmston M G C 154 Co was wounded March 5. Further reports sent on receipt [signed] Secretary War Office.

Clement recovered from his injury and wrote to his mother on 4 April 1917 wishing her a *'very happy Easter'*.

Tragically, just a few days later, on Easter Monday 9 April 1917, Clement was killed in action during the Battle of Arras. The following week another telegram from the War Office, dated 14 April 1917, was on its way to Mrs Furmston:

Deeply regret inform you 2 Lt C B Furmston M G C 154 Coy was killed in action April ninth. The army council express their sympathy [signed] Secty War Office.

The same day Clement's mother received a letter from his Commanding Officer, Major A V Board giving details of his death:

He was killed half an hour after the beginning of the action. A shell landed in the middle of his gun team whilst it was in action and instantaneously killed him and the three men with him.

Enclosed with this letter was the last letter that Clement wrote to his mother on Easter Sunday, just hours before he was killed.

A final telegram for Clement's mother arrived from Buckingham Palace on 18 April 1917:

The King and Queen deeply regret the loss you and the army have sustained by the death of your son in the service of his country. Their majesties truly sympathise with you in your great sorrow. [signed] Keeper of the Privy Purse.

Delays in transmitting the news of injury or death were not unusual. Casualty lists were compiled in the field and sent to the War Office in London, who notified next of kin.

At the start of the war, the War Office published daily casualty lists, but these ceased in August 1917 and were replaced by a weekly list, copies of which were sold for three pence. Notification of death by telegram was reserved for officers serving in the armed forces. Next of kin of other ranks were notified by a pre-printed Army form B104-82, on which details of the name, rank, date and cause of death could be entered.

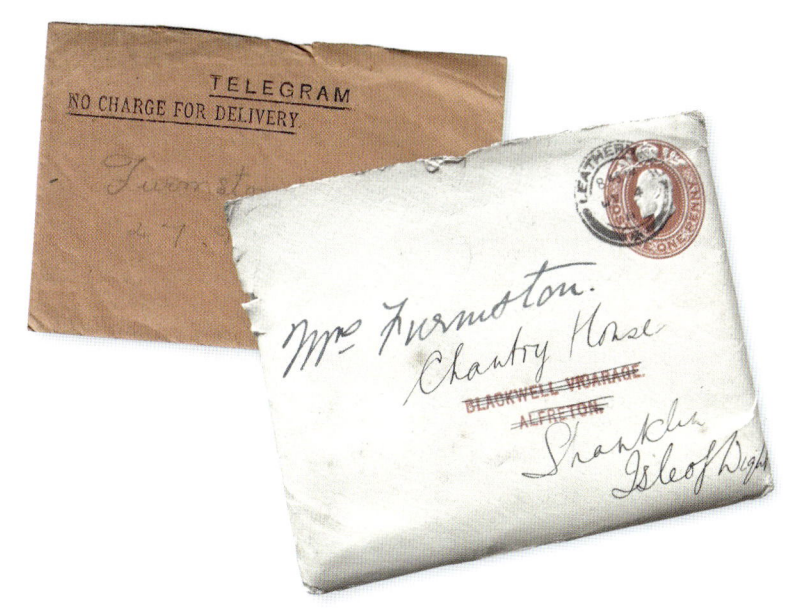

Casualty lists and obituaries also appeared in national and local papers which provided a source of information for friends and family in the wider community. News of Clement's death appeared in the *Derbyshire Times* and *Chesterfield Herald*, 21 April 1917.

2nd Lieutenant Clement Barrington Furmston

154 Company, Machine Gun Corps (Inf)
Killed in Action 9 April 1917, aged 22
St John's School, 1905-1911

Clement Barrington Furmston joined North House in 1905 as a Foundationer. He played football for his House and the School 2nd XI and earned his House colours. Clement was joined at Leatherhead by his younger brother, Wilfrid in January 1911, but they were only together for a few months as Clement left at the end of the Summer Term. He was articled, for five years, to a firm of solicitors, Wilson & Son, in Alfreton, close to the family home. Correspondence shows that the headmaster was disappointed to lose a boy that he regarded very highly (he had been awarded a Downes Prize for the academic year 1910-11).

Clement seemed destined for a future in the legal profession but on the outbreak of war, in August 1914, he joined up. Enlisting initially with the Royal Fusiliers he was commissioned into the Machine Gun Corps in 1916, joining 154 Company in France two days before Christmas 1916.

In early March 1917, a gunshot wound to his left knee kept him away from the front line for three weeks. By the end of the month he was back with the Company and able to play his part in what we now know as the Battle of Arras. The attack went in along a broad front to the east of Arras on the morning of the 9 April and the unit war diary describes the part played by its men:

At 5.30 this morning ten guns of the Company opened fire… during the period 5.30am to 10.30am, 95,000 rounds were fired.

Overall, the casualties were remarkably light with five other ranks wounded, and just one officer and three other ranks killed. The officer in question was Second Lieutenant Clement Furmston and the war diary expands on how he was killed:

During the barrage one complete team and an officer were killed by a direct hit from a 5.9.

Clement's body was recovered and buried, alongside two of his gun crew, in what is now Roclincourt Military Cemetery.

LETTERS OF CONDOLENCE

One of the sad and frequent duties of officers and army chaplains was to write letters of condolence to the grief-stricken families of those who had been killed. The language of the following letter written by S M Morgan, Chaplain to the Forces, to the father of OJ Edmund Trevennin Gray is typical of many of these letters. The idea of Christian duty and sacrifice for the greater good was prevalent among public schoolboys who served as junior officers during the war. Euphemisms relating to war and death were common. Soldiers were described as having 'died a splendid death' or were 'called to a higher service'. Phrases such as 'young heroes' 'died instantly' or 'died of wounds' only served to mask the horror of war.

Dear Mr Gray,

I feel I cannot do better than tell you the bad news straight out. Your son was killed in action last night. He was observing the fire of one of his machine guns from the parados. You may rest quite certain that he suffered absolutely no pain; his death was quite instantaneous. The doctor and I went up at once, and we buried him the same night in our cemetery in a wood. I don't know if you will see what I mean when I say it was all very wonderful and beautiful in a strange way. It was a glorious full-moon night with a slight mist. Except for the rifle fire a few hundred yards away one could hardly believe there was a war. The wood seemed to shut us in all by ourselves. There were only a few of us there: his Company Commander, Captain Taylor-Loban, the Doctor, some 10 men, and myself, and the boy who had given all he had to give. One of the men is making a cross to-day and carving his name on it. I suppose I may not tell you now where the grave is, but it is known and marked, and later on I shall be allowed, I think, to say where it is. At any rate it is a most perfect resting place, among the men of our brigade. He is a great loss to us; everyone was fond of him, and I need hardly express our sympathy with you in your great trouble.

Yours truly,

S M MORGAN, CF, 64th Brigade

Captain G T Fitzgerald also wrote a long letter to Gray's father, and these extracts illustrate the trouble that senior officers took to reassure families that their sons had been highly valued and respected by fellow officers and the men they led:

I wish to tell you how very much we all regret your son's death, and how deeply we sympathise with you in your terrible loss. But to me in particular his death has been a great shock. Very soon after he joined the Battalion I was attracted by his charming personality and by the keenness which he showed in his work and, determined to take him as my machine-gun subaltern if he would like the job, I was pleased to find that machine-gun work was exactly the work he most wished for.

Gray was very popular with all his brother officers, and also (which I know he valued far more) with his men. They appreciated that he always took every possible care for their comfort, and never put any unnecessary work on them, while at the same time he insisted on and maintained strict discipline in all respects. Several of them have since told me that 'Mr Gray was a champion officer,' and this is the highest praise our Durham miners (who seem naturally shy and reticent) ever use, and there are not many of the officers to whom they would dream of applying the term.

Gray's death in addition to all personal feeling is a real loss to the battalion. He died fighting his guns in the middle of a careful plan contrived by him to enfilade a German trench by indirect fire. In the noise of the fight he was not seen to fall but was found by his Sergeant afterwards lying in the trench. Death must have been quite instantaneous and painless. He was buried the same night in Ploegsteert Wood.

Yours sincerely,

G T Fitzgerald, Captain
15th Durham Light Infantry.

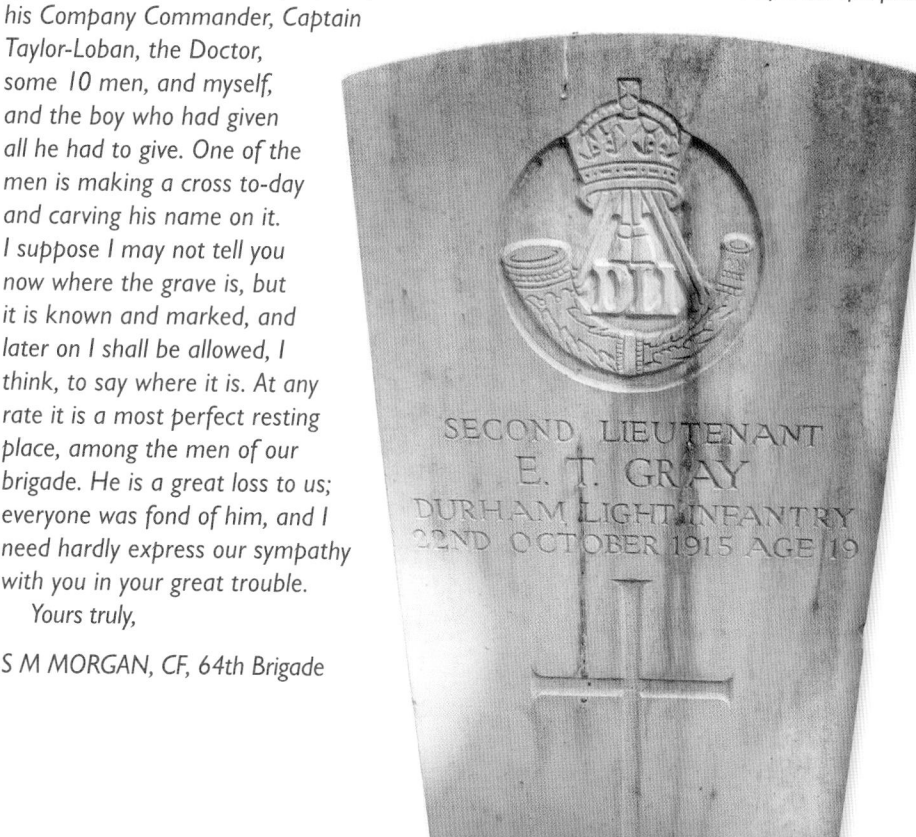

OLD JOHNIANS AT WAR

2nd Lieutenant Edmund Trevennin Gray

15th Battalion Durham Light Infantry
Killed in Action 22 October 1915, aged 19
St John's School, 1906-1914

Edmund Gray, the eldest son of the Reverend C J Gray was a Foundationer and a member of North House who excelled both in the classroom and on the playing fields. By the time he left school in the summer of 1914, he was Captain of the School, Captain of cricket and Captain of football.

With an exhibition in classics he was due to take up a place at St Catharine's College, Cambridge but when war broke out just a few weeks after leaving school he was keen to apply for a commission. He was eventually persuaded to go up, but immediately joined the University OTC. By December 1914, Gray had left Cambridge, gained a commission in the Durham Light Infantry and a posting to the 15th Battalion. When Edmund joined his battalion they were billeted, and training, at Maidenhead in Berkshire later moving to Halton Park in Hertfordshire, then to Witley in Surrey.

Deemed ready for action, the Battalion moved abroad on 11 September 1915. Just eight days 'rest' followed before, over the next four days, they marched toward the front line arriving at Houchin on 25 September 1915. Here they found themselves, along with the rest of the 21st Division, in reserve for the Battle of Loos which had just begun.

Loos was the biggest offensive action by the Allies so far in the war and by the early hours of the 26 September all was not well. The Durham's were ordered to attack a German strongpoint called Hill 70 and suffered terribly as a result with over 50 per cent of the battalion becoming casualties. Edmund however survived, left behind so that should the need arise (as it indeed now had) there was a cadre of 'experienced' officers around which to rebuild the battalion, the shattered remains of which were now withdrawn from the battle, and sent to the rear to recover.

The period out of the line was brief. On 10 October they were on the move again, this time north towards Armentieres and the next day the battalion was back in the trenches. On 19 October the battalion took over the front-line trenches in Ploegsteert Wood, on the French Belgian border. They stayed in the line for a week but when they were relieved, they left Edmund behind. On the evening of the 22 October, while observing the fire of one of the machine guns under his command he was killed, most probably by either a sniper or indirect enemy machine guns.

Edmund was buried that same night in a cemetery deep within the wood, not very far from where he fell, and he lies there still. He was 19 years old and had been in France for just over six weeks.

Ploegsteert Wood Military Cemetery, Belgium

CHAPTER 5 WAR AT SEA

At the outbreak of war, the British Grand Fleet – which consisted of 20 Dreadnoughts and the corresponding number of battle cruisers, cruisers, destroyers and other craft – was based mainly at Scapa Flow in the Orkney Islands and at Harwich. A second sizeable fleet guarded the Channel. The German fleet was smaller in size and, therefore, from the beginning of the war avoided the North Sea apart from the occasional raid on towns in the east of England. Instead, the German navy waged an aggressive submarine war in the Atlantic and English Channel with the purpose of preventing imports into Britain from the Caribbean and North America. While the German navy was attempting to blockade Britain, the Royal Navy was more successful in preventing goods reaching German ports.

Many OJs served around the world in the Royal Navy. Bernard Paul Mainprice entered the Royal Navy as an Assistant Clerk on 15 July 1912, and was assigned to HMS Agamemnon, one of the last pre-dreadnought battleships commissioned by the Navy. In February 1913 he was transferred to the new dreadnought, HMS King George V, and qualified as a Clerk in July. His service records show that he was also taking exams with a view to becoming an interpreter and he was granted six months study leave in Germany from August 1913. Returning in April 1914, he was posted to HMS Bulwark and, having passed his Acting Interpreter (German) exam, he remained with her until the outbreak of war.

On 26 November 1914, Bulwark was moored at Kethole Reach, four nautical miles west of Sheerness, in line with several other ships. Just before 8.00am, witnesses on nearby ships, including HMS Prince of Wales and Bernard's former ship, HMS Agamemnon saw smoke issuing from the stern of Bulwark. Seconds later, a series of massive explosions tore the ship apart and an eye witness account of the incident, published in the *North-Eastern Daily Gazette* on 27 November 1914, described the scene:

When the explosion occurred a great volume of flame and smoke shot into the air. The ship seemed to split in two, and then heeled over and sank. She disappeared in less than five minutes.

A Naval Court of Inquiry into the loss of HMS Bulwark found that the most likely cause was the overheating of cordite charges which were known to be stored alongside a (hot) boiler room bulk head, though other explanations have also been put forward. Out of her crew of 750, no officers and only 14 sailors survived, two of those subsequently dying from their injuries. Although some bodies were recovered for burial, Bernard Mainprice was never found and today he is remembered on the Portsmouth Naval Memorial. He was nineteen years old.

Clerk Bernard Paul Mainprice
HMS Bulwark, Royal Navy
Killed in Action 26 November 1914, aged 19
St John's School, 1906-1912

Bernard Paul Mainprice, the youngest of the Mainprice children (his brother Ernest was eighteen years his senior) joined South House in January 1906. Bernard was a keen sportsman who represented the School 2nd XI in both cricket and football. His prowess at sport was rewarded in the summer of 1911 when he was awarded Senior House colours for sport and the following term gained his School 2nd XI colours for football. His final game for the School was played against Cranleigh on 12 June 1912, and the match report notes that:

The team secured their one and only victory of the season by the narrow margin of 4 runs. The match was played in heavy rain and on a sodden pitch. Mainprice bowled well, taking 4 wickets for 25.

Bernard's academic achievements were also impressive. He was awarded 1st Class in the Cambridge Local Examination with distinction in French and German in 1909. At Speech Day in July 1910, Bernard was awarded the Upper Fifth Form prize and he gained first place in the Competitive Examination for Naval Clerkships in 1912, following in the footsteps of brother Ernest who passed the same examination in 1885.

Fleet Paymaster Ernest William Loxley Mainprice

HMS Invincible, Royal Navy
Killed in Action 31 May 1916, aged 36
St John's School, 1888-1895

Ernest William Loxley Mainprice was a keen sportsman and is described in *The Johnian* as '*a very fair bat, with some good strokes; hits hard; good field*'. He was awarded colours for 1st XI cricket in 1895.

Ernest left St John's in May 1895, having been successful in the examination for Naval Clerkships. He continued to play cricket with the Navy and in 1909 was selected to play in the annual cricket match, Navy versus Army.

JUTLAND

In January 1916, the Kaiser appointed Admiral Scheer as Commander of the German High Seas Fleet. Scheer's priority was to break the Royal Navy's blockade of German ports. In late April a German Squadron raided Lowestoft and Yarmouth and a battle cruiser squadron was sent to show itself off the coast of Denmark and Norway. In London, the German naval code was broken and the Grand Fleet, commanded by Admiral Jellicoe, set sail to engage the Germans in battle.

Fought over 36 hours between 31 May and 1 June 1916, the Battle of Jutland was the major naval battle of the war between the British Grand Fleet and the German High Seas Fleet. It took place in the North Sea just off Denmark's Jutland peninsula.

Fleet Paymaster Ernest William Loxley Mainprice was serving on HMS Invincible, the world's first battle cruiser and Flagship of the 3rd Battlecruiser squadron. During the action on 31 May 1916 she was hit by a shell which penetrated one of the turrets and the ship exploded. There were 1,021 casualties, one of whom was Ernest Mainprice, and only six survivors.

Ernest served in South Africa in the Anglo-Boer War and was awarded the Queen's South Africa Medal and King's South Africa Medal. His service record describes him as '*most efficient and zealous and extremely hardworking*'. He had a fair knowledge of French and Hindustani and it was noted that he played cricket and football well. In August 1910, his captain wrote that he was:

Strongly recommended for advancement as, in addition to his own work he has always been ready and willing to work in the plotting room, act as decoding officer during manoeuvres and in fact has done his utmost to promote the efficiency of the ship.

Promoted to Fleet Paymaster in July 1914, Mainprice was killed in action in HMS Invincible in the naval engagement in the North Sea, on the 31 May 1916 aged 36. Fleet Paymaster Ernest William Loxley Mainprice is remembered on the Portsmouth Naval Memorial in Hampshire and on the Wisborough Green Memorial in Sussex alongside his younger brother, Bernard Paul Mainprice.

To the Old Johnians on Service.

Once, long ago, we sat together
   In hall and class-room day by day,
And the same field, in wintry weather
   Or sunshine, held us all at play;

You peopled all my world. But after,
   Dawned other days that banished these;
Stray scenes, dim shapes and formless laughter
   Were all my schoolboy memories;

Blurred were the once familiar faces,
   Grown strange the names that once I knew;
Our lots were cast in far-off places
   Apart; I had forgotten you.

I had forgotten, till I saw
   The list of those by land and sea
Who fight to-day in England's war.
   . . . . Then the old names came back to me

And the old faces, fresh as ever;
   Faint pictures of the School grew plain,
And dearer for your high endeavour
   I found my boyhood's friends again.

O.J.

Anonymous poem by an OJ, published in The Johnian, October 1915

CHAPTER 6 THE MISSING

The scale and nature of the fighting in the war, particularly on the Western Front, meant that many of those killed were never found, or their terrible injuries meant that they could not be identified. Those who did not answer the roll call after a battle and whose bodies had not been discovered or could not be retrieved, were listed as 'missing' and their next of kin were informed.

Victor Leopold Stevens Bedwell received a commission in the Suffolk Regiment in June 1915. On 18 August 1916, during the Battle of the Somme, he was with the 4th Battalion of the Suffolk Regiment when they attacked across the open ground to the right of High Wood, with Wood Lane Trench their primary objective. The Germans had positioned a machine gun post on the right side of the wood which dominated the landscape here and by the time the Suffolk's had reached the trench every officer, except Victor, had become a casualty; as he led his remaining men on past the trench he too was hit and killed. The war diary for that day records that:

The assault was carried out with determination; D and C companies reached the German trenches and remained in them for some time. 2nd Lt VLS Bedwell the only surviving officer was killed in advance of the German line.

Victor's body was never identified and today his name can be found on the walls of the Thiepval Memorial to the Missing, one of nine OJs on the memorial which remembers over 72,000 men with no known grave, killed in the battles of the Somme.

Inset: VLS Bedwell bronze memorial plaque; Above: Thiepval Memorial, France

2nd Lieutenant Victor Leopold Stevens Bedwell

4th Battalion, Suffolk Regiment
Killed in Action 18 August 1916, aged 22
St John's School, 1904-1913

Victor Leopold Stevens Bedwell came to St John's in 1904 with an Albany Scholarship and showed impressive all-round ability. He won many academic prizes, excelling particularly in classical languages. A School Prefect, Victor was also an accomplished sportsman, playing 1st XI cricket for the last two years of his time at School.

Leaving St John's in 1913, he went up to Exeter College, Oxford with an Open Classical Scholarship, along with a leaving scholarship from the School. He continued to excel at Oxford, being runner up in the prestigious Gaisford Greek Verse Prize in 1914 and winning a Craven scholarship the same year. He took a first class in Classical Moderations in 1915 and was twice honourably mentioned in the Hertford Scholarship Examination.

At the outbreak of war in August 1914, Victor signed up with the University Officers' Training Corps, while continuing his studies, before receiving a commission in the Suffolk Regiment in June 1915.

Following Bedwell's death in 1916, Major E P Clarke of the 4th Suffolk's wrote to his parents:

Although I am extremely sorry that you should have been called upon to sacrifice your son for his country, I feel sure the fact that he died like a gallant gentleman would, and with the finest soldierly spirit, will be some comfort to you in your sorrow. The fact that your son was the only officer in the battalion to reach the trench at all will give you some idea of the severity of the fight. I feel sure you will feel as proud of your son's heroism as everyone in the regiment is, and while offering you my sincerest sympathy I cannot refrain from almost congratulating you at the same time.

His Chaplain wrote:

Dear Mr Bedwell,…
Your son was leading his men in action against the enemy when he was killed. I thought you would like to know that he died without pain, right in the forefront. He had got past the first trench and was on his way to the second when he was shot in the head. A week ago today, the day before they went into the line, I held a celebration of Holy Communion to which your son came with all devotion. So you may feel he died the death of a hero and strengthened with God's grace. His company mess-table, screened by boughs, was the altar. The little band knelt round on the ground. I remember how a shell burst awfully near and made me feel nervous. I asked him if it would be all right to go on, and he reassured me.

Yours faithfully,
PHILIP P W GENDALL (Chaplain).

Victor Bedwell's death was singled out for mention in the Annual Report of the Committee for 1916:

Lieutenant V L S Bedwell, who fell in action in the Bois de Fourceaux, on August 18th, after distinguishing himself among so many brave men by his bravery left £25 to the School Library. His recklessness of danger was noted by the War Correspondent of the Times, who deplored his death as that of 'one of the best officers in his regiment.' His career at our School and at Oxford, until he closed it last year by accepting a commission, was extraordinarily brilliant as well as blameless.

The families of the missing were to suffer the additional anguish of not knowing what had happened to their sons. Second Lieutenant Willingham Richard Ekins, East Yorkshire Regiment, was sent to France with the 11th (Service) Battalion in 1917. The Battalion spent six weeks training (including detailed work on fighting in woods) for the part they were to play in the Battle of Arras and, on 28 April 1917, were moved back into the lines close to the village of Oppy, north east of Arras. Oppy was protected by a wood on its western edge and a network of trenches and bunkers. It had so far defied all efforts to take it but now Willingham and the 11th East Yorkshires were given the task of advancing through the southern section of Oppy Wood and entering the village. They arrived at their position in the early hours of 3 May. Zero Hour was set for 3.45am, by which time the men had been lying out in no man's land for over two hours under continuous enemy artillery fire. Nevertheless, at the allotted time the British barrage began. All along the front, men rose to follow the bombardment as it moved through the German lines. However, in Oppy Wood the attack soon descended into chaos as the battalion war diary explains:

It was dark, the smoke and dust caused by our barrage and the hostile barrage, also the fact that we were advancing on a dark wood made it impossible to see when our barrage lifted off the German trench. Consequently, the Hun had time to get his machine guns up. Machine guns were firing from within the wood from trees, as well as from the front trench, nevertheless the men went forward...

The initial attack was unsuccessful, so officers and NCOs reorganised the men under heavy fire in no man's land, attacked again and were repulsed a second time. A few men made a third attempt but ultimately the wood and the village beyond remained in German hands. The East Yorkshires were now so scattered and casualties so high that all they could do was fall back to the assembly trench from whence they had begun the attack and assess their losses.

The war diary states that casualties exceeded 260 men of which 12 were officers, including Willingham Ekins who is listed as '*missing*'. His father, George, would have been informed within days that his son was missing but at that early stage he would still have had some hope that his son would turn up, as a wounded man or perhaps as a prisoner of war.

George Ekins contacted the British Red Cross in the hope that they might have some positive news but when they wrote to him on 28 September it was to inform him that a private in Willingham's B Company had seen him hit, shot in the left arm, about 4.30am in front of Oppy Wood. With no further news forthcoming, the War Office finally wrote to George on 6 December 1917 stating:

It is regretted that no further report has been received concerning Second Lieutenant W. R. Ekins... reported missing 3 May 1917. It is regretted that it will consequently be necessary for the Army Council to consider whether they must not now consider that this officer is dead.

George replied the same day, confirming that he had heard no more. Finally, on 14 December 1917, the Army Council wrote confirming what he most probably had known in his heart for many months:

Sir I am commanded by the Army Council to thank you for your letter of 6th December, to the effect that you have received no further information concerning Second Lieutenant W. R. Ekins... The Army Council are in consequence regretfully constrained to conclude that this officer died on or since 3rd May 1917 and I am to express their sympathy with you in your bereavement.

It must have been a bitter blow to his father to finally have to accept that his son was dead and further tragedy was to strike the family when Willingham's older brother Franklin (who went to Christ's Hospital School), a Lieutenant in the Royal Irish Regiment who had been awarded a Military Cross and Bar, died on active service in January 1919, several months after the cessation of hostilities. Franklin's grave lies in a cemetery near Cherbourg, but Willingham's body was never identified and today he is remembered on the Arras memorial, along with almost 35,000 other men with no known grave who were killed in the fighting around the town.

2nd Lieutenant Willingham Richard Ekins

3rd Battalion, attached 11th Battalion,
East Yorkshire Regiment
Killed in Action 3 May 1917, aged 20
St John's School, 1908-1914

Willingham Richard Ekins joined North House in 1908, and by the time he left school in the summer of 1914 he had been awarded House colours for gymnastics, played for the 2nd XI football team, taken part in debates, been a member of the School choir and spent two years in the School's OTC.

For North House, he played football, cricket and fives in the House competitions. He was also awarded the Special Form prize for French in 1914.

On leaving school, Ekins took the post of school master at Norwood Preparatory School in Exeter, Devon, prior to applying for a temporary commission with the East Yorkshire Regiment in March 1915.

News of Ekins' death in 1917 was not passed on to the School and so his name was not included on the School's Roll of Honour. In May 2017, almost 100 years to the day after his death at Oppy, Willingham Richard Ekins was one of six names added to the Roll of Honour boards in the School Chapel.

John Charles Raymond Godwin, Second Lieutenant Royal Sussex Regiment, was reported wounded and missing on 7 July 1916 during an attack on German trenches at Ovillers. The Company Commander wrote to Godwin's mother:

I am afraid I cannot give you any definite news of Lieut Godwin. On the 7th July, when we charged the village of____, your son was acting second-in-command of my Company. It was about 6.45am that morning when he left me to take charge of the left half-Company. We were then in the second line of trenches and had to go into the first line to double up with another Company. To reach the first line your son had to lead his half-Company through a tunnel near the left end of the second line and I had to take my half-Company through a tunnel near the right end. When in the first line I received a message that the left half-Company was in position. The trench was so crowded that it was impossible for me to travel up and down, so I did not see your son again. I was wounded twice and on reaching our lines again I heard your son was missing and in spite of various inquiries since I have been unable to obtain further news of him. Your son has proved himself a very capable officer and will certainly get his promotion if he is still safe.

It is not clear exactly how John died, though letters and official telegrams, held by the family, throw some light on what probably happened. An early War Office telegram states that, to the best of their knowledge, John was *'slightly wounded'* which must have been of some comfort to the family. However, on 28 July, Mrs Godwin received a telegram which stated that Godwin: *'previously reported wounded July 7 is now reported missing'*.

This prompted the beginning of a desperate search for John's whereabouts by his mother and his sister. Letters were sent to the War Office and to the Graves Registration Committee who were unable to find any trace of his burial. The Godwin family also wrote to a number of charitable organisations including the British Red Cross, the Young Men's Christian Association (YMCA) and the Queen Victoria Jubilee Fund Association, all of which offered assistance in tracing missing servicemen during the war. A plea for information was also inserted in the *Daily Mail*. Replies sometimes fuelled hope, with sightings at Dressing Stations, but most, including eye witness accounts, drew the inevitable conclusion that John was dead, seen to be hit and then fall on the battlefield as he

YMCA letter of acknowledgement

THE MISSING

headed for the second line of German trenches. A private who was in his platoon wrote:

The last time I saw Lieut Godwin he was just by me when we reached the second line of German trenches. I saw him hit and just before he got hit he said to me 'Come on boys!' I got hit just about the same time, or I would have seen to him.

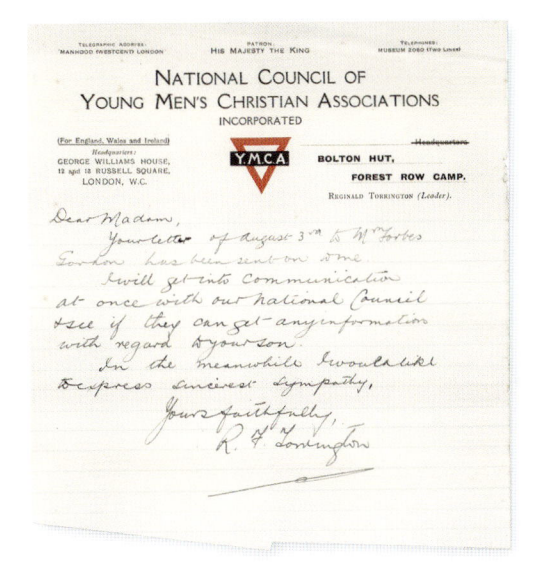

As late as January 1917, the family were still hopeful that he would turn up as a prisoner of war, but it was not to be. With no identifiable body to bury, John's name is today found on the walls of the Thiepval Memorial to the Missing of the Somme.

2nd Lieutenant John Charles Raymond Godwin
10th Battalion, attached 7th Battalion, Royal Sussex Regiment
Killed in Action 7 July 1916, aged 27
St John's School, 1899-1904

John Charles Raymond Godwin was born in Umtata, South Africa on 18 July 1888. His father, Robert Herbert Godwin was at the time a missionary in the Cape Colony where he had met and married his wife Alicia. John, known as Jack by family and friends, came to St John's in 1898, as a Supplementary Foundationer. He played cricket for South House and in 1902 was awarded a House cap and blazer. That same year he came first in the Under 14 quarter mile athletics competition.

John left the School at the end of the Summer Term, 1904 and, after a short time as an apprentice with the London and North Western Railway Company, he began to train as a wireless telegraphist before emigrating to Canada where he was employed by the Marconi Company.

When war broke out, John attested on 16 February 1915 and joined the Canadian Expeditionary Force at Winnipeg. Very soon he was on a ship, the SS Megantic, a White Star Liner on his way back to Britain. The ship docked on 24 May 1915 and two months later John sought and obtained a commission as 2nd Lieutenant in the Royal Sussex Regiment.

The following year he received orders to join the 7th Battalion, Royal Sussex Regiment in France.

On 15 March, John wrote to his mother from Vermelles, just before going into the front line for the first time. He mentioned his delight at discovering that his new company commander had been at school with his brother Harold. He also talked about his first experiences (while out on a wiring party the previous night) of artillery and machine gun fire, describing it as, *'nothing yet to speak of.'*

Early on the morning of 6 July, the 36th Brigade received orders to relieve the 37th Brigade, move into the front line trenches and be prepared to launch an attack towards Ovillers the following day. The Royal Sussex men had some initial success and, despite taking casualties from machine gun fire on their flanks, they took the first two lines of German trenches and pushed on to the third. However it proved impossible to hold on to their most advanced position and, in the face of further severe machine gun fire, any thoughts of pushing on to the final objectives were soon abandoned. The war diary, reviewing the casualties at the end of the following day 8 July 1916, records that twenty officers and over 500 men had been killed, wounded or reported missing. Such was the confusion that only one of the officers killed could be identified and named in the war diary on that day.

Godwin was among those reported missing and on 8 November 1916, Mrs Godwin received a letter from the Military Secretary at the War Office, which said that the Graves Registration Committee had made enquiries and had been unable to find any trace of the burial of 2nd Lieutenant J C R Godwin.

Example of a poster published in 1916 by the Queen Victoria Jubilee Fund Association. 2nd Lieutenant J C R Godwin is shown second row down on the left-hand side.

Private William INGLIS, 686, C. Co., 8th Brig., Australian Imperial Forces, missing July 20th 1916.

Private (or Bomber) Frederick Haydn HOBSON, 957, D. Co., Sheffield City Battn. 12th York & Lancaster Regt., missing July 1st 1916.

Private John KERSHAW, 5156 (Public Schools) Royal Fusiliers, Observation Section, C. Co., missing at Bois des Foureaux 20th July 1916.

2nd Lieut. J. C. R. GODWIN, 7th Royal Sussex Regt., missing July 7th 1916.

Lieut. Edgar HAMPSON, Lancashire Fusiliers, missing July 1st 1916.

Private H. L. FEARN, 8137, A. Co., Manchester Regt., missing at Guillemont July 30th 1916.

Private Harry ALDERTON, West Yorkshire Regt., wounded and missing July 1st 1916.

2nd Lieut. E. W. VENNER, Royal West Kent Regt., attached Manchester Regt., missing July 9th–11th 1916.

Captain Samuel WILLIS, Royal Irish Rifles, missing July 1st 1916 at Thiepval.

Private George BINNS, 22114, King's Own Scottish Borderers, missing in a wood near La Bassée 17th July 1916.

Private William OLIPHANT, 6349, 11th, transferred 2nd Argyll and Sutherland Highlanders, C. Co., missing 18th Aug. 1916.

Private William A. STEPHEN, S/13926, 1st Gordon Highlanders, B. Co., 8th platoon, missing July 18th–19th 1916 at Mametz Wood.

QUEEN VICTORIA JUBILEE FUND ASSOCIATION
for the relief of British subjects in distress at Geneva
Honorary Manager of Enquiry Branch: S. GUTMANN

MISSING BRITISH OFFICERS,
N. C. OFFICERS AND PRIVATE SOLDIERS.

Private Andrew Deuchar, 27854, Highland Light Infantry, missing Sept. 3rd 1916.

Capt. G. G. H. Batty, 6th Northamptonshire Regt., reported to have died of wounds Sept. 27th 1916.

Private Lewis Phillips, 25462, Lancashire Fusiliers, missing July 30th 1916.

Private J. M. L. Jardine, 3286, Reinforcement to 25th Battn. Australian Infantry, missing at Pozières 29th July 1916, in a bombing expedition.

2nd Lieut. George Sholto Douglas Carver, 2nd Devonshire Regt., wounded and missing July 1st 1916.

Sergt. W. E. Abbott, 625, West Yorkshire Regt., missing June 29th 1916.

Capt. Francis Maxwell Barton, Australian Imperial Force, A. Co., missing August 11th 1916 near Mouquet Farm.

Capt. Ernest Cecil MacLaren, Lancashire Fusiliers, missing July 1st 1916 at Thiepval.

2nd Lieut. Vyvyan Hope Lancelott Davenport, Leicestershire Regt. missing July 14th 1916, at Bazentin-le-Petit-Wood.

Private Willie Lawton, 4577, B. Co., 7th platoon, Duke of Wellington's West Riding Regt., wounded and missing Sept. 3rd 1916.

Private George Craig, 2833, 4th Gordon Highlanders, D. Co., 16th platoon, missing July 23rd 1916.

2nd Lieut. G. B. T. Jardine, Argyll & Sutherland Highlanders, attached Cameron Highlanders, missing at Le Sars-Bapaume Oct. 18th 1916.

Private John Scott, 3099, Highland Light Infantry, missing 15th July 1916.

2nd Lieut. Maurice Sharpe, Royal Flying Corps, disabled when flying over the Somme front Oct. 28th 1916, missing.

CHAPTER 7 THE WAR IN THE AIR

Military aviation was in its infancy when war began in 1914. The Royal Flying Corps (RFC) was established by Royal Warrant on 13 April 1912 and included a military wing and a naval wing, with the latter known as the Royal Naval Air Service (RNAS) from 1 July 1914. This meant that when the war began there were in effect two distinct air services although it was not until 1 August 1915 that the Royal Navy took full control of the RNAS. However, as the war progressed, the importance of an effective and unified air force was recognised, and a decision was made to merge the army and naval air sections to provide an air service that would be on equal standing with the Army and Royal Navy. As a result, on 1 April 1918, the Royal Air Force (RAF) was formed.

At least fifty-nine OJs and one member of staff are known to have been members of the RFC, RNAS or RAF although many of these had originally enlisted in the army before being seconded or attached to one of the air services. Seventeen OJs serving with the flying services died during the war, though it is interesting to note that more were killed in flying accidents (ten) than as a result of enemy action (seven).

FLYING ACCIDENTS

Leaving St John's in the summer of 1906, Bertram Robert Raggett went up to Durham University, despite only being sixteen years old. He attended Armstrong College where he took a BSc in Mechanical Engineering, passing with First Class Honours in 1909 before he had reached his nineteenth birthday, a remarkable achievement. When war broke out, Bertram first volunteered as a despatch rider with the Royal Engineers Signals Company. In January 1917 he was commissioned in the Royal Garrison Artillery (RGA) but a few months later, on 10 August 1917, he began training to be an observer with the Royal Flying Corps. Bertram attended several flying schools in England before completing his training and being posted to France on 4 December 1917 where he joined 10 Squadron of the RFC, based on the French/Belgian border at Abeele. One of 10 Squadron's principal roles was to 'spot' enemy artillery batteries so that they could be targeted in counter-battery fire by British artillery. They did this by looking for the muzzle flashes of the enemy guns and this type of sortie was often referred to as a 'flash recce' in official records.

On 5 January 1918, Raggett, aged 27, and his pilot, nineteen-year-old 2nd Lieutenant Ronald V Garbett, took off on a flash recce in their Armstrong Whitworth FK8 (Serial Number B320). This two-seater bi-plane was ideally suited to the role of artillery observation but on this occasion something went wrong. Accident reports state that the upper left wing of the aircraft broke away causing the plane to fall to the ground and crash, close to the airfield at Abeele; the plane was completely wrecked and both men were killed. The two bodies were recovered from the wreckage and taken to the nearby military cemetery at Lijssenthoek where they were laid to rest next to each other.

In a letter to his mother offering his condolences, Bertram's Commanding Officer wrote:

He is the man in the squadron I can least spare, for I considered him quite the best observer and one of the keenest officers I had, and the whole squadron will miss him for his continual good temper and energy. He was due to go on leave the day before, but offered to wait for a week, so that the next observer on the list, a married man, might go in his place.

The likelihood of being killed was spread across all three services. However, the risk of dying accidentally was proportionally higher for those who fought in the air. Spencer Harold Millard left St John's in 1916 and by October 1918 was a flight cadet, about to get his RAF wings when, on 16 October, he was killed in a flying accident. This was devastating news for his family and a letter from Spencer's father, the Reverend Frederick Millard, to his brother Richard who was now serving with the RAF as an observer in Egypt, shows how keenly they felt his loss. His father wrote:

Above: Bertram Robert Raggett memorial at St Lukes Church, Spital Tongues, Newcastle

THE WAR IN THE AIR

Spencer Harold Millard in uniform

My dear old Dick
I hardly know how to write to you in the midst of this great sorrow to tell you that Spencer is to be but a memory to you – but such a precious memory. He was here on leave a fortnight ago looking so well, and strong, full of the highest spirits, and life, and now battered and broken his poor body waits for me to go and consign it to its last resting place.

And his mother wrote, confirming the news they had all been dreading:

My dearest Dick, you will have got father's cable saying Spencer was killed flying early this morning it was bound to happen for he said himself his eyes misjudged the landing and he had already crashed three times.

In her next letter she described how the accident happened:

As far as is possible to know, this is the story… Spencer was practically at the end of his training and had flown a Camel for some weeks practising firing the guns regularly and they said he was quite a good pilot though his hands were heavy, but he never lost his nerve and was able to get himself, and had done, out of all sorts of very dangerous positions. Well on Thursday morning at 9.00am several went up on Camels to fire guns and do stunts – Spencer went up to 2,000 feet firing at interval and when at 2,000 feet up they think that the guns must have recoiled and struck his head as he bent forward to adjust the engines for the machine nose-dived from that height and turned on its back at about 200 feet from the ground.

They feel quite sure Spencer must have lost consciousness when the gun struck him and only had time to shut off the engine before he was unable to do anything, for they say there was plenty of time at that height to recover his position and correct the machine so that he could have landed. His face was cut on the cheek and forehead by the guns and his neck was broken but nothing else and they think he would be dead before he crashed.

A military funeral was held at Andover Parish Church at 2.00pm on Monday 21 October 1918 and Spencer was buried in Andover Cemetery, Hampshire.

First plane crash 1918. Spencer standing in the middle of the group

The following day, 22 October 1918, the last OJ to be killed before the armistice, Captain Kenneth Carlyle Gill, MC, of 22 Squadron RAF (formerly 1st Battalion, Cambridgeshire Regiment) died in a flying accident in France. He is buried in Fillievres British Cemetery, Pas de Calais, France and the inscription on his gravestone reads:

AND IF WE FALL
WE FALL FOR THEE
GLAD TO DIE IF THOU ART FREE
ENGLAND

Captain Kenneth Carlyle Gill
22 Squadron RAF (formerly 1st Battalion, Cambridgeshire Regiment)
Killed in Action 22 October 1918, aged 25
St John's School, 1907-1912

Kenneth Gill came from a large family in West Wittering, Sussex where his father was Vicar. He excelled at School, where he was in South House, and was awarded School colours for football, cricket and running. He sang in the choir and was made a prefect in his final year. Kenneth spent two years at St Catharine's College, Cambridge and planned to enter the Church and become a missionary. Instead, he joined the Cambridgeshire Territorial Force in September 1914.

Kenneth enlisted in the Cambridgeshire regiment as a private and was commissioned in October 1914. He was quickly promoted to lieutenant and received praise for his skill and coolness in patrol duty. Awarded an MC in 1915 for trying to bring in a fellow officer who had been mortally wounded, he was himself wounded. Kenneth spent many months in hospital and after rejoining his old regiment in 1916 was attached to the RFC, becoming a flying instructor in September 1917. He married Louie Cullen on 3 April, 1918, but six months later died of wounds in France on 22 October 1918 following a flying accident.

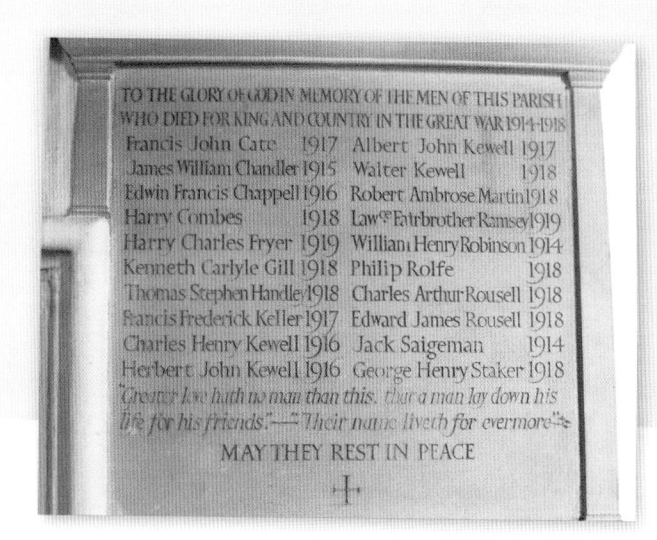

His younger brother, Cecil Ernest Gaspar Gill was also an OJ. On leaving School in 1915, he also joined the Cambridgeshire Regiment and then transferred to the RFC. After the war, Cecil qualified as a doctor and for a while was a medical missionary in Papua New Guinea, becoming ordained in 1930. In 1934, he was accepted into the Roman Catholic Church and from 1936 practised as a Doctor in Cardiff.

One of Kenneth's older brothers was the sculptor Eric Gill, and another was Leslie Macdonald Gill (Max Gill) the graphic designer and cartographer who designed the lettering used on headstones and war memorials by the Imperial War Graves Commission. Eric Gill carved the Parish War Memorial at St Peter and St Paul's Church West Wittering on which Kenneth's name is recorded.

Great War memorial, St Peter and St Paul's Church, West Wittering, carved by Eric Gill

A·M·D·G· In loving memory of KENNETH CARLYLE GILL M·C· Capt. Camb. Regt. Atd R·A·F·

Killed in France 22 Oct 1918 This window is given by his wife Louie Gwendolen

Kenneth Carlyle Gill is also commemorated in a stained-glass window in the south aisle, given by his wife Louie Gwendolen.

Kenneth Gill memorial window at St Peter and St Paul's Church, West Wittering

A·M·D·G· In loving memory of KENNETH·CARLYLE·GILL M·C· Capt. Camb. Regt. Atd R·A·F·

FLYING ACES

In the early days of the war, aircraft were chiefly used for reconnaissance and observation but, as the war progressed, pilots began to engage in aerial battles and dog fights with German pilots. Fighter pilots who shot down five or more enemy aircraft gained considerable celebrity status and became known as 'Aces'.

Wing Commander Frederick James Powell OBE, MC, served in both the First and Second World Wars. He left St John's in 1911, at the age of 18, having spent five years at the School. Powell joined the Duke of Lancaster's Own Yeomanry in August 1913 and on 21 September 1914, soon after the outbreak of the war, he transferred to the 18th (Service) Battalion (3rd City) the Manchester Regiment, as a second lieutenant. He immediately volunteered for service in the RFC and transferred as an observation officer in November 1914. Powell then started training as a pilot, obtained his certificate and quickly attained efficiency. He was awarded the Military Cross in January 1916 and *The Johnian* for February 1916 published an account of his activities, saying:

In June 1915 he went to France. His work there has met with approval and commendation. He has had frequent combats in the air with hostile aircraft and has been very successful. On one occasion he engaged four German machines single-handed, and forced them all down, but as the engagement was fought over the German lines it could not be definitely ascertained what damage had been done to the enemy, though observers stated that two aeroplanes were destroyed. He was mentioned in Sir John French's last dispatch for gallant and distinguished service, and later was awarded the Military Cross and promoted to Captain and Flight-Commander.

Powell quickly gained recognition as a British 'air ace' with six confirmed and nine unconfirmed aerial victories.

In February 1917, Powell was appointed chief fighting instructor in the RFC's Northern Group and was made a squadron commander with the temporary rank of major on 16 May 1917. He returned to France on 2 August 1917 as Commander of 41 Squadron. However, on 2 February 1918 he was wounded during a dog fight, made a forced landing on a German airfield and was captured. Powell spent the rest of the war as a prisoner of war and was repatriated after the armistice. Powell remained in the RAF after the war, relinquishing his commission in 1931. He returned to military service

Lieutenant Arthur Elsdale Boultbee
25 Squadron Royal Flying Corps
and Northamptonshire Regiment
Killed in Action 17 March 1917, aged 19
St John's School, 1908-1909

Arthur Elsdale Boultbee came to St John's in May 1908 where he joined one of his older brothers, Beauchamp St John Boultbee who had been at the School since 1906. Both boys left at the end of the Summer Term 1909 to continue their education at The King's School, Ely.

From Ely, Arthur gained a history exhibition to St Catharine's College, Cambridge in 1915 but, in December 1915, after one term, he applied for a commission and joined the Northamptonshire Regiment. In 1916 he transferred to the RFC and began flight training, finally being posted to 25 Squadron for active service on 30 December 1916, joining the squadron at Auchel (Lozinghem) on New Year's Day 1917. Less than three months later he was dead, shot down by the Red Baron along with his observer.

Arthur's brother, Beauchamp St John Boultbee also served, in the East Yorkshire Regiment and then the RFC, winning a Military Cross in 1917.

during the Second World War and was promoted to acting Wing Commander at the end of 1942. Mentioned three times in despatches between 1943 and 1945 he was made an Officer of the Order of the British Empire (OBE) on 14 June 1945, in the King's Birthday Honours. He died in 1992 aged 96.

Powell's aerial victories took place between 1915 and 1916. The following year, two OJs also serving in the RFC, Arthur Elsdale Boultbee and Frank Guy Buckingham Pascoe, fell victim to the German 'ace' Manfred von Richthofen, (also known as the 'Red Baron') when they were shot down within four months of each other.

On 17 March 1917, Boultbee and his observer Frederick King took off from Lozinghem, one of nine FE2bs of 25 Squadron taking part in a reconnaissance and photographic mission between Annouellin and Vitry, north east of Arras. German fighters took to the air to confront them and several aircraft on both sides were either shot down or forced to land, including Arthur's FE2b which became the 27th victim of the legendary 'Red Baron'. Arthur was 19 years old and Frederick was 22 years old.

The two airmen were laid to rest in the village cemetery at Oppy, but the British authorities were unaware that the two men had been found and buried so they were listed as missing and remained so for many years after the war. Commonwealth War Graves Commission records show that the two bodies were found in the cemetery at Oppy in 1930 and subsequently identified by their clothing. As a result, both men were given a named burial in Canadian Cemetery No 2, Neuville-St Vaast.

Second Lieutenant Frank Guy Buckingham Pascoe was the observer for pilot Sergeant Hubert Arthur Whatley flying in an RE8. They were escorting another aircraft from the squadron on a photographic mission when they were shot down by the Red Baron on 2 July 1917. Von Richthofen's combat report said:

I attacked the foremost plane of an enemy squadron. The observer collapsed with the first shots. Shortly thereafter, the pilot was mortally wounded. The RE reared up and I fired on the rearing aircraft from a distance of 50 metres with a few more shots until flames shot out of the machine and the opponent crashed burning.

Both bodies were recovered and buried by Australian troops who were nearby. The graves were lost in the subsequent battles and both Pascoe, who was aged 20, and Whatley, aged 19, are commemorated on the Arras Flying Services Memorial in France.

2nd Lieutenant Frank Guy Buckingham Pascoe
53 Squadron RFC and 9th Battalion Royal Irish Fusiliers
Killed in Action 2 July 1917, aged 20
St John's School, 1907-1915

Frank left School at the end of the Easter term 1915 to take up a commission with the Royal Irish Fusiliers and then applied for transfer to the RFC. At St John's he was a School Prefect, a member of the choir and a corporal in the OTC. He won the Lower Sixth prizes for Greek composition and Latin composition for the Autumn Term 1914 and in February 1915 was elected a member of the Literary and Dramatic Society in place of Edward Rowley Kelly, who had left the previous term to enlist. He was also appointed to Kelly's position as assistant editor of *The Johnian*.

Frank's father, the Reverend Frank Pascoe, Vicar of St George's, Millom received a telegram from the war office on Friday 6 July 1915 with the news that his son had been missing since 2 July.

Confirmation of his death came at 10am on Sunday 8 July, just as he was preparing to take the morning service at St George's Church. The *Millom Gazette* dated Friday 13 July 1915 records that the curate, the Reverend G W Arnold informed the congregation saying that:

They would all learn with regret that the Vicar's son had been killed in action, and he invited the congregation to join with him in special prayer. The hymn 'Peace, Perfect Peace' was sung and after the lessons were read the congregation dispersed.

CHAPTER 8
CONSCRIPTION AND CONSCIENTIOUS OBJECTORS

During 1915 it became clear to the British government that the system of relying on volunteers to fight was not producing sufficient recruits to replace the mounting casualties so, reluctantly, they decided to introduce conscription or compulsory active service.

The Military Service Act passed in January 1916 imposed conscription on all single men aged between 18 and 41. The medically unfit, clergymen, teachers and some in reserved occupations were exempt, but a second act passed in May 1916 extended conscription to married men.

Conscientious objectors, who objected to fighting on moral grounds were also exempted but were expected to take civilian or non-combatant roles.

Many of St John's former pupils could claim legal exemption: those who were ordained and many who were resident abroad would fall into this category. Nevertheless, forty-three OJs served as Chaplain to the Forces and of these six were killed in action. Nineteen OJs are known to have served with the Royal Army Medical Corps (RAMC) which was often the service of choice for those who preferred not to bear arms, but there is no evidence that any of these OJs was a conscientious objector.

Patriotism ran high throughout the war and there was huge social pressure on all eligible men to enlist. On 20 May 1916 the *Dorking and Leatherhead Advertiser* published a statement from the headmaster listing the number of OJs and masters who had already signed up. The Reverend Downes made special mention of the distinctions gained in the war by former pupils and took pains to point out that all masters who were within the age bracket had attested and that four had been rejected on medical grounds. He said that there was only one for whom he had claimed exemption on the grounds that he was doing very useful work preparing boys for the Army and Navy in the Army class.

CHAPTER 9
MASTERS SERVING IN THE GREAT WAR

Of the 16 masters shown in this photograph, ten of those standing in the back row served in the armed forces between 1914 and 1918 and three (Alderson, Bourne and Driffield) lost their lives and are listed on the School's Roll of Honour boards.

Albert Evelyn Alderson was appointed to the teaching staff at the beginning of 1912. His arrival coincided with the formation of the School's OTC and he and the Reverend Clarence White Ingram assisted Lancelot Townshend Driffield in running the Corps. Albert was a keen cricketer, coaching the junior boys and playing locally for Leatherhead Cricket Club. In 1913 he became President of the Protestants Club (the name given to the School debating society between 1910 and 1914) and in 1914 he was appointed House Tutor of East House. But this appointment was to be short lived; on the outbreak of war in August 1914 Albert informed the headmaster that he had applied for a commission in the army and on 4 September 1914 received a probationary commission as a Second Lieutenant in the Queen's (Royal West Surrey) Regiment.

Albert's commission was confirmed in the London Gazette of 9 March 1915 and by April 1915 he was with 3rd Battalion Queens at Rochester, Kent. Albert soon received the news that he was to be sent or 'attached' to the 1st Battalion of the King's Own Yorkshire Light Infantry, arriving in France on 11 May 1915, before heading up to the Ypres Salient where his new battalion were involved in the ongoing Second Battle of Ypres. In September the battalion moved south, into France and into action once more at the Battle of Loos. Within days of the battle grinding to a halt in October 1915, the 1st KOYLI, along with the rest of 28 Division prepared to sail for Salonika (now known as Thessalonika) where they remained for the majority of the war. Albert was twice promoted during this time, eventually attaining the rank of Captain before he drowned in what appears to have been an unfortunate accident.

Masters' Group, Summer 1914

St John's School, Leatherhead and the Great War, 1914-1919

The events leading to his death are described in a letter from his Colonel:

On the 11th of March, 1918, Captain Alderson and a brother officer were returning to their post in the dark; to reach his post he had to cross a barbed wire fence which ran down to the river bank, and it seemed certain that he either tripped in the wire or the bank gave way, and threw him into the river, which was in flood at the time. Lieutenant Mottley, who was with him, made two attempts to save him, but failed. His body was found, and he was buried in the military cemetery at Salonika.

I should like to add that his death was a great blow to me personally, as I had known him since the day he joined this Battalion in France. I felt the greatest esteem for him as his Commanding Officer, and I can only say that I have lost one of my best company commanders.

Albert Evelyn Alderson now lies in Struma Military Cemetery, Greece.

Albert Alderson at St John's School, 1913

2nd Lieutenant Cyprian Bourne

When Albert Alderson left to take up his commission in 1914, his place as Sergeant in the School's OTC was taken by another teacher, Cyprian Bourne. Cyprian was the fifth member of the family to come to St John's, having been preceded by his four cousins who were pupils at the School.

At St John's he took up the post of Lower Fifth master in 1913 but at the end of 1915, Cyprian followed Albert Alderson into The Queen's (Royal West Surrey) Regiment, and his commission was confirmed on 20 January 1916. Several months of training at various depots around the country followed, including time in Ireland during the Easter Rising of 1916 and at the bombing school on Clapham Common where he qualified as a bomb (grenade) instructor.

The following extract from his obituary in *The Johnian*, June 1917 describes his subsequent war service and death, aged 29, on 11 April 1917:

In November 1916 he went to France to join the 6th Battalion of The Queen's. Whilst there he attended a musketry course, gained the highest marks possible and was appointed Brigade Musketry Officer. At various times he held the posts of Second in Command, Company Commander, Transport Officer, and Quarter-Master. Last of all he was made Bombing Officer, and it was in this capacity that he met his death. In the early morning of Easter Day he led a bombing party into the German trenches, was wounded and taken prisoner. For two days he lay in a German dug-out where he was well treated by the Germans, and when they surrendered to an attack of our men two days later, he was brought over by them to the English lines, too late however to save his life. He died of his wounds on the 11th April.

All who knew him will readily confirm his commanding officer's estimate of him:

'He was a splendid fellow in every way, a gallant gentleman, and absolutely to be relied on in everything he undertook.'

MASTERS SERVING IN THE GREAT WAR

Lancelot Townshend Driffield, Captain, St John's School OTC

The sudden death at the School of Lancelot Townshend Driffield on 9 October 1917 at the age of 37, came as a terrible shock to the whole community. A tall, athletic and popular teacher, Driffield had been a pupil at the School from September 1890 to November 1899 when he won a classical scholarship to St Catharine's College, Cambridge. At Cambridge he was awarded a *'blue'* for both cricket and football and later played county cricket for Northamptonshire. Lancelot Driffield returned to his old School as a master in September 1911 and quickly proved himself to be a valuable member of staff. He was appointed Housemaster of East House in 1912, coached and managed the School cricket team and was Contingent Commander of the OTC. Holding the rank of Captain in the Special Reserve, Lancelot Driffield remained in Leatherhead when war broke out. The headmaster explained the reason for this in his monthly report to the Committee dated 18 September 1914, saying that the masters who held commissions in the OTC had applied for a commission but *'had received notice from the War Office to the effect that OTC officers were not being taken as the military authorities considered their work of training the OTC contingents so important.'*

A heartfelt tribute was paid to him in the October issue of *The Johnian*:

It is with feelings of the deepest sorrow that we have to report the death of Lancelot Townshend Driffield, whose body was found lying just outside his rooms at the School on the evening of Tuesday, October 9th.

Lancelot's grief-stricken widowed mother was also in their thoughts. Her husband, George Townshend Driffield, died in April 1901 when Lancelot was eleven and her only other child, Herbert George Driffield, had been killed in action just two months previously:

Deeply as we regret his loss for our own sakes, our chief thoughts must be for his Mother. Her family consisted of Mr Driffield and a younger brother, and the latter was killed in France only a few weeks ago.

At the inquest held two days later the doctor, who conducted the 'post-mortem' examination, said that he had found *'a very diseased condition of the heart'*. The jury returned a verdict of *'Death from natural causes'*.

The whole of the Senior School and staff attended the funeral in the School Chapel at 8.30am on Saturday 13 October. Those who were in the OTC wore their uniforms and a detachment from the 10th Surrey Volunteer Regiment provided a firing party. The second part of the service took place in the afternoon at Northampton General Cemetery, attended by some of Lancelot Driffield's family and representatives from the Northamptonshire County Cricket Club. A special memorial service was held in the School Chapel and an appeal to OJs raised fifteen pounds and nine shillings for a brass memorial plaque which was put up in the Chapel in 1918.

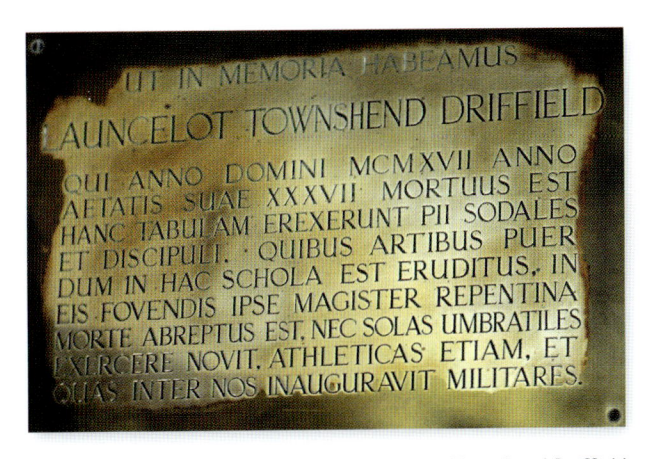

Brass memorial plaque for Lancelot Townshend Driffield in St John's School Chapel

CHAPTER 10 BROTHERS IN WAR

Many families suffered terrible losses during the Great War. Receiving news of the death of one child was shocking, but much worse was the repeated arrival of a telegram to say that yet another son had been killed in action. St John's families experienced this pain and sorrow no less than many hundreds of others all over the country. At least ten pairs of OJ brothers died in the war, and many of their parents lost further sons who were educated elsewhere.

The Reverend Prince William Thomas Beechey, a Lincolnshire vicar and his wife Amy Reeve Beechey had fourteen children in 22 years, eight boys and six girls. Amy was widowed in 1912 and between 1914 and 1918 saw all eight of her sons sign up to fight in the war. Only three survived. Two of her boys were educated at St John's and both died in the war. Barnard, the eldest, came to the School as a Foundationer in September 1886, the recipient of the very first Albany Scholarship, and was followed in 1897 by one of his younger brothers, Frank Collett Reeve Beechey.

Barnard excelled at mathematics and it was no surprise that he left school in 1896 with an Open Scholarship to St John's College, Cambridge. He graduated in 1899 and went on to teach at various schools before taking the position of assistant master at Dorchester Grammar School in 1908. Besides teaching mathematics Barnard coached the football 1st XI and helped to set up the School's OTC. He left Dorchester in 1912, the same year his father died, and returned to the family home. In August 1914, Barnard was 37 years old, and he joined the 9th Battalion of the Lincolnshire Regiment as a private. By the time he was posted to France in July 1915 Barnard Beechey was a lance sergeant and soon found himself on the front line. He was the first of the brothers to die, killed on 25 September 1915.

Barnard Reeve Beechey

His grave was subsequently lost and today his name is inscribed on the walls of the Ploegsteert Memorial in Belgium.

Frank left St John's in 1904 and went on to De Aston School at Market Rasen. He took up teaching and by 1912 he was an assistant master at the Lincoln Cathedral Choir School, where he remained until just a few weeks before the outbreak of hostilities when he resigned his position and announced he was to be married. But the war, when it came, brought about a dramatic change of heart. Frank abandoned plans for marriage and instead announced he intended to join up.

On 12 August 1914 (the day after Lord Kitchener's 'Your King and Country Need You' appeal) he was at the recruiting office. Two days later, in the town of Beverley, he applied for a temporary commission in the East Yorkshire Regiment. The commission however failed to materialise and, frustrated by the delay, Frank instead enlisted as a private in the Lincolnshire Regiment on 7 September 1914. Posted to the 7th Battalion he eventually received his commission as a signals officer in May 1915. Training continued for a further year before, in May 1916, Frank was posted to France, to the 13th Battalion of the East Yorkshire Regiment (a Hull 'Pals' Regiment).

In November 1916, as the weather deteriorated, the British determined to make one final attempt to take objectives in the north of the Somme front in an attack now known as the Battle of the Ancre. This time the East Yorkshires were to spearhead the assault against Serre but once again it was destined to fail; an adjacent battalion's attack faltered, leaving the 13th East Yorkshires flank exposed. Despite some men reaching as far as the German third trench line the advance first stalled and then began to collapse as German counter attacks pushed

Frank Collett Reeve Beechey

them back or cut them off completely. Frank's signallers tried in vain to maintain telephone lines to the forward troops and as a group suffered heavy casualties. Frank himself, having left the forward trench to help his men, was severely wounded in the legs by a shell blast. It proved impossible to get Frank back into the trench as enemy fire swept no man's land, but the Battalion Medical Officer bravely crawled out to dress Frank's wounds.

Remarkably, it turned out that the Medical Officer, Captain Harold Ernest Pierpoint Yorke, though five years younger than Frank, had been at St John's with him between 1901 and 1904 and it may have been some comfort to Frank to see a familiar face from his schooldays. Frank was finally brought in at dusk and taken to the Casualty Clearing Station, but it was too late to save him and he died the next day, 14 November 1916. Aged 30, he was the second of the five Beechey brothers to die between September 1915 and the end of December 1917.

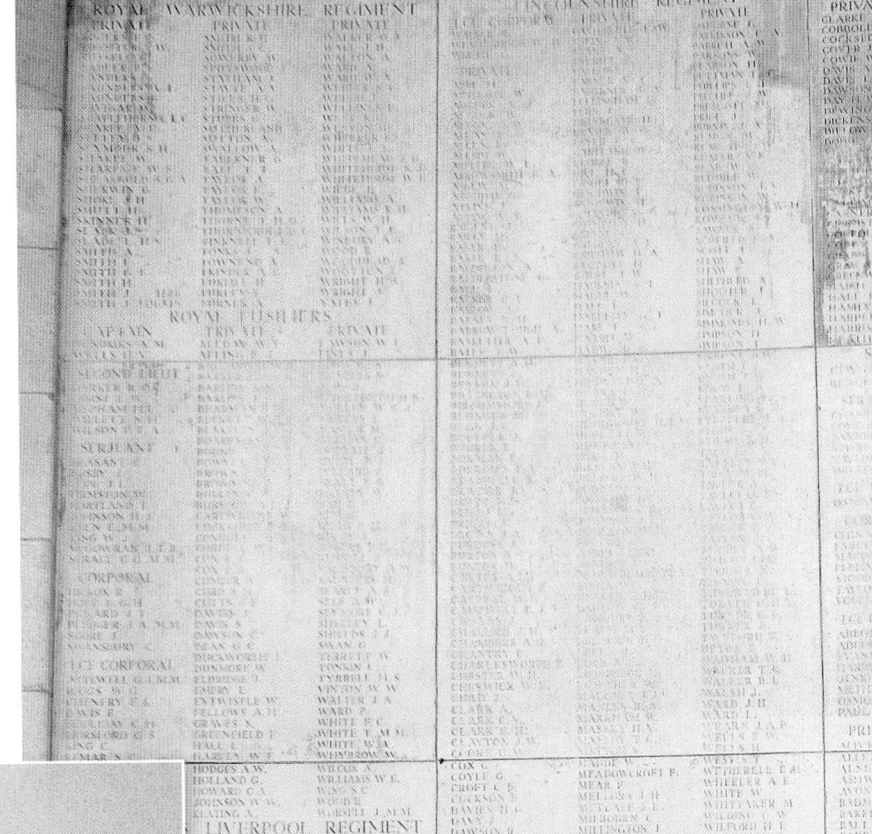

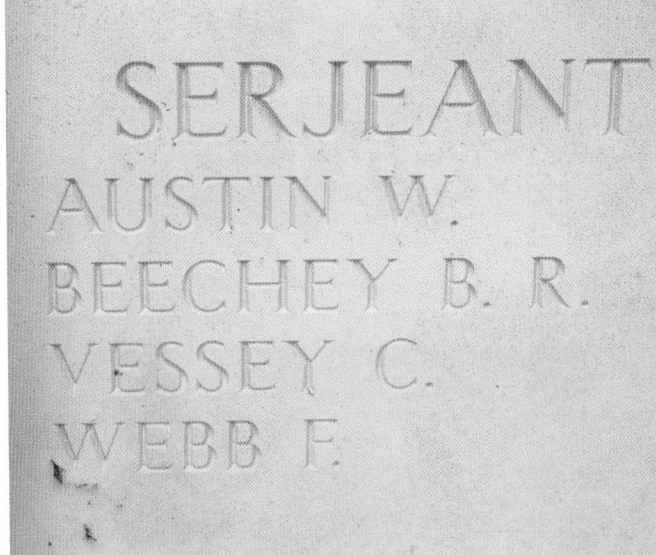

B R Beechey, Ploegsteert Memorial

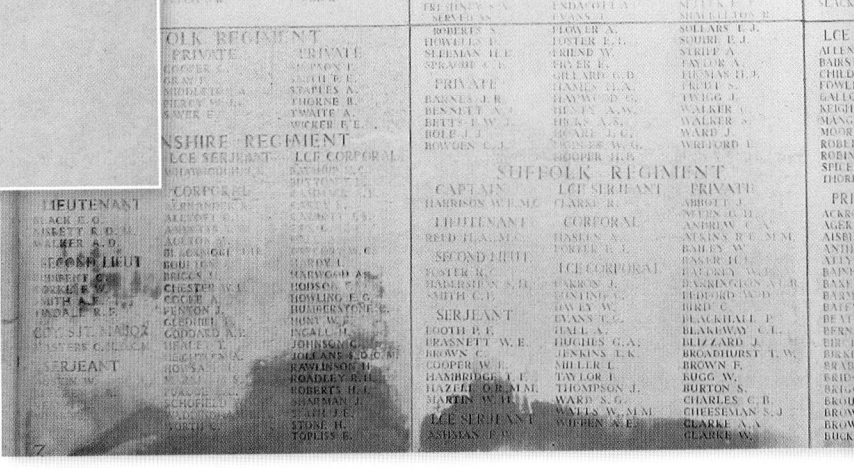

Ploegsteert Memorial in 2009, prior to restoration work

CHAPTER 11 OLD JOHNIANS IN THE RAMC

Boys in the OTC at St John's were taught very little about army medical routine so, in 1916, the editor of *The Johnian* wrote to an OJ serving with the Royal Army Medical Corps (RAMC) saying '*Tell us something about RAMC work at the front.*' He duly received and published a lengthy article describing the system currently in place in France. Living and working conditions were explained in the article:

Every battalion in the field, and most other units of any size, have a Regimental Medical Officer, generally a subaltern or captain, who accompanies and lives the life of his unit. His first aid post is established as near the front-line trenches as possible; it may be in the support trench, it may be in a dug-out, or perhaps a shell-battered house.

Wounds were initially treated with 'first field dressings' which consisted of two dressings, along with safety pins for fastening them in a brown fabric wrapper. Stretcher bearers carried wounded men to the Advanced Dressing Stations (ADS) between a quarter and half a mile from the front line and then on to the Main Dressing Station (MDS) run by the headquarters of the Field Ambulance. Wounded soldiers were given warm food and, after their wounds had been reassessed, were taken to the Casualty Clearing Station (CCS):

The first thing that Tommy asks for when he is wounded is a cigarette; his second want is supplied at the ADS in the shape of a good warm feed. Then,

generally under cover of night, he sets out on the next stage of his journey in horse – or motor-ambulance to the 'Headquarters of the Field Ambulance,' of which that particular ADS is a part. This is situated from one to two miles in the rear. Here his wound is looked at again, and classification labels checked. Then up come the cars of the 'Motor Ambulance Convoy', and our friend finds himself deposited at the first of anything approaching the popular idea of a hospital, namely, the 'Casualty Clearing Station'. This is situated usually in a town some six miles or so further back, in the most convenient building available.

At the Casualty Clearing stations, the wounded were tended by nurses and eventually despatched to the General Hospital at the base. A 'Blighty' wound was an injury serious enough to warrant being sent home to England or 'Blighty' in popular slang:

If our friend has not been fortunate enough to get a 'Blighty' wound, he is kept at the hospital until he is fit to look after himself and is rather less comfortable under canvas than he was in hospital. When he is fit for general duty again, he is sent to another camp called 'Base Details.' Here he returns to the old life of 'ordinary diet' and mother earth for his pillow.

If, on the other hand, Thomas has obtained a 'Blighty' wound, he is placed as soon as he is fit to travel, on a hospital ship, and in a few hours he finds himself in bed in an English hospital at home – that Paradise of a wounded man's imagination.

Wilton House Hospital 1916. Richard Millard aged 18, sitting on the ground, third from the left

Richard Millard, who suffered a 'Blighty' wound to his arm on 1 July 1916, was evacuated back to England. He had sustained a fairly large flesh wound in his left arm which would not seem serious nowadays but gas gangrene was always a risk before the days of antibiotics. Richard was sent to Wilton House Hospital, a stately home near Salisbury in Wiltshire which opened some of its rooms for convalescing officers during the war.

Several of the eighteen OJs who served with the RAMC providing first aid and emergency treatment for servicemen on the front line and in casualty clearing stations, had medical qualifications. One such OJ was John Wilfred Stokes who came to St John's with his two younger brothers in 1888. Leaving in 1890, he trained at University College, London and qualified as a surgeon in 1895. John was house surgeon at the Sheffield Children's Hospital and house physician at the Sheffield Royal Infirmary. Later he became anaesthetist to the Royal Infirmary and demonstrator of anatomy at the University of Sheffield. After war broke out in August 1914, John Wilfrid Stokes became Lieutenant Colonel and Commanding Officer of the 3rd West Riding Field Ambulance. He went to France in 1915 but was twice invalided home suffering from shell shock. He died on 10 February 1916 in the hospital for officers at Latchmere, Ham Common.

Others in the RAMC were to survive the war. Jeffrey Alexander Amherst Orlebar left St John's in 1894 for Magdalene College, Cambridge and then studied medicine at St Thomas's Hospital, qualifying as a surgeon in 1905. Jeffrey practised in Edmonton in London and served as a ship's doctor with the Orient Line. He moved to Hove in Sussex in 1914 and then served as a Captain in the RAMC in Salonika and Gallipoli from 1914 to 1919 and was subsequently medical officer for Brighton Dispensary and house physician at the Royal Sussex Hospital. He died in January 1936 at the age of 56.

Orlebar survived without physical injury, but proximity to the front line meant that many in the RAMC were injured while serving at the front.

Captain Harold Ernest Pierpoint Yorke, who went to the aid of Frank Beechey on the battlefront in France in 1916, was a medical student at St Bartholomew's Hospital before the war. Joining the RAMC in December 1915, Harold first served in Egypt and later in France. In January 1917 he was awarded the MC for conspicuous gallantry and devotion to duty. His citation reads:

He displayed great courage and determination in tending the wounded under very heavy fire. Later, although himself wounded, he continued to carry out his work.

After the war, Harold Yorke continued to serve with the RAMC as a doctor and was promoted to the rank of Major in 1930.

Captain Harold Ernest Pierpoint Yorke, RAMC

CHAPTER 12 CHAPLAIN TO THE FORCES

The chaplain's role in the Great War was much the same as that of a present-day army chaplain:

To provide spiritual support, pastoral care, and moral guidance to all, irrespective of religion or belief…

To conduct religious services at sea or in the field.

In August 1914, there were just 117 full-time army chaplains and 129 naval chaplains serving with the armed forces.

With the huge expansion of the armed forces from 1914, as men and boys answered the call to defend their country, there was a similar growth in numbers in the Army Chaplain's Department to meet the demand for chaplains to accompany the troops abroad. By 1918, over 3,000 Anglican clergymen had been granted temporary commissions with the army. A further 150 Church of England chaplains joined the Navy between 1914 and 1918.

Forty-six former pupils, three assistant masters, the School Secretary and a Governor served as chaplains in the Army and Royal Navy between October 1914 and November 1918. The Chaplain-General, Bishop John Taylor Smith, who was responsible for the recruitment of Church of England army chaplains, interviewed the majority of applicants at the War Office. He asked them a series of questions to determine their suitability to serve abroad. Their age, fitness, marital status, population of their parish (where applicable), ability to preach without notes and ability to ride a horse, were all taken into consideration. Those who were accepted had their names recorded in the 'Army List' and published in *The London Gazette*. Little or no training was given to temporary chaplains before 1917, and their role was ill-defined. Apart from conducting religious and burial services, a chaplain, more generally known as 'Padre', would also write to the next of kin of those who had died, assist with censoring letters home or even help to write letters for men who were illiterate. Chaplains were non-combatant, did not carry arms and in the previous war, the Boer War, the War Office decreed that they should not be in the front line but remain with the field ambulance or at the casualty clearing station. However, many chaplains felt that their duty was to be with their men and, increasingly, as the war progressed, they worked on the front line and assisted with bringing in wounded soldiers and administering first aid.

ARMY CHAPLAINS

Many chaplains recorded their war experiences in some detail. Henry Robert Cooke kept a detailed war diary from the date of his appointment in May 1915 until 2 January 1919, when he was demobilised. He spent his first few months in France visiting wounded soldiers, writing letters for some of the men, taking services in hospital wards, and conducting funerals. On 22 September 1915, Henry was ordered to join the 12th Field Ambulance 4th Division at Acheux in the Somme region where he was billeted in a local curé's house. Here he experienced his first visit to the trenches. The diary entry for Tuesday 28 September records:

Then on to Auchonvillers, visited our advance dressing stations. This village is a wreck. Here we entered the communication trench 2nd Avenue and so down to the front line. Through this we went for about 9 miles, most interesting walk, but quiet only our own shells and snipers on each side. We gave away cigarettes and writing paper and talked to men and at two points had short services. We left trenches by a trench, which brought us into the ruined village of Hamel where we had lunch.

A week later, Henry describes a visit he made to the town of Albert where the statue on the top of the Basilica of Notre Dame de Brebières was badly damaged by a shell on 15 January 1915:

The town was a most sad sight, in some parts as badly destroyed as Ypres… The most notable sight was the great bronze image of the Virgin and child still hanging from the top of the church tower although the tower was half shot away.

Henry was soon on the move and, on 24 November 1915, sailed with the RFA for Salonika, Greece. Transferred to the 100th Brigade RFA, Henry spent his first Christmas abroad celebrating Holy Communion with his Brigade in a bell tent and describes their Christmas dinner as a great success:

Sardines, soup, turkey (roasted in the sergeants field oven) plum pudding and fruit.

A blizzard on 15 January forced the cancellation of the usual Sunday programme of services and the following week Henry was busily engaged in digging headquarters dug-outs for battle positions:

Three dug-outs, one for telephone instruments and orderlies 12 x 6 foot and 7 foot deep, another 18 x 6 x 7 foot for living room and a smaller one 12 x 6 x 7 foot for officers sleeping quarters.

The Reverend Henry Robert Cooke

Chaplain to the Forces, 1915-1919
St John's School, 1896-1904

Henry left St John's in 1904 for Queen's College, Cambridge with a £50 scholarship. He gained his Batchelor of Arts degree in 1907 and was ordained in 1908.

Henry volunteered for army service in 1914, while a curate at St Luke's Church, Torquay. He was interviewed at the War Office on 4 May 1915 where it was noted that he had his vicar's approval, could preach without notes and was available for service immediately. He was appointed Temporary Chaplain to the Forces, 4th Class, with effect from 12 May 1915. Temporary Chaplains did not have standard officer ranks but instead were given equivalent grades. His grade, 4th Class, equates to the rank of captain.

Henry's first posting was as Chaplain at 10 General Hospital, Rouen in France and then Chaplain to 12 Field Ambulance, France. In November 1915, he sailed with the Royal Field Artillery from Marseilles and landed at Salonika in Greece. There he was Chaplain with the Gunners on active operations on the Salonika Front, against the Germans and Bulgarians.

After a short period of leave he returned to Salonika where he was twice mentioned in despatches and awarded the Military Cross in January 1918. Henry was then posted to Basra, sailing via the Suez Canal. From March 1918 until the end of hostilities he served as Chaplain with the Cavalry Division and 13th Hussars. He was wounded in April 1918 but was able to return to duty a month later.

Henry returned to England in January 1919, having accepted the offer from the then Prince of Wales of the appointment of Vicar of Princetown with Postbridge and Dartmoor. Later he was vicar of King's Teignton, Devon and vicar of Seaton in Devon. On his retirement in 1956, Henry was appointed Prebendary of Exeter Cathedral. He died on 11 November 1968, aged 82.

Over the next few months Henry continued to take Sunday services, he visited local churches and rode on horseback in the hills distributing cigarettes and sweets. He experienced several Zeppelin raids and his diary entries show that the fighting had increased with more frequent bombardments and trench raids. On 26 November 1916, he writes:

The climax to a three days heavy bombardment of the Bosch [sic] lines, I carried out my mornings work and in the afternoon went round the batteries. Some of them had a very hot time of it, especially where there was an ammunition explosion. Luckily, only one man was killed in our forward wire-cutting batteries. I buried him at 8.00pm. Some infantry kindly dug the grave and also came to the funeral to form a congregation.

Right: Henry Cooke in Army Chaplain's uniform, 1919

Below: Henry Cooke outside Buckingham Palace, 19 May 1919, after being presented with the Military Cross, accompanied by his sister

CHAPLAIN TO THE FORCES

Clifford Salisbury Woodward c.1934

The Reverend Canon Clifford Salisbury Woodward, Chaplain to the Forces, and a member of the Committee of Governors, was awarded the Military Cross in November 1916, for his work on the Somme. His citation in the *London Gazette* said:

He tended and brought in wounded under very heavy shell fire and continued this gallant work for 36 hours without stopping. He showed an utter disregard of danger and gave confidence to many.

Canon Woodward wrote a long article for *The Johnian* in 1917, describing two days during one of the big attacks during the Battle of the Somme. These short extracts show the difficult conditions they endured:

We had been stationed a couple of miles or so behind the line, and on the morning of the fight we moved off at about 9.00am to take up our position in support of the main attack. The roads were hopelessly congested with traffic of every conceivable kind, and we were very slow in getting along...

At last we reached the place where we were to leave the road and strike across country to our trench...'

I went along the trench to see how the companies were getting on. When I got back I found lunch in progress, and I regaled myself on a plate of cold beef followed by the inevitable tinned fruit, which is the staple pudding at every mess in France...

Punctually to the moment, the guns began; we were a little way in front of them, so the noise did not sound quite so bad as it sometimes does. But the sight in front was terrific: the German trenches were about three quarters of a mile away, and within two or three minutes of the opening of the bombardment their whole line was a solid mass of smoke and flying earth. Shell after shell burst with tremendous effect all along their front, while overhead the explosions of shrapnel formed a white pall, which gradually overhung the whole field of battle. Very soon, it was impossible to distinguish anything in the inferno, which the guns were creating, but we could just see our men leaving their trenches and advancing steadily across the open to the attack. At the same time two of the famous 'tanks' lumbered slowly forward. It was a wonderful sight, but one which I could not watch for long, as my place was now at the dressing station, at which the wounded would soon be arriving.

On his way back to his previous position, Canon Woodward found that his battalion had moved on and no one knew exactly where it was. Eventually he managed to re-join his unit, and by 10.00pm they were hoping to settle down for the night:

But it was not to be; things had not gone too well up in front, and new plans had to be made involving the employment of our battalion very early next morning...

As the morning wore on and the wounded began to trickle back, we learnt that the attempt had not been successful; machine gun fire had been exceedingly heavy, and it had been impossible to advance.

To add to the general discomfort, it began to rain heavily and continued so for hours, with the result that tracks and trenches became hopeless quagmires.

It had been fairly miserable all day for those of us who spent it in the comparative comfort of the headquarters trench. What it had been for the bulk of the battalion lying out until dusk under the pouring rain in shell-holes or crammed together in an overcrowded trench is unthinkable.

Clifford Salisbury Woodward was elected Vice Chairman of St John's School Council in 1930. He was consecrated Bishop of Bristol in 1933 and in 1946 became Bishop of Gloucester. He died on 14 April 1959.

NAVAL CHAPLAINS

It was not just on land that chaplains served. The Reverend Ivor Morgan Lewis, who died when HMS Goliath was sunk in the Dardanelles in 1915, was a junior curate at Uttoxeter Parish Church before the war. His obituary in the *Derbyshire Advertiser* of 21 May 1915 remarked that, even before the war broke out:

It was generally known that the Reverend Lewis had leaning towards a naval chaplaincy.

The newspaper commented that:

It is, of course a chaplain's duty to remain on a sinking ship to the last, and those who knew him best are confident that Mr Lewis faithfully performed his duty and remained with those who were unable to leave the sinking ship, offering words of comfort and solace to the men until the warship disappeared beneath the waves of the Dardanelles.

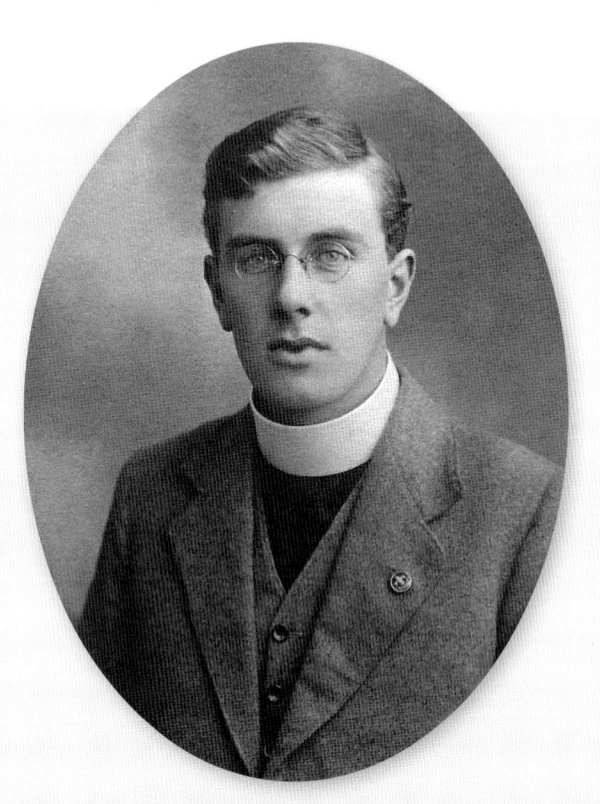

Ivor Morgan Lewis
Chaplain HMS Goliath, Royal Navy
Killed in Action, 13 May 1915, aged 26
St John's School, 1899-1908

Ivor Morgan Lewis joined West House in 1899 and played in the 2nd XI football team for his last two years. He left at Easter 1908 with a place at Jesus College, Oxford. He gained his BA in 1912, was ordained and accepted the post of junior curate at Uttoxeter Parish Church.

In August 1914, Ivor was appointed Chaplain with the fleet, and was posted to the battleship HMS Goliath. In November 1914, HMS Goliath was diverted to East Africa where she took part in the operation to blockade the German Light Cruiser Königsberg in the Rufiji River and also bombarded Dar Es Salaam.

Then, in March 1915, Goliath was ordered to the Dardanelles where, on 25 April, she covered the Allied landings at Cape Helles, Gallipoli. Although she received some damage from Turkish coastal batteries that day, and over the subsequent weeks, Goliath's high calibre armament allowed her and other battleships to remain out of range of the shore based guns.

On the night of the 12-13 May 1915 a Turkish torpedo boat managed to avoid detection as it slipped down the Dardanelles and closed in on Goliath who spotted the danger too late. The Turk fired three torpedoes, all of which hit the battleship; the subsequent explosions caused her to roll over and sink in a matter of minutes. Of the 750 men aboard around 570 lost their lives and among the dead was 26 year old Ivor Morgan Lewis.

His body was never identified and today he is commemorated on the Chatham Naval Memorial, one of 18,625 men with no known grave other than the sea.

His obituary in the *Derbyshire Advertiser* of 21 May 1915 says that he was popular man with the community where, aside from his clerical duties, he was Scout Master and an enthusiastic playing member of the Uttoxeter Rugby Club.

Ivor's younger brother, John Gordon Lewis, also attended St John's School. He was killed in action on the first day of the Battle of Messines, 7 June 1917.

CHAPTER 13 PRISONERS OF WAR

Thousands of British and Commonwealth servicemen were taken prisoner between 1914 and 1918, and many endured harsh conditions in prisoner of war camps in Germany and Turkey. Forced labour, cold weather, insanitary conditions, disease and starvation all contributed to the death of many of these prisoners. At least 16 OJs are known to have been captured during the war and four of these subsequently died in captivity.

Robert Leslie Harvey joined St John's in 1891. Leaving in 1896, he found employment as a clerk with the London County and Westminster Bank. In June 1917 he joined the Queen's Westminster Rifles, a battalion of the London Regiment, with whom he had served as a volunteer for several years. After training at Richmond, Robert went to France with his battalion in September 1917.

Early in 1918, Robert was posted as missing. Family and friends were anxiously waiting for news when, in April 1918, his wife received a postcard from him dated 24 March 1918, which said that he was a prisoner of war (POW) in Germany. Robert suffered much ill health as a POW and was eventually admitted to the German Military Hospital at Trier suffering from dysentery and heart trouble. In the third week of November 1918, news reached his family that he had died at the hospital on 24 September 1918. He was 38 and left a wife and two small children. His obituary in the *Middlesex Chronicle* dated 23 November 1918 said:

> Letters from him have appeared in these columns from time to time and there can be no doubt but that the hardships he endured and of which he spoke, undermined his constitution and left him too weak to battle against the disease which has killed so many of our soldiers. There is, however, proof that he received kind treatment at the hospital, and that he at least had a peaceful crossing over…

Although Robert was treated well in hospital, many POWs suffered considerable privation, especially towards the end of the war. Cedric Septimus Ireland, who left St John's in 1903, was an electrician and wireless operator living in Southend-on-Sea when he signed up with the Royal Naval Volunteer Reserve (RNVR) on 7 August 1914. He was attached to the Royal Navy's Hawke Battalion that was sent to assist in the defence of Antwerp in September 1914. The operation was a failure and the British forces withdrew on 9 October with few casualties but many men, including Cedric Ireland, were captured. By 5 December 1914 he was being held at the Döberitz Prisoner of War camp near Berlin.

In August 1915, Cedric sent a postcard home to his sister Mildred, the front of which shows the funeral of a fellow Royal Naval Division (RND) seaman at Döberitz. It is likely that Cedric is one of the group of British prisoners shown standing near the front of the photograph.

On 8 May 1916, Germany sent around 1,000 prisoners from Döberitz to carry out forced labour on the Russian Front, as a reprisal for the British allegedly employing German prisoners of war for work on the Western Front. Cedric was among those who endured the three-day journey in cattle trucks from Döberitz to Libau in Russian Latvia where, for several months, the prisoners were mostly employed in the docks. Then, on 23 February 1917, Cedric and hundreds of other prisoners, including Company Sergeant Major (CSM), Alexander Gibb (2nd Argyll & Sutherland Highlanders) who was the senior 2nd Class Warrant Officer with the group, left Libau for Mitau and were marched along the frozen River Aa to a camp in the village of Latchen, where they experienced atrocious conditions and treatment. War Office files (WO 161) held at The National Archives, reveal that accommodation at this camp was: *'one tent for all 500 NCOs and men, pitched on a frozen swamp'*.

There was no fuel for heating the tent and no light. Prisoners had to use melted snow for drinking or washing water and rations were barely enough to keep the men alive. Hours of work were from 5.30am to 5.30pm in freezing weather, with no food during this time and just two breaks of 20 minutes during the day. Work included felling and carrying timber to be used for machine-gun emplacements, road making, ice breaking and trench digging. The British NCOs were not forced to work, but they accompanied the men everywhere, and the trench parties were constantly under Russian shell fire.

CSM Alexander Gibb described the conditions in the camp:

> Towards the end of March, the party was in a terrible state. The men were so weak from starvation that they were simply crawling about, and many were covered with sores, chiefly on the face and hands, from frostbite. Several had died already.

A postcard sent home by Cedric Ireland in August 1915 showing a funeral at the Döberitz camp. Foreground shows men of the Royal Naval Division, one of whom is probaby Cedric

A small cottage, which held about 20 men, was used as a hospital, but little or no medical treatment was given to them. Others who were sick remained in the tent and were still expected to go to work each morning. Alexander Gibb wrote:

About 25 per cent of the remainder had to be assisted to their work in the morning and we had to carry most of them home in the evenings.

Twenty-eight-year-old Cedric Septimus Ireland died on 26 March 1917 in his comrades' arms while they were carrying him back to the camp. Cedric's service record, held by The National Archives, notes that he died of *'heart failure after rheumatism'* but his obituary in *The Johnian* magazine, October 1919, attributes his death directly to the treatment he received as a prisoner, saying that he died *'as the result of brutality and starvation'*.

KUT

In early May 1916, nine days before Cedric Ireland was sent to the Russian Front, another OJ, the Reverend Harold Elwyn Spooner (St John's School, 1890-1895) was taken prisoner by the Turks following the Siege of Kut-al-Amara where he had been serving as Chaplain to the 6th Division of the Indian Army under General Townshend.

British and Indian troops had been besieged by Turkish forces in Kut, a town on the banks of the river Tigris, about 100 miles south of Baghdad, for 147 days between December 1915 and April 1916. The Reverend Harold Spooner was the only Church of England Padre in Kut when the troops surrendered to the Turks on 29 April 1916 and he declined safe conduct to India to remain with his Division. He was marched 2,000 miles into captivity at Kastamuni on the Black Sea coast and detained for nearly three years.

THE INCOMPARABLE PADRE

A fascinating article headed 'The Rev H Spooner: His Heroism in the Field' appeared in *The Johnian* in 1918. Re-published from an Indian newspaper, *The Statesman, Calcutta*, 30 July 1917, Harold Spooner was described as:

This incomparable Padre who volunteered to stay with the wounded that had been collected in a particular field ambulance that we almost had to relinquish.

The story continued:

The clergyman who volunteered to stop with the wounded was the Rev Harold Spooner, AC, MC, whose heroism on this and several other occasions came under my personal observation. In this particular instance, the time was about 4.00pm, the 23rd November 1915. The Turks were developing a counter-attack against our main force and at that moment their extreme left flank was in a line with the field ambulance under reference, and finally was between 300 and 400 yards away from where the seriously wounded were accumulated. The position of the field was marked by the usual Red Cross flag and two tents and must have been known by the Turks. The counter-attack fizzled out and the Turks retired just before dawn next morning.

The wounded in the trenches, however, endured a night of terrible apprehension. During that long night I was afterwards told Spooner was indefatigable in cheering up and nursing the wounded. He, the medical officer and the assistant surgeon, who remained with the wounded, were decorated for their courageous behaviour and devotion to duty on this occasion.

One afternoon during the siege of Kut, I was passing through the British General Hospital (located in the covered bazaar, the hospital wards consisting of a double row of cubicles arranged on either side of a colonnade), and I saw Spooner kneeling beside a dangerously wounded case. A shell came through the next cubicle, but he never moved nor interrupted his prayers'.

Spooner is one of the very finest types of soldiers' parsons in the field. He won our affection, respect and reverence by his complete devotion to his sacred duties and the manner in which he brought comfort and relief to the sick and wounded. He is now a prisoner in the hands of the Turks. God grant him an early and safe return to his friends.'

The Reverend Harold Spooner was awarded the MC at the Battle of Ctesiphon in 1915 and the MBE for his services at the Siege of Kut-al-Amara. He survived the war and remained in India as Chaplain until 1928. Following his retirement, he stayed active to the end of his life. He appeared on BBC2 in the 'Great War' series in 1964 and, at the time of his death on 17 December 1964, was an assistant priest at Kendal Parish Church in the Lake District.

SPIES AND SECRET AGENTS

Writing to *The Johnian* in 1964, Harold Spooner commented:

By the way, Leonard Woolley was in the same POW Camp as I was, but he was not in the Siege of Kut.

Charles Leonard Woolley was a contemporary of Harold Spooner at St John's in the 1890s, and the older brother of VC winner Geoffrey Harold Woolley. Before the war Leonard Woolley spent three years carrying out archaeological work with T E Lawrence (later known as 'Lawrence of Arabia') in the Middle East. In his memoir, *As I Seem to Remember*, Woolley describes how, in the winter of 1913-14, he and Lawrence were sent to Sinai because the Palestine Exploration Fund wanted some archaeologists to help make a definitive map of the Holy Land. This led them into the Turkish part of Sinai and the expedition they joined was headed by Captain Stewart Newcombe, who was conducting a military topographical survey. While collecting their archaeological data, Woolley and Lawrence helped Captain Newcombe by obtaining valuable military information for the War Office about the construction of a German railway near Carchemish (the Berlin-Baghdad Railway).

The British Government and Foreign Office had long recognised the contribution that archaeologists could make to intelligence work. A report sent to the Foreign Office from Cairo in 1918, said:

The enemy has been making quite as much use as we have of the archaeologists who were engaged in the excavation and exploration of Ottoman territory before the war. Their familiarity with out-of-the-way localities and with native ways and means of transport which such men possess and the close relations, generally much more intimate than a consul's, which they have held to native populations, obviously fit them for special missions and agencies.

Shortly after war broke out in August 1914, Woolley contacted the Foreign Office to offer his services. In a letter dated 29 August 1914 he wrote:

Dear Sir

I fancy that my name has come before you in connection with work in North Syria; and during the last winter I assisted in the survey of South Palestine up to the Egyptian frontier, carried out by Captain Newcombe RE. Should the present troubles extend in the near East and the Turkish empire take sides against us, I think that, as I know the language, the people and the country, I might perhaps be of some use to the Government.

Woolley also wrote that he intended to join the army and, in September 1914, joined the Inns of Court Officers Training Corps. He was given a commission in the RFA in October 1914, was assigned to the Intelligence Service and posted to Port Said in Egypt, where he was made head of the Intelligence Department. Here he had charge of the eastern Mediterranean spy ships of the British and French navies and was actively involved in covert operations, surveying fortifications, running agents and arranging drops.

Sir Charles Leonard Woolley
1880-1960
St John's School, 1891-1899

Leonard Woolley came to St John's as a Foundationer in January 1891, shortly before his eleventh birthday. Within two years he had gained a distinction in Latin in the Cambridge Local examinations, the Gatehouse Divinity Prize and the Soames' Reading Prize. Further academic prizes followed and in 1898, Leonard was awarded a prestigious £80 open scholarship to New College, Oxford and a Special Prize for the best candidate for Higher Certificates in the Oxford and Cambridge Board Examination. Speech Day that year was a grand occasion as it was the first to be held in the new Dining Hall and the prizes were presented by the guest of honour, HRH the Duchess of Albany.

In his final year at School, Leonard was Head Monitor and an editor of *The Johnian*. He took part in lively debates and played numerous roles in scenes from classical Greek and French plays on Speech Day.

After graduating from Oxford, Leonard went to France and Germany for a year to study modern languages. In 1905, he was appointed assistant keeper at the Ashmolean Museum in Oxford. He left the museum in 1907 to pursue an active career in archaeology in Egypt and the Middle East.

The School followed Leonard's career with interest and he visited St John's on many occasions, giving lectures on aspects of his archaeological finds. In 1927 Leonard married Katharine Keeling, widow of Lieutenant Colonel Bertram Keeling, and she worked alongside him as artist and draughtswoman. An extract from the *Daily News, 20 March 1929*, appeared in *The Johnian*:

Years spent in digging under the desert sun have led up to the discoveries at Ur of the Chaldees which Mr Woolley has made regarding the story of the Flood. As leader of the joint expedition of the British Museum and Philadelphia University, Mr. Woolley has made a series of finds almost unparalleled in their historical and artistic importance. He is a man of medium height, with brown hair, and is the possessor of a most magnetic personality, by means of which he infects all around him with his own intense enthusiasm. His wife accompanies him on his expeditions.

Leonard Woolley was knighted in 1935 for his contributions to archaeology and in 1937 was made President of the Old Johnian club.

In 1939 Sir Leonard Woolley was re-commissioned into the Intelligence Division at the War Office and in 1943 he became part of the Monuments, Fine Arts and Archives Section of the Allied Armies which was set up to help protect and safeguard historic monuments from war damage and, towards the end of the war, to find and return works of art and other items that had been stolen or hidden for safe keeping.

After his death on 20 February 1960, a tribute in *The Johnian* said:

St John's lost one of its most distinguished sons when Sir Leonard Woolley died at the age of 79.

CAPTURE AND IMPRISONMENT

Leonard Woolley's intelligence work came to a sudden end in August 1916, when the yacht, Zaida, which he used for landing spies on the enemy coast and taking them off again, hit a mine in Ayas Bay. There was a tremendous explosion and the yacht went down in under a minute. Thirteen men were killed or drowned but Woolley, and eighteen others, survived by clinging to the wreckage of the charthouse roof. Four hours later they were rescued by a Turkish vessel and were taken into custody. Woolley and three of his fellow officers were sent to Kastamuni, a Turkish prisoner of war camp near the Black Sea, where his old school friend, Harold Spooner, and other prisoners from the Siege of Kut were being held.

OFFICERS IN CAPTIVITY

Officers held as prisoners of war were not required to take part in the gruelling working parties, to which other ranks were assigned, and they received more favourable treatment. They were allowed to receive letters via the Red Cross and *The Johnian*, April 1917, published a plea from Leonard Woolley for news from his former school friends:

C L Woolley, who is a prisoner in the hands of the Turks, is very anxious to receive letters from his OJ friends, as he is so cut off from everything.

Letters should be only two sides of a sheet of paper, and no stamps are required.

PRISON CAMP ACTIVITIES

Food was a constant concern to prisoners at the camp, so Woolley and another officer were appointed to run the mess facilities. Woolley also occupied his time by giving lectures on ancient history and took classes in Italian. He contributed to the camp magazine, *Mastik*, which contained satirical verse, drawings, fake advertisements, regular columns and letters to the editor and the single handwritten copy was passed from one prisoner to another.

MUSIC AND DRAMA

Improvised concerts and dramatic productions were also a feature of camp life. One of the officers crafted banjos out of spare pieces of wood and wire, other instruments were purchased in the town and the Kastamuni Orchestral Society was formed.

Leonard Woolley helped with the organisation of the concerts, but his chief contribution was to the scenery and costume design for plays such as *Twelfth Night* and original revues, with topical songs, dances and sketches, where the dresses and wigs were credited to 'CL Woolley and Co'. These are described in detail in *From Kastamuni to Kedos*, a collection of reminiscences, drawings and poems edited by Woolley and published shortly after the war:

All the songs were very good, some very good indeed; the dancing delightful, the dresses an even greater triumph for Woolley & Co, who once more created out of scraps and fragments the effect of a first-rate London musical comedy.

During captivity, Woolley also found time to finish his memoir *Dead Towns and Living Men*. In his preface he wrote:

Probably I should never have started on this book had I not found myself a prisoner of war, with many hours of enforced idleness to overcome. The war brought the archaeologist out in a new light, and his habit of prying about in countries little known, his knowledge of peoples, and his gift of tongues, were turned to uses far other than their wont.

At the end of the war, Woolley was awarded the Croix de Guerre by the French and was repatriated to England for a period of leave. In 1919 he was ordered back to Syria under the command of Field Marshal Allenby to serve as a Political Officer with the temporary rank of Major. He continued with his excavations under extreme difficulties due to guerrilla warfare and some opposition from the French. By the end of the year Woolley had been demobilised and his contract with the British Museum to resume digging at Carcamesh began on 1 December 1919. His fame as an archaeologist grew rapidly in the inter-war years; he made important discoveries while excavating the royal tombs of the Sumerians at Ur in present day Iraq, finding paintings, gold and silver jewellery and other priceless treasures.

CHAPTER 14 ARMISTICE 1918

News that the armistice had been signed reached the town of Leatherhead soon after 11.00am on the morning of Monday 11 November 1918 and, as reported in the *Dorking and Leatherhead Advertiser, 16 November 1918*, flags could soon be seen flying from shops, businesses and private houses. The parish church bells rang out in the evening and the bugle band of the Church Lad's Brigade paraded in the town. The following day many local residents took a day's holiday and, in the evening, a bonfire was lit in front of the Bull Inn to celebrate the end of the hostilities.

THANKSGIVING SERVICE

A special service of thanksgiving was held in the School Chapel at 5.00pm on Sunday 17 November 1918. The editorial in *The Johnian* for December 1918 said:

Our School shared in the national joy on the signing of the armistice, just as it has shared in the national sacrifices during the long years of war, and it was with feelings of deep gratitude to the giver of Victory and of pride in those of our Old Boys who by their courage and devotion had helped to win for us the final success that we assembled in our School Chapel at 5 o'clock on Sunday, November 17th, for our special service of thanksgiving.

But, while many families celebrated the armistice with rejoicing, for some there was tragedy still to come.

INFLUENZA PANDEMIC

Very few members of the School were able to join in the local celebrations on Armistice Day. Some weeks earlier an outbreak of influenza, which had caused other local schools to close, was considered serious enough for boys of St John's School to be sent home for a month. The Johnian for December 1918 commented:

The week beginning Sunday, October 20th, saw the beginning of an influenza epidemic, which by Tuesday and Wednesday was spreading rapidly. Owing to the impossibility of obtaining nurses in the event of a serious outbreak, it was decided that the School should be sent home, and by Friday all boys except the victims had departed. There were about thirty cases among the boys, while Miss Rice had to look after several members of her staff in the west wing; fortunately, none of the cases proved serious. The School returned again on Friday, November 15th, and discovered that in their absence few had escaped the scourge, the headmaster and his family being among the victims.

The influenza virus persisted throughout 1919 and was responsible for over 50 million deaths worldwide, far more than the number of those killed in combat in the war. Many servicemen who survived the fighting on the battlefields found themselves struck down by the virus and died of complications such as pneumonia. Towards the end of November 1918, Harold Mowatt Maxwell Crofton, who left St John's in 1913 to pursue a career in the Royal Navy, was on board HMS Curacoa and about to be made Acting Paymaster, when he became ill. He died on 29 November 1918 at Shotley Naval Hospital at the age of 22, after developing bronchopneumonia. Admiral Tyrwhitt wrote to Harold's mother:

'Curacoa' December 1, 1918.
Dear Mrs Crofton,
I cannot refrain from writing to express my deepest sympathy to you and Mr Crofton and your family. Your son's death is a great blow to us all, and to me in particular. I shall miss him dreadfully after five years in the same ship. I always hoped to keep him with me. He has done splendid work during the war and was always the life and soul of the ship, and a general favourite wherever he went. My children will be dreadfully sorry, as he was always so good to them, and they were so fond of him. I would have come to see you, but I have been so busy that I have had no opportunity. With deepest sympathy.
Yours very sincerely,
Reginald Tyrwhitt

One of Harold Crofton's friends wrote:

Dear Mr Crofton,
As an old messmate and friend of your son, I want to express my sincere sympathy with you and your family. I have been with him since 'Arethusa' days, and I feel a keen loss. He was a good friend to me and my wife, and a good messmate. It seems particularly hard after over four years' strenuous work with Admiral Tyrwhitt and special promotion just come for the same, he should be taken away, a mere boy, I feel more than I can express to you.
Yours very sincerely,
Henry Burns (Surgeon, Lieutenant-Commander)

Paymaster Sub-Lieutenant, Harold Mowatt Maxwell Crofton

HMS Curacoa, Royal Navy
Died 29 November 1918, aged 22
St John's School, 1906-1913

Harold joined St John's as a Foundationer and proved to be a good all-rounder. He won the Fourth Form prize in 1910 and a choir prize in 1911. He played second violin in the School orchestra and sang a solo in the School concert in 1912. Harold also played fives, cricket, and football at school and was awarded 2nd XI colours for football in 1913.

Harold gained a Naval Clerkship in 1913 and left St John's at the end of the Christmas Term, joining the Royal Navy as an assistant clerk on 15 January 1914. He was posted to the newly commissioned HMS Arethusa at the beginning of August 1914. Harold wrote a series of long letters home, describing his time on the Arethusa, the first of which tells of his excitement of taking part in the first naval battle of the war, the Battle of Heligoland, on 28 August 1914:

HMS ARETHUSA.
Chatham, 7th September 1914.

I am extremely sorry that I have been so long in writing, but I have never been so hard-worked in my life as during the past week. However, now that things are a bit squarer I will just write you a line about the action off Heligoland that I had the great fortune to be in. You can imagine how proud Chatham is of 'the saucy Arethusa' when I tell you that we had taken part in the first naval action when we had been in commission less that a fortnight. I have the luck to be in a ship that thousands of naval officers would give pounds to be in…

He sent a further two letters home, the first describing the memorable air raid on German naval forces at Cuxhaven on Christmas day 1914 and the final letter, dated 26 January 1915, told of sinking of the German battle cruiser, SMS Blücher, on 24 January during the Battle of Dogger Bank. Harold remained with the Arethusa until February 1916, when she struck a mine off Felixstowe, drifted on to a shoal while being towed back, and was irreparably damaged. He then spent some time on office duty in Maidstone before joining HMS Curacoa. Harold's service record shows that he was very highly regarded by his superior officers. In August 1915, Commander Arbuthnot wrote:

Able to render valuable services in translating intercepted German wireless and conversing with prisoners.

and, on 3 January 1917, Commander Reginald Tyrwhitt wrote of Harold in glowing terms:

Very willing and loyal, hardworking. Takes the keenest interest in his work, has improved greatly in judgement and decision during the last year. Is conscientious and with more experience will be a very suitable officer for employment in an admiral's office. A good messmate, rather sensitive, very musical, physique very good. Good at games.

Harold is buried in Shotley (St Mary) Churchyard, Suffolk. He was just 22 years old when he died.

HMS Curacoa alongside possibly at Chatham, 1918

Others also succumbed to the influenza virus. Chaplain to the Forces, the Reverend Gerald James Lester had been in France for just over two months when he caught influenza and died of pneumonia on 16 December 1918. *The Western Times* and *North Devon Journal* for 20 December 1918 carried the sad announcement of his death:

The passing-bell announced to the parish of Rackenford on Wednesday morning the distressing news of the death of its Rector, Rev G J Lester BA, in France, from pneumonia following influenza. A wire came on Friday last that he was critically ill in hospital at Rouen, but as no further news was heard, it was hoped that the reverend gentleman was better.

Mr Lester was held in the highest respect and esteem and he will be much missed. It is less than two short years that he was inducted into the living by the present Bishop, in succession to the late Rev H G Gifford. Mr Lester was accepted for work as an Army Chaplain, leaving the parish early in October and had been in France about a month.

All hearts go out in deepest sympathy with Mrs Lester.

Mr and Mrs W H Woods, of Fetcham, Surrey lost their only son, Captain Leslie Woods, MC, when he died of pneumonia following influenza on 25 February 1919, aged 27. Leslie left St John's in 1905 and before the war was employed as an apprentice engineer. He was serving with the RFA in Belgium when he died. Leslie is buried in the Halle Communal Cemetery, Belgium and his obituary in *The Johnian* describes him as:

A loving and dutiful son, a good soldier, and the best of fellows.

Leslie's name is also inscribed on the parish memorial in St Mary's Church, Fetcham.

Gerald James Lester

MURDER AND MALARIA

Further deaths in service occurred during 1919 and 1920. Lieutenant Kenneth Leslie Stewart Hartigan, 35th Scinde Horse, attached, 36th Jacob's Horse, died of malaria on 2 November 1919, at the Military Hospital, Ras-el-Tin, Alexandria, aged 20. Lieutenant Frank Dawson-Smith of the King's African Rifles and Military Governor of North Jubaland was murdered by Somali mutineers on 11 January 1920. Frank enlisted as a private with the York and Lancaster Regiment in August 1914. He obtained a commission as 2nd Lieutenant with the Oxford and Buckinghamshire Regiment in 1917 and was posted to the King's African Rifles in 1918. An obituary published in *The Johnian*, February 1920, described Frank Dawson-Smith as a '*brilliant and capable officer, fearless and resourceful*' and ended:

His men adored him and would follow him anywhere. Added to this he was a great-hearted man with a most lovable and attractive personality. He has been taken in the zenith of his youth. He was indeed 'a very gallant gentleman' and the nation is the poorer for his loss. RIP.

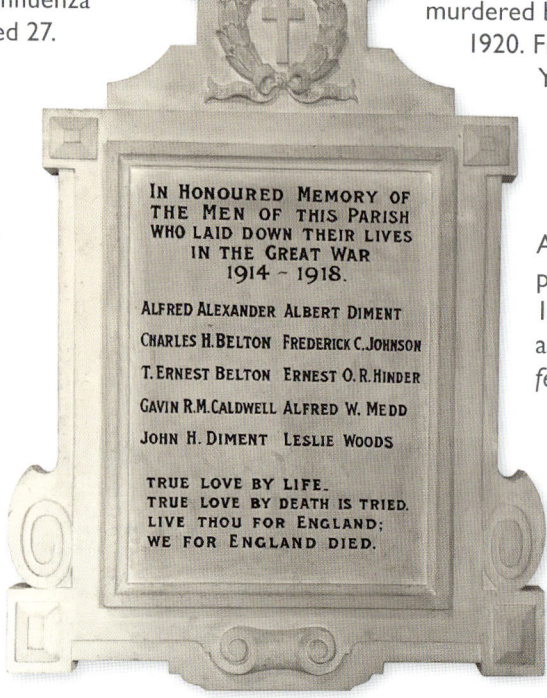

Great War memorial plaque at St Mary's Church, Fetcham

CHAPTER 15 PEACE CELEBRATIONS 1919

While the fighting on the Western Front ended in November 1918, many months of negotiations followed at the Paris Peace Conference to determine the terms of the peace. It was not until 28 June 1919 that the Treaty of Versailles, which brought the war between Germany and the Allied Powers to an end, was signed. To mark the end of the war, Saturday 19 July 1919 was declared a public holiday and celebrations and victory parades took place in towns and villages across the country.

In Leatherhead, St John's hosted a lunch for 350 returning servicemen in the Dining Hall, as part of the town's celebrations. The headmaster wrote to the Committee on 18 July 1919, to inform them of this event:

The Committee will be interested to hear that I have put the use of our School Dining Hall for the dinner to be given tomorrow to the demobilised sailors and soldiers of Leatherhead and that, at the request of the local committee, I have given permission for our School OTC and Band to take a prominent part in the afternoon and evening processions. The choir are also singing in the Parish Church on Sunday evening.

Following the lunch, a procession which included the Leatherhead Silver Band, demobilised soldiers and sailors, St John's School Cadet Corps and Band, the Red Cross Society, the Church Lads' Brigade, Scouts and children from local schools, formed outside the School. Over 2,000 people made their way down Epsom Road to Randall's Park via The Crescent, High Street and North Street. At Randall's Park there were sports, dancing and tea for all. Later, as dusk fell, the Silver Band led a procession to Yarm Court and the townspeople continued their celebrations with fireworks and a bonfire.

Peace procession outside St John's School, Epsom Road, Leatherhead, 19 July 1919

Invitation to OJs to the festival day at St John's, Saturday 21 June 1919

FESTIVAL WEEKEND FOR OLD JOHNIANS

A month before the national Peace Day celebrations, the School extended a warm welcome home to OJs who had been on active service during the war. Around 120 old boys accepted the headmaster's invitation to spend the weekend of Saturday 21 and Sunday 22 June 1919, at their old school. The proceedings started with a short memorial and thanksgiving service in the School Chapel, conducted by the headmaster and the Right Reverend Edward Talbot, Bishop of Winchester. Afterwards, friends of the School, the Reverend Thomas Frederick Hobson, vicar of Leatherhead, School Governors and old boys gathered together on the School playing fields where a cricket match between the School and the Old Boys was in progress. (A cricket match against Cranleigh was advertised on the invitation card, but this was replaced by the match against OJs).

The Field Gun.
(With apologies to Gunga Din.)

When you're standing on Parade
Wishing rifles were not made
And that there was no such beastly thing as war,
Will you spare a thought, my son,
For the very ancient Gun
Given to us by the courage of the Corps?

'Twas 'way back in old '18,
When we'd licked the German clean
And had put an end to Kaiser Wilhelm's rule,
That some brass-hat just for fun
Thought that something should be done
To show the love of England for our School.

Now we're proud to think of days
When we clambered o'er the maze
Of all its nuts and bolts and wheels and things,
When we drank our bottled booze
Near a gun that fought at Loos
And which may have changed the destiny of kings.

Alas! It's gone away
To join once more the fray,
And we'll watch its progress with a loving eye.
We'll all help to win this war
And, like the gun that's gone before,
We too shall never be afraid to die.

EL CABALLERO VIGILANTE.

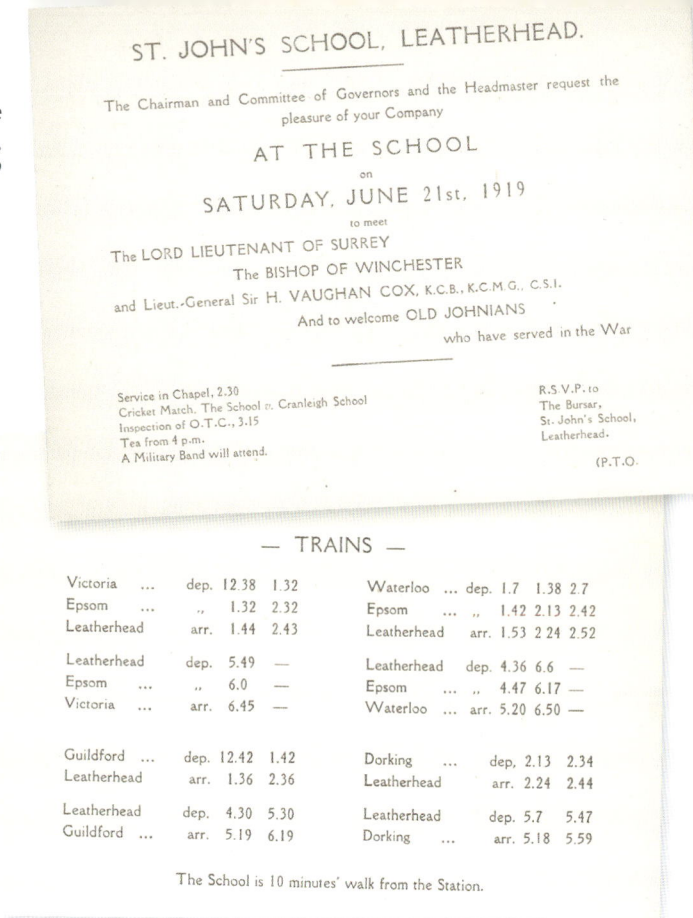

WAR TROPHY PRESENTED

During a break in the cricket, Lieutenant-General Sir Herbert Vaughan Cox accompanied by Geoffrey Woolley VC and other OJs who had been decorated during the war, inspected the OTC. Then Lord Ashcombe, the Lord Lieutenant of Surrey, presented the School with a German field gun which had been allotted to the OTC by the War Trophies Committee at the War Office, in recognition of the part played by OJs in the war. *The Johnian* reported:

The Lord Lieutenant said he understood they hoped to get something more imposing, but at any rate this would be something to go on with and would be sure to remind them of the great deeds which had been done in the war by those who had gone from that school.

The boys then gave 'three hearty cheers' for the Lord Lieutenant, the cricket match was resumed and resulted in a win for the School, and the visitors were entertained to tea. The German field gun depicted in this 1925 etching of the Chapel is probably the one that Lord Ashcombe presented to the School. In 1940, war trophies such as this were recalled by the War Office and the scrap metal used to make weapons for a new war effort. The March 1940 issue of *The Johnian* mourned the loss of 'The Field Gun', which had graced the main entrance to the School for 20 years, with a poem.

PEACE CELEBRATIONS 1919

About eighty OJs attended a dinner in the Dining Hall in the evening and toasts were raised to 'The King' and 'The Fallen'. After dinner, a concert was held in front of the pavilion, illuminated by fairy lights.

MEMORIAL SERVICE

On Sunday 22 June 1919, a memorial service was held in the School Chapel. The Reverend G Vernon Smith, MC, began his sermon with the words:

This is a great day in the history of the School. A day on which we look back with thanksgiving for the achievements of the past: and forward with thanksgiving too for the hope and promise of the future.

The School may indeed be proud of its record in the War. All the Public Schools of England gladly gave of their best: and a Roll which shows that every Old Boy of military age joined up or volunteered is indeed a tribute to the spirit with which St John's School inspires its sons.

ANNUAL MEETING

The festival weekend at the School was considered to be a great success. It was the first time that all OJs had been invited back to their old school. Plans were soon being made for an OJ Festival Day in 1920, with a chapel service, cricket match, garden party and OJ dinner in the evening, though it proved impossible to offer hospitality for the night. The Committee wrote in their report for 1920:

The institution of 'Old Johnians' Day' as the annual School Festival at Leatherhead has contributed greatly towards fostering the continuing interest of old boys in the School, and the Committee propose to make it a permanent fixture.

Etching of the Chapel (1925) showing the field gun presented to the School as a war trophy

CHAPTER 16 THE SCHOOL AFTER THE WAR

CHANGES TO THE SCHOOL CONSTITUTION

The financial difficulties suffered by the School over the four years of war were noted by the Committee in their report for the year ending 1919 in which they said:

The war which has now ended in complete victory, has among its countless other ills brought the School into serious financial difficulties, both by diminishing our receipts and enormously increasing our necessary expenses.

The decision in 1917 to raise the age of entry to eleven had the desired effect of reducing numbers in the School and thus saving money. At the start of the war in 1914 there were 264 pupils but by 1919, after the closure of Block A, the School had just 242 pupils, of whom ten were day boys as dormitory accommodation was limited to 232 boys. The number of Foundationers receiving free board and tuition went down from 143 to 102. These and other changes in the constitution of the School, such as the reorganisation of the House system, appointment of House Captains and School Prefects in 1914 (see page 31) were made permanent in 1919. Full details were published in *The Johnian* for October 1919:

The War has affected a number of changes in the constitution of the School, and now that it has at last been possible to make permanent arrangements with regard to it, we think the time has come to print in The Johnian the following complete list of the School Governing Body and the Tutorial and Domestic Staff, together with the most important details of the School Constitution, as this information will be likely to be of interest to many Old Johnians.

Under the new arrangements no boy is allowed to enter the School if he is under 11 or, except in special circumstances, over 15. Every boy in the School has to be out of Upper Fourth before he is 16, and out of the Lower Fifth before he is 17, and if he fails to do so, he is superannuated and must leave at the end of term of his 16th or 17th birthday.

APPOINTMENT OF SCHOOL BURSAR

Another significant change was made in the administration of the School by the appointment in 1918 of John Harold Burnside, an assistant master, as the first Bursar of the School. The Committee said in their report the following year:

This relieves the headmaster of work which does not properly belong to his office, and which war conditions had made intolerably heavy, and enables him to devote more time and energy to his proper duties of education. This change has so far worked excellently.

FINANCIAL COST OF THE WAR

The School struggled to make ends meet throughout the war and in the years immediately following the armistice. The Annual Reports show that during the war years (1914-1919), despite receiving a total of £12,382 from appeals and legacies, there was a deficit of £5,565. This was met by realising a considerable part of the capital accumulated from legacies received in earlier years. At the end of 1920, the Committee reported a further deficit in the balance sheet of £2,723. Appealing to friends, benefactors and OJs to give generously, and to remember the School in their will, the Committee said:

Assuredly the time has come when we can no longer realise our few remaining securities, the saleable value of which has greatly depreciated. There must be a halt called in that 'Road to Ruin'.

The School remained in financial crisis throughout the 1920s and, in retrospect, it is possible to see the devastating fire of 1913 as a blessing in disguise. The wide-ranging improvements made to the fabric of the School during the rebuilding programme would have been unthinkable both during and immediately after the war. Baths, showers, hot water and electric light would have been considered a luxury in those times of austerity.

RUGBY FOOTBALL

On the sports fields, at the start of the 1919-20 season, the School reverted to playing rugby rather than 'soccer' as the main winter game. The headmaster explained the reasons for the change to the Committee in March 1919, saying:

The Committee will be interested to hear that after the most careful consideration we have decided to change next Autumn from Association to Rugby football. One of the chief reasons being that nearly all the schools we play have already done so and it is therefore becoming increasingly difficult to arrange for the right kind of matches in Association.

The Johnian report on the 1918-1919 football season noted that:

The last of the School 'Soccer' seasons was not marked by any outstanding features; perhaps the play suffered a good deal from the anticipation of the coming change of game. On paper the 1st XI had all the makings of a good side, but it certainly failed to live up to the hopes entertained in the early days of the season. The principal fault lay, as it has done for several years past, with the forwards – lack of dash, want of proper combination and lamentable weakness in front of goal once more told their old story.

The 2nd XI proved a better side than we have had of recent years only losing one of its matches by the odd goal in five.

As in 1885 when soccer was first introduced, the change to rugby was not greeted with enthusiasm, but the performance of the 1st XV who won their first fixture against Christ's Hospital helped to quell the criticism. John Burnside was one of those who had reservations about the change. E M P Williams, who played for the 2nd XI football team in 1918 and the 1st XV rugby team in 1919, paid tribute to Burnside in *The Quest Goes On* (Williams 1951, p.35) saying:

As a young man, Burnside was a fine Soccer player, and he continued to coach the First Eleven until the School reverted to Rugger. The change must have been a great blow to him, although at a later date he confessed it was for the best.

Top: 1st XV, 1919-1920
Bottom: John Harold Burnside, 1922

CHAPTER 17 WAR MEMORIALS AND REMEMBRANCE

In the early days of the war, Fabian Ware, the commander of a British Red Cross ambulance unit in France, was struck by the huge number of casualties and devised a way of recording all the graves that he and his unit could find. The War Office soon recognised the value of his work and the Graves Registration Commission was established. In 1917 his organisation was given a Royal Charter and became the Imperial War Graves Commission, the forerunner of the present Commonwealth War Graves Commission. By 1918, around 587,000 graves had been recorded and another 559,000 of the dead also had no known grave. For the missing, memorials such as the Menin Gate in Ypres and Thiepval on the Somme carry the names carved in stone of those who were never identified. After the war, families were allowed to visit these graves to pay their respects, lay a wreath, and say goodbye. But thousands of families, unable to travel to the cemeteries in France or Belgium or farther afield, had no grave or memorial to visit.

Arras Flying Services Memorial to the Missing, France

COMMUNITY WAR MEMORIALS

Across Britain, local communities raised money for memorials which were to become a focal point for national mourning and remembrance. From 1919 onwards, war memorials were planned, commissioned, built and unveiled. They were normally constructed where people could grieve individually and collectively. The emphasis of many of the memorials was the universal sense of loss. And they were re-affirmations of community, often in towns and villages which had been ripped apart by the loss of so many.

ST JOHN'S WAR MEMORIAL

A War Memorial Fund appeal was launched towards the end of 1914, with the plea,

It is hoped all OJs will subscribe in memory of those Old Boys who by their act of devotion, have brought credit to the School.

The appeal fund was kept open throughout the war and names of subscribers were published in *The Johnian*. Details of all those known to be serving in the armed forces were recorded and obituaries for OJs killed in action were published under the heading 'Pro Patria'. The War Memorial Committee met on 31 January 1919 to discuss what form the commemoration should take. It was decided that the memorial should be in two sections, the first 'Commemorative' and the second 'Utilitarian'. The committee agreed that the commemorative portion should consist of a cross in the Chapel, a cross in the quadrangle, and a record of names of all who served in the war. It was decided that the utilitarian part of the memorial should be a 'swimming bath' which would benefit the pupils and fulfil a long-felt need. A further appeal was addressed to the whole body of OJs, parents of old boys and of those in the School, the members of the Governing Body, and the past and present masters:

To commemorate in a fitting manner the part taken in the Great War by the hundreds of Old Johnians who have served in the Navy, Army or Air Force.

The proposed commemorative memorials were described:

A Stone Cross about 20 feet high with inscription – to be erected in the centre of the Inner Quadrangle; secondly a Cross and Tablet – to be placed in a suitable position in the Chapel; and thirdly, a Roll of Honour on Vellum bearing the names of all who have served in any capacity in the Navy, Army, or Air Force, and with a distinguishing mark against the names of the fallen, and of those who have gained any War distinction – to be placed in an oak case in the library for all to see. The cost of this commemorative Memorial will be about £400.

War Memorial, St John's College, Leatherhead.

St John's School, Leatherhead and the Great War, 1914-1919

And the utilitarian part of the memorial was outlined:

After the most careful deliberation, we have decided by an unanimous vote to issue an appeal for an Outdoor Swimming Bath – to be built in what was formerly called 'The Matron's Garden' – the cost of which has been estimated at about £2,700. Towards this object, the sum of £500 has already been contributed from another source, and so the actual amount required is about £2,200. Anyone who knows St John's School will recognise that this is undoubtedly a most urgent need, and we therefore trust that all who have the true interest of the School at heart will, by their own liberal response, do everything within their power to help in providing this part of the proposed Memorial, which would confer so great a benefit on every succeeding generation of Johnians.

By December 1919, £1,100 had been raised and the following commemorative memorials were commissioned at the cost of £500:

- A Cross in the Quadrangle;
- A Floor-Cross in the Chapel;
- Oak Panelling in the Ante-Chapel carved with names of those who died;
- Names of all OJs who served in all the armed forces up to the end of 1918 to be handwritten on vellum and displayed in the library.

The balance of the fund was invested and was intended to be used towards the new swimming pool. However, that project was postponed due to lack of funds. The War Memorial Committee decided that a covered pool which could be used throughout the year would be of more use to the School than an open-air pool and the estimated cost for a covered pool in 1919 was around £4,500.

Architect Sir Charles Nicholson was appointed to

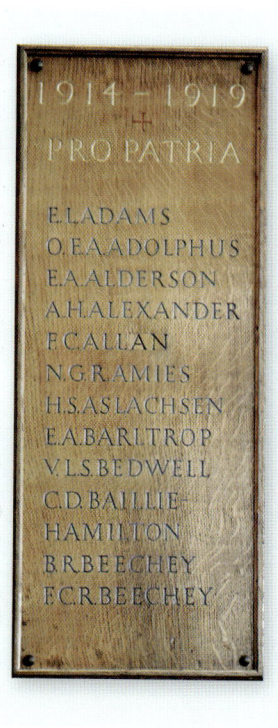

Roll of Honour – Oak panels inscribed with the names of the fallen

WAR MEMORIALS AND REMEMBRANCE

design the various commemorative memorials and the War Memorial Committee minutes, published in *The Johnian*, show that in October 1919:

The Chairman was empowered to represent to the Architect the Committee's criticisms on his design for the Floor-Cross in the Chapel and to ask for a 'plainer design as more in keeping with the position of the Cross together with an estimate for the same'

The designs were approved in December 1919, subject to two small alterations, and

The Chairman was asked to urge upon the Architect the advisability of getting the work on the Commemorative Memorial started as soon as possible.

DEDICATION OF THE WAR MEMORIALS

The second annual OJ Festival Day took place on 19 June 1920, when the war memorials were dedicated by OJ Edward Domett Shaw, the Bishop of Buckingham. Joining St John's at Clapton in 1871 aged 11, Shaw was among the first group of pupils who moved with the School to Leatherhead the following year. Edward Shaw left Leatherhead in 1876 to continue his education at Forest School, Walthamstow and Oriel College, Oxford. He was headmaster of Bishops Stortford School in 1887 and ordained two years later. After a period as vicar of High Wycombe and Archdeacon of Buckingham, Shaw became the first Bishop of Buckingham in 1914. As the first OJ Bishop it was eminently fitting that he should be asked to perform this ceremony and there was an added poignancy, as Shaw and his wife had suffered the unbearable pain of losing three of their four sons in the war.

The Johnian described the events of the festival day in detail:

There were two impressive ceremonies at the School on Saturday afternoon, June 19th. The first was the dedication of a floor Cross in the chancel of the Chapel, and the second the unveiling of a Cross in the Inner Quadrangle. Both Crosses were in memory of the 150 old boys of the School who were killed on war service.

The Cross in the Chapel was dedicated during a short service by the Bishop of Buckingham, in the presence of a congregation so large that, there was not room in the School Chapel for all who wished to attend.

The memorial in the chapel consisted of a brass Cross with a border of brass on the floor of the chancel. The inscription was: Our Glorious Dead, 1914-1919. All live unto Him.

Major Henry Herbert Gordon Clark, Treasurer of the Committee and High Sheriff of Surrey, stood in for Admiral Lord Jellicoe at the unveiling of the Cross in the Quadrangle:

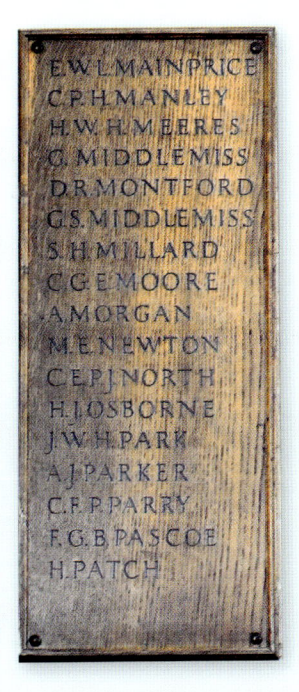

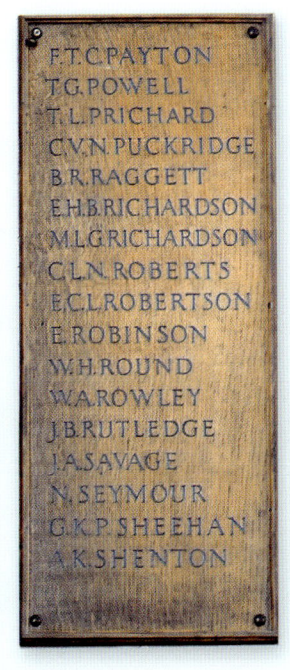

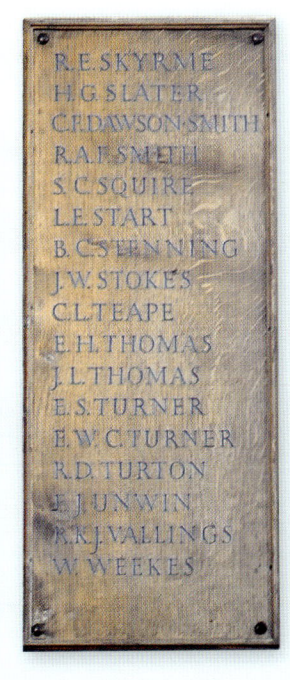

The last panel was updated in 2017 to include six newly discovered names

The Cross in the Inner Quadrangle was next unveiled. Admiral Lord Jellicoe had arranged to be present to perform this duty, but, owing to illness, he was prevented from fulfilling the engagement. Major H H Gordon Clark, High Sheriff and Deputy Lieutenant, acted in his stead. A guard of honour, composed of a company of the School OTC, lined the path through the Quadrangle in the centre of which the Cross had been erected. The Union Jack covering the Cross was removed by Major Gordon Clark, and the dedicatory prayers were said by the Bishop of Buckingham.

The Last Post was sounded by the buglers of the OTC, while the Guard of Honour presented arms, and the spectators assembled round the Quadrangle stood in silence. The poignant notes of the call reverberated through the cloisters of the Quadrangle as if they were an ethereal echo from the gallant dead to whom tribute was being paid. These moments were deeply impressive.

The surpliced choir sang the hymn 'Ten thousand times ten thousand', and the ceremony concluded with the National Anthem, played by the drum and fife band of the OTC.

Finally, in 1925 a long-held dream was realised when the swimming pool was opened. The cost of the building, designed by architect Leonard Martin, had risen to over £8,000 and was funded by a legacy from T S Whitaker and the balance of the Old Johnian War Memorial Fund.

Above: Dedication of the War Memorial, 1920

WAR MEMORIALS AND REMEMBRANCE

RESTORATION OF THE WAR MEMORIAL

Over the years, the weather took its toll on the war memorial in the Quad. Ninety years after it was unveiled, the memorial was in need of repair and the cross on the top was found to be crumbling. Generous donations from OJs helped to fund the restoration of the war memorial in 2013. The monument was cleaned and repaired, damaged areas of stone were renewed, and the cross was replaced with an exact replica. After the School's 94th annual Service of Remembrance on Sunday 10 November 2013, the Right Reverend Ian Brackley, Bishop of Dorking, rededicated the fully restored War Memorial in honour of the many OJs who have died in war.

STAINED GLASS WINDOW

In 2014 to mark the centenary of the start of the war a memorial window, designed by stained glass artist Jude Tarrant, was installed in the School Chapel. A gift to the School from a donor, this contemporary stained glass window features the symbolic poppy that came to represent the sacrifice of those who fought in the Great War and in subsequent conflicts. The red poppies, shown rising and swirling above the cornfield towards heaven, are also a symbol of rebirth and regeneration.

The inscription in the bottom right hand corner is taken from Psalm 23:

Even though I walk through the valley of the shadow of death I will fear no evil for You art with me.

ROLL OF HONOUR UPDATED

In 1920, the number of OJs thought to have died in the war was about 150 and 157 names were originally carved on the oak Roll of Honour panels in the Chapel.

Considerable efforts were made at the time to identify those who died, but almost inevitably there were some oversights. News often travelled slowly, and in some cases the School had lost touch with the former pupils concerned.

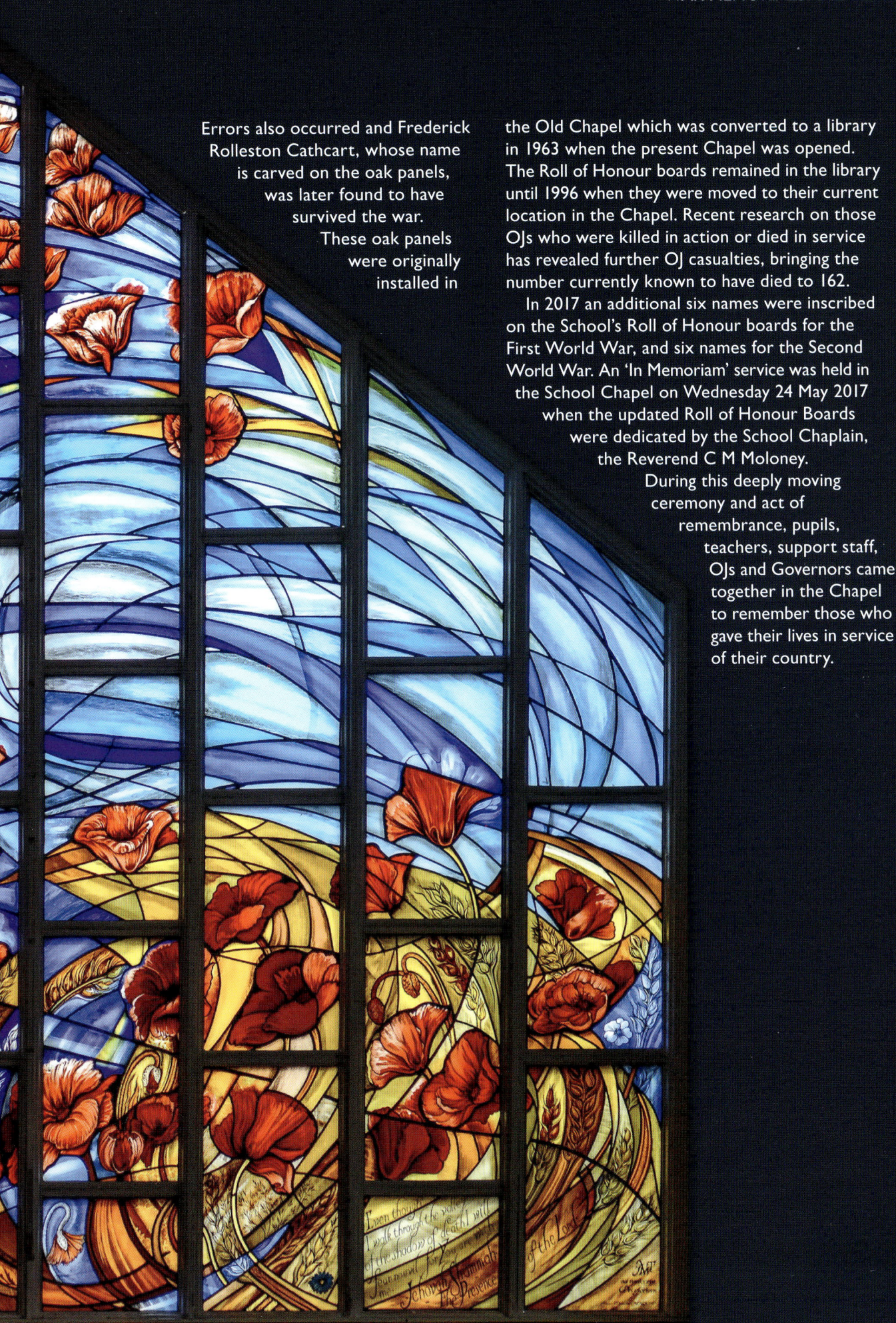

WAR MEMORIALS AND REMEMBRANCE

Errors also occurred and Frederick Rolleston Cathcart, whose name is carved on the oak panels, was later found to have survived the war.

These oak panels were originally installed in the Old Chapel which was converted to a library in 1963 when the present Chapel was opened. The Roll of Honour boards remained in the library until 1996 when they were moved to their current location in the Chapel. Recent research on those OJs who were killed in action or died in service has revealed further OJ casualties, bringing the number currently known to have died to 162.

In 2017 an additional six names were inscribed on the School's Roll of Honour boards for the First World War, and six names for the Second World War. An 'In Memoriam' service was held in the School Chapel on Wednesday 24 May 2017 when the updated Roll of Honour Boards were dedicated by the School Chaplain, the Reverend C M Moloney. During this deeply moving ceremony and act of remembrance, pupils, teachers, support staff, OJs and Governors came together in the Chapel to remember those who gave their lives in service of their country.

ABBREVIATIONS

AC	Army Chaplain
ADS	Advanced Dressing Station
BBC	British Broadcasting Corporation
CCS	Casualty Clearing Station
CF	Chaplain to the Forces
CSM	Company Sergeant Major
DCM	Distinguished Conduct Medal
DORA	Defence of the Realm Act
HMC	Headmasters' Conference
IWM	Imperial War Museum
KOYLI	King's Own Yorkshire Light Infantry
MBE	Member of the Order of the British Empire
MC	Military Cross
MDS	Main Dressing Station
OBE	Officer of the Order of the British Empire
OJ	Old Johnian
OTC	Officer Training Corps
POW	Prisoner of War
RAF	Royal Air Force
RAMC	Royal Army Medical Corps
RE	Royal Engineers
RFA	Royal Field Artillery
RFC	Royal Flying Corps
RGA	Royal Garrison Artillery
RND	Royal Naval Division
RNVR	Royal Naval Volunteer Reserve
SMS	Seiner Majestät Schiff – His Majesty's Ship (German)
UOTC	University Officer Training Corps
VC	Victoria Cross
YMCA	Young Men's Christian Association

ROLL OF HONOUR

SURNAME/FIRST NAME	REGIMENT/SERVICE	RANK	DATE OF DEATH	AGE	CEMETERY/MEMORIAL	YEARS AT SCHOOL
ADAMS, Edgar Lainson	London Regiment (Artists' Rifles)	Private	27/09/1918	21	SUCRERIE BRITISH CEMETERY	1911-1912
ADOLPHUS, Otto Ernest Augustus	Royal Fusiliers	Private	09/11/1916	19	EUSTON ROAD CEMETERY	1908-1915
ALEXANDER, Alfred Herbert	Hampshire Regiment	Second Lieutenant	03/12/1917	23	CAMBRAI MEMORIAL	1905-1913
ALLAN, Frank Cecil	Durham Light Infantry	Second Lieutenant	29/09/1916	20	ST SEVER CEMETERY	1906-1915
AMIES, Nathaniel George Read	The Buffs (East Kent Regiment)	Private	20/08/1915	30	CALVAIRE (ESSEX) MILITARY CEMETERY	1896-1901
ASLACHSEN, Hector Shields	The King's (Liverpool Regiment)	Second Lieutenant	25/04/1917	20	COJEUL BRITISH CEMETERY	1908-1915
BAILLIE-HAMILTON, Charles Douglas	1st Canadian Mounted Rifles	Private	02/06/1916	35	TYNE COT CEMETERY	1890-1894
BARLTROP, Eric Arthur	Royal Flying Corps	Lieutenant	23/04/1917	27	JEANCOURT COMMUNAL CEMETERY EXTENSION	1900-1908
BAYLAY, Charles R.	The Buffs (East Kent Regiment)	Private	03/05/1917	41	ARRAS MEMORIAL	1886-1895
BEDWELL, Victor Leopold Stevens	Suffolk Regiment	Second Lieutenant	18/08/1916	22	THIEPVAL MEMORIAL	1904-1913
BEECHEY, Barnard Reeve	Lincolnshire Regiment	Sergeant	25/09/1915	38	PLOEGSTEERT MEMORIAL	1887-1896
BEECHEY, Frank Collett Reeve	East Yorkshire Regiment	Second Lieutenant	14/11/1916	30	WARLINCOURT HALTE BRITISH CEMETERY	1897-1904
BENNETT, Joseph Victor	Royal Berkshire Regiment	Corporal	26/08/1918	40	PERONNE ROAD CEMETERY	1891-1896
BLANDFORD, William Arthur Innocens	Northumberland Fusiliers	Private	26/10/1917	27	TYNE COT MEMORIAL	1900-1906
BOISSIER, William Arthur Marshall	Royal Marine Artillery	Lieutenant	27/07/1917	27	COXYDE MILITARY CEMETERY	1900-1905
BOTT, Francis George	35th Scinde Horse	Lieutenant	20/08/1920	20	BASRA WAR CEMETERY	1910-1917
BOTT, William Ernest	Royal Fusiliers	Captain	18/09/1918	25	EPEHY WOOD FARM CEMETERY	1904-1910
BOULTBEE, Arthur Elsdale	Royal Flying Corps	Lieutenant	17/03/1917	19	CANADIAN CEMETERY No. 2	1908-1909
BOURNE, Austin Spencer	South Staffordshire Regiment	Second Lieutenant	23/04/1917	25	ARRAS MEMORIAL	1903-1910
BRAMLEY, Cyril Richard	King's Own Yorkshire Light Infantry	Captain	20/03/1917	25	ANCRE BRITISH CEMETERY	1901-1910
BRAMLEY, Harold	King's Own Yorkshire Light Infantry	Second Lieutenant	13/05/1915	21	YPRES (MENIN GATE) MEMORIAL	1905-1910
BUCKNALL, Marc Antony	Duke of Cornwall's Light Infantry	Second Lieutenant	06/03/1917	26	DERNANCOURT COMMUNAL CEMETERY EXTENSION	1901-1907
BULLER, Arthur Edward Adderly	Inns of Court Officer Training Corps	Captain	21/09/1918	35	RAMLEH WAR CEMETERY	1892-1899

SURNAME/FIRST NAME	REGIMENT/SERVICE	RANK	DATE OF DEATH	AGE	CEMETERY/MEMORIAL	YEARS AT SCHOOL
BULLER, Richard Francis Montague	Middlesex Regiment	Major	24/08/1918	33	VIS-EN-ARTOIS MEMORIAL	1896-1903
CALLEY, Oliver John	Wiltshire Regiment	Lieutenant	12/03/1915	22	LA LAITERIE MILITARY CEMETERY	1906-1908
CARDEW, Basil St Merryn	Royal Navy	Clerk	01/11/1914	19	PLYMOUTH NAVAL MEMORIAL	1904-1913
CARRE, Maurice Tennant	Australian Infantry AIF	Private	02/09/1915	30	SHRAPNEL VALLEY CEMETERY	1897-1899
CARVER, Lionel Henry Liptrap	Irish Guards	Second Lieutenant	26/05/1918	34	AYETTE BRITISH CEMETERY	1894-1902
CHANNER, Edward Winter	Leicestershire Regiment	Private	07/07/1917	30	PHILOSOPHE BRITISH CEMETERY	1897-1906
CLARKE, Arthur Frederick	York and Lancaster Regiment	Private	01/07/1916	21	THIEPVAL MEMORIAL	1905-1911
COLLINS, Neville Lancelot	Royal Sussex Regiment	Second Lieutenant	15/08/1916	22	CATERPILLAR VALLEY CEMETERY	1908-1909
COLNETT, Richard Daunteshey	Essex Regiment	Captain	13/08/1918	23	JERUSALEM MEMORIAL	1908-1910
COOKE, Hans Hendrick Anthony	Connaught Rangers	Captain	24/01/1917	32	NAIROBI BRITISH AND INDIAN MEMORIAL	1897-1903
COPEMAN, Robert George Henry	Essex Regiment	Second Lieutenant	12/01/1916	21	BETHUNE TOWN CEMETERY	1905-1913
CROFTON, Harold Mowatt Maxwell	Royal Navy	Paymaster Sub-Lieutenant	29/11/1918	22	SHOTLEY (ST MARY) CHURCHYARD	1906-1913
CRUTTWELL, Hugh Lockwood	Royal Garrison Artillery	Second Lieutenant	12/10/1917	36	THE HUTS CEMETERY	1893-1897
D'ALBERTANSON, Ronald	East Surrey Regiment	Second Lieutenant	08/08/1916	22	DERNANCOURT COMMUNAL CEMETERY	1903-1905
DAVIES, David Ethelston	Royal Welsh Fusiliers	Second Lieutenant	18/06/1917	23	FEUCHY CHAPEL BRITISH CEMETERY	1904-1909
DAVIES, Walter Llewellyn	King's Shropshire Light Infantry	Second Lieutenant	15/07/1916	34	LA NEUVILLE BRITISH CEMETERY	1893-1899
DAWSON SMITH, Frank	Oxford. and Bucks Light Infantry	Lieutenant	11/01/1920	33	WAJIR CEMETERY	1897-1903
DEACON, Ernest Cecil Watson	Royal Air Force	Second Lieutenant	22/04/1918	19	GODEWAERSVELDE BRITISH CEMETERY	1908-1915
DEWAR, David Sonnie	Machine Gun Corps (Infantry)	Lieutenant	22/03/1918	24	GRAND-SERAUCOURT BRITISH CEMETERY	1903-1912
DIXON, Charles Penrose	Royal Flying Corps	Second Lieutenant	25/10/1917	19	MENDINGHEM MILITARY CEMETERY	1908-1908
EDWARDS, Frank Glencairn De Burgh	Royal Horse Artillery	Lieutenant	12/10/1914	29	VIEUX-BERQUIN COMMUNAL CEMETERY	1895-1903
EKINS, Willingham Richard	East Yorkshire Regiment	Second Lieutenant	03/05/1917	19	ARRAS MEMORIAL	1908-1914
ELLABY, Cecil Annesley	Wellington Regiment NZEF	Private	08/08/1915	26	CHUNUK BAIR (NEW ZEALAND) MEMORIAL	1899-1906
ELTON, George Kenward	Hampshire Regiment	Second Lieutenant	18/10/1916	18	THIEPVAL MEMORIAL	1911-1914
EVANS, Neville Vernon	South Wales Borderers	Second Lieutenant	16/08/1917	19	ARTILLERY WOOD CEMETERY	1909-1913

ROLL OF HONOUR

SURNAME/FIRST NAME	REGIMENT/SERVICE	RANK	DATE OF DEATH	AGE	CEMETERY/MEMORIAL	YEARS AT SCHOOL
EVERETT, John Eric Murray	Royal East Kent Yeomanry	Private	12/10/1915	20	PINK FARM CEMETERY	1906-1911
FLETCHER, Robert Ronald Rawcliffe	South Lancashire Regiment	Lieutenant	29/10/1919	34	KIRKEE 1914-1918 MEMORIAL	1899-1905
FRENCH SMITH, Robert Arthur	Canadian Field Artillery	Gunner	08/06/1917	33	LA TARGETTE BRITISH CEMETERY	1895-1900
FURMSTON, Clement Barrington	Machine Gun Corps (Infantry)	Second Lieutenant	09/04/1917	22	ROCLINCOURT MILITARY CEMETERY	1905-1911
GEDGE, Joseph Theodore	Royal Navy	Staff Paymaster	06/08/1914	36	PLYMOUTH NAVAL MEMORIAL	1888-1895
GILL, Kenneth Carlyle	Royal Air Force	Captain	23/10/1918	25	FILLIEVRES BRITISH CEMETERY	1907-1912
GODWIN, John Charles Raymond	Royal Sussex Regiment	Second Lieutenant	07/07/1916	27	THIEPVAL MEMORIAL	1899-1904
GORE-BROWNE, Eric Antony Rollo	Dorsetshire Regiment	Major	03/07/1918	28	MOMBASA BRITISH MEMORIAL	1905-1905
GRAY, Edmund Trevennin	Durham Light Infantry	Second Lieutenant	22/10/1915	19	PLOEGSTEERT WOOD MILITARY CEMETERY	1906-1914
GREENLEES, Charles Fouracres	The Queen's (Royal West Surrey Regiment)	Second Lieutenant	01/07/1916	21	AUCHONVILLERS MILITARY CEMETERY	1904-1914
GRIFFIN, Basil Walker	Lincolnshire Regiment	Second Lieutenant	02/12/1917	21	TYNE COT MEMORIAL	1906-1911
GRIGSON, Lionel Henry Shuckforth	Devonshire Regiment	Second Lieutenant	09/05/1917	19	ARRAS MEMORIAL	1908-1916
HALL, Arthur James Melville	London Regiment	Second Lieutenant	15/09/1916	24	THIEPVAL MEMORIAL	1903-1905
HALL, The Reverend William	Royal Navy	Chaplain and Naval Instructor	04/11/1916	49	FORD PARK CEMETERY	1878-1881
HAMLEY, William Walter	Dorsetshire Regiment	Second Lieutenant	26/03/1918	24	DOULLENS COMMUNAL CEMETERY EXTENSION No.1	1909-1912
HAMMOND, William Cecil	Duke of Cornwall's Light Infantry	Captain	24/04/1917	19	DOIRAN MILITARY CEMETERY	1907-1913
HARDING, Herbert Oliver Denman	Judge in Trichinopoly, Madras India	District Judge	22/02/1916	50	ST GEORGE'S CATHEDRAL, MADRAS	1876-1880
HARDING, The Reverend Wilfrid John	Army Chaplains' Department	Chaplain 4th Class	31/10/1917	31	TYNE COT MEMORIAL	1900-1904
HARTIGAN, Kenneth Leslie Stewart	35th Scinde Horse	Lieutenant	02/11/1919	20	ALEXANDRIA (HADRA) WAR MEMORIAL CEMETERY	1910-1917
HARVEY, Robert Leslie	London Regiment	Private	24/09/1918	38	COLOGNE SOUTHERN CEMETERY	1891-1896
HEMSTED, John	Royal Field Artillery	Second Lieutenant	16/04/1917	33	ARRAS MEMORIAL	1894-1901
HOCKING, William	Royal Naval Air Service	Flight Sub-Lieutenant	21/04/1916	24	CHATHAM NAVAL MEMORIAL	1902-1907
HOCKLEY (HOCKLY), Nigel Alan	Mercantile Marine	Apprentice	27/02/1917	17	TOWER HILL MEMORIAL	1909-1915
HOPKINS, Lawrence Hilton	Huntingdon Cyclist Battalion	Captain	07/10/1918	25	SUCRERIE CEMETERY	1904-1908

SURNAME/FIRST NAME	REGIMENT/SERVICE	RANK	DATE OF DEATH	AGE	CEMETERY/MEMORIAL	YEARS AT SCHOOL
HOULT, Robert Percy	West Yorkshire Regiment (Prince of Wales's Own)	Second Lieutenant	16/08/1917	19	TYNE COT MEMORIAL	1911-1914
HOWIS, Francis Thackeray	Essex Regiment	Second Lieutenant	08/12/1915	23	HILL 10 CEMETERY	1902-1908
IRELAND, Cedric Septimus	Royal Naval Volunteer Reserve	Able Seaman	26/03/1917	28	NIKOLAI CEMETERY	1899-1903
JACKSON, Henry Stewart	King's Own Yorkshire Light Infantry	Lieutenant	01/07/1916	20	THIEPVAL MEMORIAL	1905-1908
JAMES, Frank Clifford	Royal Berkshire Regiment	Lieutenant	04/05/1917	19	DOUAI COMMUNAL CEMETERY	1908-1913
JENKINS, Edward Tuberville Llewellin	Royal Engineers	Second Lieutenant	25/07/1916	34	CORBIE COMMUNAL CEMETERY EXTENSION	1892-1898
JENKINS, Richard	Manchester Regiment	Second Lieutenant	11/11/1916	24	THIEPVAL MEMORIAL	1902-1911
JOHNS, Bradley Cooper	Royal Garrison Artillery	Second Lieutenant	22/10/1918	38	BROOMFIELD (ST MARY) CHURCHYARD	1891-1899
JONES, Hywel Herbert Saunders	The Queen's (Royal West Surrey Regiment)	Second Lieutenant	04/03/1917	19	PERONNE COMMUNAL CEMETERY EXTENSION	1909-1915
JOYCE, Frank Postlethwaite	Border Regiment	Lieutenant	29/05/1917	26	BROWN'S COPSE CEMETERY	1901-1909
JUKES, Arthur Starr	London Regiment	Second Lieutenant	06/03/1917	46	SUEZ WAR MEMORIAL CEMETERY	1881-1883
KAY, Melville Herbert	Durham Light Infantry	Second Lieutenant	05/11/1916	25	WARLENCOURT BRITISH CEMETERY	1901-1907
KELLY, Edward Rowley	Border Regiment	Second Lieutenant	07/07/1915	17	YPRES (MENIN GATE) MEMORIAL	1911-1914
KEMP, Percy Vickerman	Durham Light Infantry	Captain	31/05/1918	25	ETAPLES MILITARY CEMETERY	1902-1910
KYNASTON, John Valentine	Royal Air Force	Lieutenant	15/07/1919	25	DURRINGTON CEMETERY	1903-1909
LAMPEN, Charles Alexander Stephen Dudley	Australian Infantry AIF	Lance Corporal	13/09/1915	24	ALEXANDRIA (CHATBY) MILITARY AND WAR MEMORIAL CEMETERY	1904-1908
LANE, Eric Arthur Milner	Manchester Regiment	Second Lieutenant	08/03/1916	24	BASRA MEMORIAL	1903-1907
LEE, Richard Henry Driffield	Royal Flying Corps	Captain and Flight Commander	23/06/1917	29	WOODTON (ALL SAINTS) CHURCHYARD	1899-1906
LESTER, Gerald James	Army Chaplains' Department	Chaplain 4th Class	16/12/1918	33	ST SEVER CEMETERY EXTENSION, ROUEN	1895-1901
LEWIS, Ivor Morgan	Royal Navy	Chaplain	13/05/1915	26	CHATHAM NAVAL MEMORIAL	1900-1908
LEWIS, John Gordon	London Regiment (City of London Rifles)	Rifleman	07/06/1917	26	YPRES (MENIN GATE) MEMORIAL	1902-1907
LITTLE, Howard Vaughan Whitchurch	King's Royal Rifle Corps	Rifleman	12/12/1916	18	THIEPVAL MEMORIAL	1908-1913
LOGSDAIL, Hugh	Royal Garrison Artillery	Second Lieutenant	19/09/1918	30	Y FARM MILITARY CEMETERY	1899-1905
MADDRELL, John Denys Hugh	Duke of Cornwall's Light Infantry	Lieutenant	13/12/1916	20	ETAPLES MILITARY CEMETERY	1908-1914

ROLL OF HONOUR

SURNAME/FIRST NAME	REGIMENT/SERVICE	RANK	DATE OF DEATH	AGE	CEMETERY/MEMORIAL	YEARS AT SCHOOL
MAINPRICE, Bernard Paul	Royal Navy	Clerk	26/11/1914	19	PORTSMOUTH NAVAL MEMORIAL	1906-1912
MAINPRICE, Ernest Wiliam Loxley	Royal Navy	Fleet Paymaster	31/05/1916	38	PORTSMOUTH NAVAL MEMORIAL	1888-1895
MANLEY, Charles Percival Henry	Queen's Own (Royal West Kent Regiment)	Second Lieutenant	04/10/1918	20	TERLINCTHUN BRITISH CEMETERY	1909-1917
MEERES, Henry William Hugh	London Regiment (Royal Fusiliers)	Lance Corporal	19/03/1915	35	FERME BUTERNE MILITARY CEMETERY	1890-1899
MIDDLEMISS, Godfrey Stewart	London Regiment (London Rifle Brigade)	Rifleman	18/06/1917	23	TANK CEMETERY	1908-1912
MIDDLEMISS, Guy	Ceylon Planters Rifle Corps	Rifleman	06/05/1915	24	BEACH CEMETERY	1904-1909
MILLARD, Spencer Harold	Royal Air Force	Flight Cadet	16/10/1918	18	ANDOVER CEMETERY	1911-1916
MONTFORD, Douglas Raymond	98th Indian Infantry	Captain	30/03/1918	28	JERUSALEM MEMORIAL	1899-1908
MOORE, Cyril George Ettrick	Canadian Infantry	Private	14/06/1916	26	YPRES (MENIN GATE) MEMORIAL	1900-1904
MORGAN, Ashton	Royal Flying Corps	Lieutenant	04/02/1918	26	FIGHELDEAN (ST MICHAEL) CHURCHYARD	1903-1908
NEWTON, Murray Edell	Royal Flying Corps	Lieutenant	18/06/1917	22	ARRAS FLYING SERVICES MEMORIAL	1904-1912
NORTH, Charles Edward Philip James	London Regiment (Artists' Rifles)	Private	28/08/1918	19	BAGNEUX BRITISH CEMETERY	1908-1915
OSBORNE, Harold John	Hampshire Regiment	Lieutenant	04/08/1915	21	BASRA WAR CEMETERY	1904-1910
PALMER, Robert Daniel Cecil	Royal Air Force	Flying Officer	02/08/1920	22	BAGHDAD (NORTH GATE) WAR CEMETERY	1909-1915
PARK, James Wilfrid Haynes	22nd Sam Browne's Cavalry	Captain	14/01/1917	28	AMARA WAR CEMETERY	1901-1907
PARKER, Arthur John	Mercantile Marine	Wireless Operator	23/12/1918	16	TOWER HILL MEMORIAL	1912-1918
PARRY, Claud Frederick Pilkington	Royal Field Artillery	Lieutenant Colonel	20/08/1918	48	BIENVILLERS MILITARY CEMETERY	1880-1885
PASCOE, Frank Guy Buckingham	Royal Flying Corps	Second Lieutenant	02/07/1917	20	ARRAS FLYING SERVICES MEMORIAL	1907-1915
PATCH, Henry	Royal Flying Corps	Captain	19/10/1917	23	HARLEBEKE NEW BRITISH CEMETERY	1908-1911
PAYTON, Frederick Thomas Croydon	Royal Engineers	Corporal	01/07/1916	20	CARNOY MILITARY CEMETERY	1906-1912
POWELL, Thomas Gerald	Canadian Infantry	Private	15/08/1917	31	VIMY MEMORIAL	1896-1901
PRICHARD, Thomas Lewis	Royal Welsh Fusiliers	Captain	09/11/1914	32	BOULOGNE EASTERN CEMETERY	1892-1897
PUCKRIDGE, Cyril Vincent Noel	Gloucestershire Regiment	Second Lieutenant	21/07/1916	21	THIEPVAL MEMORIAL	1906-1914
RAGGETT, Bertram Robert	Royal Flying Corps	Second Lieutenant	05/01/1918	27	LIJSSENTHOEK MILITARY CEMETERY	1901-1906
RICHARDSON, Edric Hugh Barnstey	Wiltshire Regiment	Captain	15/06/1915	22	LE TOURET MEMORIAL	1907-1910

SURNAME/FIRST NAME	REGIMENT/SERVICE	RANK	DATE OF DEATH	AGE	CEMETERY/MEMORIAL	YEARS AT SCHOOL
RICHARDSON, Maurice Lewis George	South Lancashire Regiment	Second Lieutenant	28/02/1917	19	HEATH CEMETERY, HARBONNIERES	1908-1909
ROBERTS, Cecil Llewellyn Norton	Royal Warwickshire Regiment	Captain	09/10/1917	23	TYNE COT MEMORIAL	1905-1914
ROBERTSON, Ernest Cecil Lennox	London Regiment	Lieutenant	18/10/1915	23	DUD CORNER CEMETERY	1903-1910
ROBINSON, Ernest	Royal Naval Reserve	Lieutenant	15/10/1914	34	CHATHAM NAVAL MEMORIAL	1891-1895
ROUND, William Haldane	Sherwood Foresters (Notts and Derby Regiment)	Captain	01/07/1916	23	FONCQUEVILLERS MILITARY CEMETERY	1903-1913
ROWLEY, Walter Austin	Leicestershire Regiment	Second Lieutenant	16/07/1917	25	ARRAS MEMORIAL	1901-1911
RUTLEDGE, John Bedell	East Yorkshire Regiment	Captain	01/07/1916	33	FRICOURT NEW MILITARY CEMETERY	1892-1897
SAVAGE, John Ardkeen	Northamptonshire Regiment	Captain	17/09/1914	31	LA FERTE-SOUS-JOUARRE MEMORIAL	1895-1899
SEYMOUR, Neville	Royal Navy	Sub-Lieutenant	31/05/1916	20	PORTSMOUTH NAVAL MEMORIAL	1906-1911
SHEEHAN, Gordon Keith Patrick	Northamptonshire Regiment	Lieutenant	28/08/1918	21	LA TARGETTE BRITISH CEMETERY	1907-1915
SHENTON, Austin Kirk	Royal Engineers	Captain	26/07/1918	22	CROUY BRITISH CEMETERY	1908-1910
SKYRME, Richard Edward Elcho	Wiltshire Regiment	Second Lieutenant	06/02/1917	21	PLOEGSTEERT WOOD MILITARY CEMETERY	1906-1914
SLATER, Henry Godfrey	2nd Canadian Mounted Rifles	Private	10/08/1918	37	BOUCHOIR NEW BRITISH CEMETERY	1893-1900
SQUIRE, Stanley Charles	Gloucestershire Regiment	Lieutenant	09/08/1915	22	HELLES MEMORIAL	1903-1912
START, Lesingham Eden	Durham Light Infantry	Second Lieutenant	23/02/1915	38	ALDERSHOT MILITARY CEMETERY	1889-1895
STENNING, Bernard Clement	East Surrey Regiment	Second Lieutenant	26/07/1917	35	GODEWAERSVELDE BRITISH CEMETERY	1895-1899
STOKES, John Wilfred	Royal Army Medical Corps	Lieutenant Colonel	10/02/1916	44	HAMPSTEAD CEMETERY	1888-1890
TEAPE, Charles Lewarne	Devonshire Regiment	Second Lieutenant	04/09/1916	20	DELVILLE WOOD CEMETERY	1909-1914
THOMAS, Eric Hand	Duke of Wellington's (West Riding Regiment)	Second Lieutenant	08/12/1917	19	ARRAS MEMORIAL	1909-1917
THOMAS, James Leonard	Royal Flying Corps	Captain	28/02/1917	27	FIGHELDEAN (ST MICHAEL) CHURCHYARD	1899-1905
TURNER, Edmund Sanctuary	Royal Garrison Artillery	Second Lieutenant	21/08/1916	30	DANTZIG ALLEY BRITISH CEMETERY	1896-1903
TURNER, Eric Walter Carpenter	Hampshire Regiment	Lieutenant	09/08/1916	21	BEDFORD HOUSE CEMETERY	1907-1912

ROLL OF HONOUR

SURNAME/FIRST NAME	REGIMENT/SERVICE	RANK	DATE OF DEATH	AGE	CEMETERY/MEMORIAL	YEARS AT SCHOOL
TURTON, Richard Dacre	York and Lancaster Regiment	Lieutenant	24/10/1917	20	THE HUTS CEMETERY	1912-1914
UNWIN, Francis John	Royal Air Force	Lieutenant	17/09/1919	22	ARCHANGEL MEMORIAL	1909-1914
VALLINGS, Ranulph Kingsley Joyce	Royal Navy	Flight Sub-Lieutenant	13/01/1917	23	MIKRA BRITISH CEMETERY	1909-1910
WEEKES, Walter	Lincolnshire Regiment	Second Lieutenant	23/04/1917	23	ARRAS MEMORIAL	1904-1909
WHALEY, Oswald Stanley	Hampshire Regiment	Second Lieutenant	10/08/1915	25	HELLES MEMORIAL	1901-1903
WILKINS, John Christopher Martin	Duke of Cornwall's Light Infantry	Lieutenant	24/03/1918	21	ARRAS MEMORIAL	1907-1912
WILLIAMS, Noel Griffith	The King's (Liverpool Regiment)	Private	13/04/1918	19	LOOS MEMORIAL	1910-1915
WILLIAMS, Theodore Edward	Somerset Light Infantry	Second Lieutenant	01/07/1915	25	TALANA FARM CEMETERY	1900-1907
WINDLE, Michael William Maxwell	Devonshire Regiment	Lieutenant	25/09/1915	22	LOOS MEMORIAL	1902-1903
WOFFINDIN, Longley Evans Martin	Mercantile Marine	Cadet Apprentice	16/08/1918	17	GREAT GONERBY (ST SEBASTIAN)	1912-1916
WOODS, Leslie	Royal Field Artillery	Captain	25/02/1919	26	HALLE COMMUNAL CEMETERY	1903-1905
WRIGLEY, Willoughby Thornton	Wiltshire Regiment	Captain	15/08/1920	25	BAGHDAD (NORTH GATE) WAR CEMETERY	1905-1912
YOUNG, Robert Percival	Royal Sussex Regiment	Lieutenant	17/12/1917	27	JERUSALEM WAR CEMETERY	1900-1906

TEACHING STAFF

SURNAME/FIRST NAME	REGIMENT/SERVICE	RANK	DATE OF DEATH	AGE	CEMETERY/MEMORIAL	YEARS AT SCHOOL
ALDERSON, Albert Evelyn	The Queen's (Royal West Surrey Regiment)	Captain	11/03/1918	34	STRUMA MILITARY CEMETERY	1912-1918
BOURNE, Cyprian	The Queen's (Royal West Surrey Regiment)	Second Lieutenant	11/04/1917	29	DUISANS BRITISH CEMETERY	1913-1917
DRIFFIELD, Lancelot Townshend	St John's School OTC Territorial Force (Unattached)	Captain	09/10/1917	37	NORTHAMPTON CEMETERY	OJ 1890-1899 Staff 1911-1917

SUPPORT STAFF

SURNAME/FIRST NAME	REGIMENT/SERVICE	RANK	DATE OF DEATH	AGE	CEMETERY/MEMORIAL	YEARS AT SCHOOL
HAYWARD, Leslie William George James	Royal Army Medical Corps	Private	17/09/1916	22	DELVILLE WOOD CEMETERY	c.1911

SCHOOL GOVERNOR

SURNAME/FIRST NAME	REGIMENT/SERVICE	RANK	DATE OF DEATH	AGE	CEMETERY/MEMORIAL	YEARS AT SCHOOL
WALROND, The Hon. William Lionel Charles	Army Service Corps	Lieutenant	02/11/1915	39	BRADFIELD (ALL SAINTS) CHURCHYARD	1913-1915

DISTINCTIONS AWARDED

VICTORIA CROSS
E G Robinson ~ Royal Navy
G H Woolley ~ Queen Victoria's Rifles

COMPANION OF THE MOST HONOURABLE ORDER OF THE BATH
J E V Morton ~ Royal Navy

COMPANION OF THE MOST DISTINGUISHED ORDER OF ST MICHAEL AND ST GEORGE
H S Measham ~ Royal Navy

COMPANION OF THE MOST EMINENT ORDER OF THE INDIAN EMPIRE
C B Stokes ~ Indian Army

DISTINGUISHED SERVICE ORDER
M E S Boissier ~ Royal Navy
R H Bowell ~ Leicestershire Regiment
J W B Grigson ~ Royal Air Force
B F Hood ~ Royal Navy
A M Kerby ~ Royal Field Artillery
C J Low ~ London Scottish
S Mildred ~ Royal Engineers
I C Montford ~ Rifle Brigade
P C R Moreton ~ Royal Monmouthshire Engineers
C F P Parry ~ Royal Field Artillery
L E Pearson ~ Royal Navy
C E V K Peberdy ~ West Yorkshire Regiment
F C Platt ~ Royal Navy
C B Stokes ~ Indian Army
T M Wakefield ~ Royal Garrison Artillery

ORDER OF THE BRITISH EMPIRE
J L Adams ~ Royal Engineers
L C E Ayre ~ Royal Navy
H A Boys ~ Army Service Corps
I A S Cooke ~ Connaught Rangers
N W A Edwards ~ Army Chaplains' Department
J D Irving ~ West Yorkshire Regiment
S Mildred ~ Royal Engineers
O L Parsons ~ Royal Navy
E. G. Robinson ~ Royal Navy
C B Stokes ~ Indian Army
E L Sturdee ~ Royal Naval Division
J H Thorpe ~ Manchester Rifles

MEMBER OF THE BRITISH EMPIRE
H J Donkin ~ Army Service Corps
D Rea ~ Suffolk Regiment
H Spooner ~ Ecclesiastical Establishment Bengal

DISTINGUISHED SERVICE CROSS
E G Boissier ~ Royal Naval Division

MILITARY CROSS
O St P Aitkens ~ Canadian Infantry
G P R Alsop ~ Dragoon Guards
A B Barltrop ~ Indian Army
B St J Boultbee ~ Royal Air Force
P N M Boustead ~ Hampshire Regiment
E L Bowley ~ Royal Field Artillery
C B Campbell ~ Highland Light Infantry
C F E Clarke ~ Gloucester Regiment
H R Cooke ~ Salonika Field Force
R D'Albertanson ~ East Surrey Regiment
H Alban Davies ~ Royal Welsh Fusiliers
B V Davis ~ Royal Engineers
N W A Edwards ~ Divisional Artillery
V B C de la P Eldrid ~ Wiltshire Regiment
J L Fairclough ~ York and Lancaster Regiment
C N C Field ~ Tank Corps
A P Fry ~ Royal Army Medical Corps
K C Gill ~ Cambridgeshire Regiment
J K L Graham ~ Royal Field Artillery
C Grellier ~ Hampshire Regiment
E J M Griffiths ~ Cheshire Regiment
R H Griffiths ~ Cheshire Regiment
W J Harding ~ Royal Naval Division
V St Clare Hill ~ Machine Gun Corps
M G Hogg ~ Royal Garrison Artillery
K H Hopkins ~ Rifle Brigade
J Hughes ~ Royal Welsh Fusiliers
J D Irving ~ West Yorkshire Regiment
H C James ~ Welsh Regiment
W A Jones ~ Army Chaplains' Department
A M Kerby ~ Royal Field Artillery
R Knight ~ Middlesex Regiment
G F Laycock ~ Royal Engineers
T R Low ~ Machine Gun Corps
C P H Manley ~ Royal West Kent Regiment
O C Marris ~ Cheshire Regiment
K R Napier ~ Royal Air Force
W H Park ~ Royal Air Force
A L Pavey ~ Wiltshire Regiment
C E V K Peberdy ~ West Yorkshire Regiment
F R Peirson ~ Northumberland Fusiliers
T G Perry ~ Durham Light Infantry
G Phillips ~ Royal Field Artillery
F J Powell ~ Royal Air Force
T A Lloyd Rees ~ Machine Gun Corps
W F Roach ~ Gloucestershire Regiment
E H Sharp ~ New Zealand Infantry Brigade
A K Shenton ~ Royal Engineers

MILITARY CROSS CONTINUED...

H Spooner ~ Indian Army
T H L Stebbing ~ Notts and Derbyshire Regiment
G R Tadman ~ Egyptian Camel Transport
H J Thomas ~ Liverpool Regiment
A R Tudor-Craig ~ Royal Irish Fusiliers
L H T Walker ~ Welsh Regiment
O Q Warren ~ Tank Corps
C R Webb ~ Royal Engineers
P G Whitefoord ~ Royal Field Artillery
B M Williams ~ Durham Light Infantry
L Woods ~ Royal Field Artillery
C S Woodward ~ Army Chaplains' Department
G H Woolley ~ London Regiment
W T Wrigley ~ Wiltshire Regiment
H E P Yorke ~ Royal Army Medical Corps
E Young ~ Gloucestershire Regiment
R P Young ~ Royal Sussex Regiment

BAR TO THE MILITARY CROSS

W A Jones ~ Army Chaplains' Department
F R Peirson ~ Northumberland Fusiliers

DISTINGUISHED FLYING CROSS

A H A Alban ~ Royal Air Force
J W B Grigson ~ Royal Air Force
W H Park ~ Royal Air Force
D L P S Stuart-Shepherd ~ Royal Air Force

BAR TO THE DISTINGUISHED FLYING CROSS (TWICE)

J W B Grigson ~ Royal Air Force

AIR FORCE CROSS

F H M Maynard ~ Royal Air Force

MILITARY MEDAL

J F Head ~ Canadian Field Artillery

ORDER OF THE NILE

E G Robinson ~ Royal Navy
J N Soden ~ Indian Army

COMMANDER OF THE LEGION OF HONOUR

J E V Morton ~ Royal Navy

CROIX DE GUERRE (FRENCH)

R H Griffiths ~ Cheshire Regiment
G W Husband ~ British Red Cross
H G Howell-Jones ~ Welsh Regiment
T R Low ~ Machine Gun Corps
B M Williams ~ Durham Light Infantry
C L Woolley ~ Royal Field Artillery

CROCE DI GUERRA (ITALIAN)

C E G Gill ~ Royal Air Force

CRUZ DE GUERRA (PORTUGAL)

E R Stagg ~ Royal Field Artillery

CAVALIER OF THE ORDER OF THE CROWN OF ITALY

A J Mellor ~ Royal Marine Light Infantry

MEDALS FOR MILITARY VALOUR CONFERRED BY THE KING OF ITALY

H G St G Morgan ~ Royal Marine Artillery (Silver Medal)
A J Peareth ~ East Kent Regiment (Silver Medal)
V M Silvester ~ British Red Cross in Italy (Bronze Medal)

CHEVALIER OF THE ORDER OF THE CROWN OF ROMANIA

C G Cavalier ~ Army Chaplains' Department

OFFICER OF THE ORDER OF THE CROWN OF ROMANIA

J C Farmer ~ Royal Marine Light Infantry

CROSS OF ST. ANNE (RUSSIAN)

J C Farmer ~ Royal Marine Light Infantry

ORDER OF ST. STANISLAUS (RUSSIAN)

W J Bocking ~ Royal Air Force
J E V Morton ~ Royal Navy

ORDER OF THE WHITE EAGLE (SERBIAN)

J Edgell ~ London Regiment
C Grellier ~ Hampshire Regiment

ORDER OF ST SAVA (SERBIAN)

N A Rhys ~ Royal Air Force

SPECIAL PROMOTIONS FOR DISTINGUISHED SERVICE

M E S Boissier ~ Royal Navy
I A S Cooke ~ Connaught Rangers
A J Davies ~ Royal Navy
C Grellier ~ Hampshire Regiment
R H Griffiths ~ Cheshire Regiment
B F Hood ~ Royal Navy
J D Irving ~ West Yorkshire Regiment
S Mildred ~ Royal Engineers
D R Montford ~ Indian Army
J W H Park ~ Indian Army
E G Robinson ~ Royal Navy
G Rutledge ~ Royal Marine Artillery
C B Stokes ~ Indian Army
G H Woolley ~ Queen Victoria's Rifles

St. John's Fou[ndation]

for

Gratuitous Education of Th[e]

Architects' sketch of proposed new buildings for St John's Foundation School at Leatherhead, 1870

DATION SCHOOL,

SONS OF POOR CLERGYMEN.

PICTURE CREDITS

Every effort has been made to identify and recognise all copyright holders but, if we have inadvertently omitted anyone, we invite them to make contact so that credit can be added to future editions.

CHAPTER 1

p1: St John's Foundation School, Kilburn by kind permission and © Illustrated London News Ltd/ Mary Evans

p3: Construction Workers at St John's 1871 by Richard Huck, Leatherhead, courtesy of the Leatherhead & District Local History Society

p4: St John's Foundation School 1874 by Carl Stackemann, Esher, Surrey

p4: Group photograph 1875 by Richard Huck, Leatherhead

p4: J H Browne 1875 by Richard Huck, Leatherhead

p7: Prince Leopold, Duke of Albany; Princess Alice, Countess of Athlone; Princess Helen, Duchess of Albany by Hills & Saunders, by kind permission and © National Portrait Gallery, London

p15: The Library, c.1910 by P A Buchanan & Company, Chiswick

p17: Henry Boldero's grave © Sally Todd

CHAPTER 3

p22: The Dining Hall c.1910 by P A Buchanan & Company, Chiswick

p25: The Big School Room c.1910 by P A Buchanan & Company, Chiswick

p27: The Gymnasium c.1910 by P A Buchanan & Company, Chiswick

p30: One of the Big Dormitories c.1910 by P A Buchanan & Company, Chiswick

p30: Chapel Interior c.1910 by P A Buchanan & Company, Chiswick

p34: Royal Fusiliers marching through Ashtead Park, Johnson's Ashtead P.O. Series

CHAPTER 4

p42: Victor Silvester in uniform 1914 by kind permission of Christopher Silvester

p42: Richard Millard, August 1914 by kind permission of the Millard family

p44: Victor Silvester with Vera Clarke by kind permission of Christopher Silvester

p47: A S Jukes CWGC memorial headstone photo by kind permission and © The War Graves Photographic Project

pp46-47: Photographs and documents of A S Jukes by kind permission of Richard Jukes

pp48-49: Photographs and documents of J C R Godwin by kind permission of Michael Godwin

p51: G H Woolley © Fred Spalding and Sons, Chelmsford

p54: Oswald Whaley by kind permission of The Royal Hampshire Regiment Museum

pp56-57: Photographs and documents by kind permission of the Millard family

p59: H S Jackson by kind permission and © Barts Health NHS Archives and Museums

p59: F T C Payton by kind permission of The Ellesmerian Club

p61: Foncquevillers Military Cemetery, France by kind permission and © Neil Pudney

p61: John Rutledge grave, Fricourt New Military Cemetery by kind permission and © Neil Pudney

p63: R P Hoult by kind permission of Anthony Hayward

p64: C L N Roberts by kind permission of the Warden and Fellows of Keble College, Oxford

p64: Tyne Cot Memorial inscription by kind permission and © Neil Pudney

p69: J W H Park by kind permission of the Warden and Fellows of Keble College, Oxford

p70: W T Wrigley memorial, St Andrew's Church, Hartburn, Northumberland by kind permission of Janet Brown.

p72: E T Gray gravestone by kind permission and © Neil Pudney

p73: Ploegsteert Wood Military Cemetery, Belgium by kind permission and © Neil Pudney

CHAPTER 6

p77: Thiepval Memorial inscription by kind permission and © Neil Pudney

p80: W R Ekins portrait by kind permission of Stephen Parfitt

pp81-82: Photographs and documents of J C R Godwin by kind permission of Michael Godwin

CHAPTER 7

p84: Bertram Robert Raggett memorial at St Lukes Church, Spital Tongues, Newcastle by kind permission and © Hassan Rizvi

PICTURE CREDITS

p85: Photographs of S H Millard by kind permission of the Millard family

p86: Great War memorial, St Peter and St Paul's Church, West Wittering by kind permission and © Alison Wren

p87: Kenneth Gill memorial window at St Peter and St Paul's Church, West Wittering by kind permission and © Alison Wren

p88: Military Cross photograph by kind permission and © Sara Azzopardi & Pete Smith

p89: A E Boultbee by kind permission of St Catharine's College, Cambridge

CHAPTER 8
p90: Military Service Act poster, 1916 by kind permission of the Imperial War Museum. © IWM (Art.IWM PST 5161)

CHAPTER 10
p94: B R Beechey, courtesy of Michael Walsh

p94: F C R Beechey, courtesy of Michael Walsh

p95: Ploegsteert Memorial by kind permission and © Neil Pudney

CHAPTER 11
pp96-97: Wilton House Hospital 1916 by kind permission of the Millard family

p98: H E P Yorke by kind permission of Alex Yorke

CHAPTER 12
p100: Photographs of The Reverend H R Cooke, by kind permission of the Cooke family

p101: C S Woodward by Veale & Co, by kind permission and © National Portrait Gallery, London

p102: I M Lewis, by kind permission and © Jesus College, Oxford

CHAPTER 13
p104: C S Ireland, postcard by kind permission of Richard van Emden

p106: Sir Leonard Woolley by Bassano Ltd, by kind permission and © National Portrait Gallery, London

CHAPTER 14
p109: HMS Curacoa by kind permission of the Imperial War Museum. © IWM (FL 5370)

p110: G J Lester, reproduced by permission of Durham University Library

p110: Great War memorial plaque at St Mary's Church, Fetcham by kind permission and © Sally Todd

CHAPTER 15
p111: Peace procession outside St John's School, Epsom Road, Leatherhead, 19 July 1919 by Albert Warren, Leatherhead, courtesy of the Leatherhead and District Local History Society

p113: The Chapel exterior 1925 by J R Hutchinson

CHAPTER 17
p116: Arras Flying Services Memorial to the Missing, France, by kind permission and © Neil Pudney

p189: The War Memorial by P A Buchanan & Company, Thornton Heath, Surrey

p119: Restoration of the War Memorial by Rob Ambrose

pp122-123: Stained glass memorial window by Rob Ambrose

BIBLIOGRAPHY

PRIMARY SOURCES
HELD IN ST JOHN'S SCHOOL ARCHIVES

Cooke, the Reverend H. R., *Great War Diary, May 1915 to January 1919*. Copy of unpublished typescript.

Furmston Archive. Letters, documents and photographs relating to Clement Barrington Furmston and Wilfrid Lewis Furmston.

Rose, Douglas. Letters and documents.

St John's Foundation School: Annual Reports of the Committee.

St John's Foundation School: Headmaster's Monthly Reports to the Committee.

St John's Foundation School: Minute Books of the Committee.

The Johnian magazine.

The Old Johnian magazine.

Whitefoord, H. P., 1988. *St John's School, 1914-1918*. Unpublished memoir.

OTHER PRIMARY SOURCES

Leatherhead and District Local History Society Archive and Museum.

Leatherhead Parish Magazines 1914-1920

PUBLICATIONS

Baker, C., 2019. *The Long, Long Trail: Researching Soldiers of the British Army in the Great War of 1914-1919*. [online] Available at: https://www.longlongtrail.co.uk/ [Accessed 16 March 2017].

British Newspaper Archive, 2019. *Findmypast Newspaper Archive Limited 2019*. [online] Available at: https://www.britishnewspaperarchive.co.uk/ [Accessed 16 July 2019].

British Red Cross, 2018. *First World War volunteers*. [online] Available at: https://vad.redcross.org.uk/ [Accessed 3 March 2018].

Brown, A. M., 1996. *Army Chaplains in the First World War*: A Thesis Submitted for the Degree of PhD at the University of St Andrews. [online] Available at: http://hdl.handle.net/10023/2771 [Accessed 20 June 2018].

Cave, N., 2003. *Beaumont Hamel: Newfoundland park*. Barnsley: Leo Cooper.

Census & Electoral Rolls. [online] Available at: https://www.ancestry.co.uk/search/categories/35/ [Accessed 10 May 2019].

Commonwealth War Graves Commission. *Casualty Database*. [online] Available at: https://www.cwgc.org/find/find-war-dead [Accessed 15 October 2018].

Commonwealth War Graves Commission. *History of the CWGC*. [online] Available at: www.cwgc.org/about-us/history-of-the-cwgc [Accessed 15 October 2018].

Desplatt, Dr J., 2014. *Digging for King and Country. National Archives Blog*, [blog] 18 November. [online] Available at: https://blog.nationalarchives.gov.uk/blog/digging-king-country/ [Accessed 19 August 2018].

Donaldson, W. L., 1938. *A Register of St John's School, Leatherhead, 1852-1937*. Croydon: Roffey & Clark.

Emden, R. V., 2014. *Meeting the Enemy: The Human Face of the Great War*. London: Bloomsbury.

Epsom and Ewell History Explorer: *Woodcote Park Camp*. [online] Available at: http://www.epsomandewellhistoryexplorer.org.uk/WoodcoteParkCamp.html [Accessed 10 April 2018].

Franks, N. L. R., Giblin, H. and McCrery, N., 1998. *Under the guns of the Red Baron: the complete record of Von Richthofen's victories and victims fully illustrated*. London: Grub Street.

From our Special Correspondents, 1914. Territorial Camps. *The Times* [online] Wednesday, Jul 29, 1914; pg. 13; Issue 40588. Available at: https://www.thetimes.co.uk/archive/ [Accessed 12 December 2018].

Fussell, Paul, 2000. *The Great War and Modern Memory*. New York: Oxford University Press.

Gedge, J. T., 1914. *Letter from Joseph Theodore Gedge*. [online] Available at: The Great War Archive, University of Oxford / Primary Contributor via First World War Poetry Digital Archive, http://ww1lit.nsms.ox.ac.uk/ww1lit/gwa/document/8956 [Accessed 12 July 2014].

Gilbert, M., 1994. *First World War*. London: Weidenfeld and Nicolson.

Great Britain, Royal Aero Club Aviators' Certificates, 1910-1950. [online] Available at: https://www.ancestry.co.uk/search/collections/royalaeroclub/ [Accessed 9 May 2018].

BIBLIOGRAPHY

Great Britain, Royal Naval Division Casualties of The Great War, 1914-1924. [online] Available at: https://www.ancestry.co.uk/search/collections/royalnavydeaths/ [Accessed 10 December 2018].

Hart, P., 2014. *Gallipoli.* Oxford: Oxford University Press.

Hope, C., 2014. *Chaplains (Padres) at War.* [online] Available at: https://irp-cdn.multiscreensite.com/a8bb8484/files/uploaded/Chaplains%20at%20War%20r.pdf [Accessed 7 November 2018].

Hughes, R., 2001. *Those Things Which Are Above: The History of St John's School, Leatherhead.* Oxford: Gresham in Partnership with St John's School, Leatherhead.

IWM, 2018. Voices of the First World War: *War In The Air,* 5 June 2018. [online] Available at: https://www.iwm.org.uk/history/voices-of-the-first-world-war-war-in-the-air [Accessed 15 August 2018].

IWM, 2018. *Voices of the First World War: Prisoners of War.* [online] Available at: https://www.iwm.org.uk/history/voices-of-the-first-world-war-prisoners-of-war [Accessed 20 August 2018].

Jefford, C. G., 2001. *RAF Squadrons: A Comprehensive Record of the Movement and Equipment of All RAF Squadrons and Their Antecedents since 1912.* Shrewsbury: Airlife.

Jones, H., 2014. *Prisoners of War.* British Library, 29 Jan 2014. [online] Available at: https://www.bl.uk/world-war-one/articles/prisoners-of-war# [Accessed 5 November 2018].

Lewis-Stempel, J., 2011. *Six Weeks: The Short and Gallant Life of the British Officer in the First World War.* London: Orion.

Malinovska, A., and Joslyn, M., 2006. *Voices in Flight: Conversations with Air Veterans of the Great War.* Barnsley: Pen & Sword Aviation.

McCarthy, Chris., 1996. *The Somme: The Day-by-day Account.* London: Greenwich.

McKay, R., 1973. *John Leonard Wilson:* Confessor for the Faith. London: Hodder and Stoughton.

Museum of Army Chaplaincy. *1914-18 Chaplain Interview Record cards.* [online] Available at: https://www.chaplains-museum.co.uk/ [Accessed 4 November 2018].

North East War Memorials Project, 2013. [online] Available at: http://www.newmp.org.uk/ [Accessed 4 May 2019].

Old Cranleighan Society, 2014. *OTC camp, Tidworth July/August 1914.* [online] Available at: https://www.ocsociety.org/2014/08/eve-war/ [Accessed 17 May 2017].

Parker, L, 2018. *Naval chaplains in the First World War.* [online] Available at: http://www.linda-parker.co.uk/blog/post.php?s=2018-01-29-naval-chaplains-in-the-first-world-war [Accessed 7 November 2018].

RAF Museum Storyvault, 2019. *Casualty Card archive.* [online] Available at: http://www.rafmuseumstoryvault.org.uk/pages/raf_vault.php [Accessed 26 August 2019].

RAMC (2007) *RAMC in the Great War.* [online] Available at: http://www.ramc-ww1.com/index.html [Accessed 18 September 2019].

Ruvigny, Marquis De, 1922 (2003 reprint). *De Ruvigny's Roll of Honour, 1914-18. A Biographical Record of Members of His Majesty's Naval and Military Forces Who Have Fallen in the War.* 5 vols. Uckfield: Naval & Military Press Ltd.

St John's School Leatherhead, 2019. *War Memorial Archive.* [online] Available at: http://stjohnsleatherheadatwar.co.uk/ [Accessed 20 August 2019].

Seldon, A., and Walsh, D., 2013. *Public Schools and the Great War: The Generation Lost.* Barnsley: Pen & Sword Military.

Silvester, V., 1958. *Dancing Is My Life, an autobiography.* London: Heinemann.

Snape, M., 2011. Church of England Army Chaplains in the First World War: Goodbye to 'Goodbye to All That'. In *Journal of Ecclesiastical History,* Vol. 62, No. 2, April 2011. Cambridge University Press.

Spindler, L., 2016. *Leatherhead in the Great War.* Barnsley: Pen & Sword Military.

Spooner, H., 1916. Extract from the diary of the Reverend Harold Spooner, 2-6 February 1916. *The National Archives.* 76/115/1. [online] Available at: http://www.nationalarchives.gov.uk/pathways/firstworldwar/battles/p_diary_kut.htm [Accessed 10 November 2018].

Stevens, P., 2012. *Great War Explained: A Simple Story and Guide.* Barnsley: Pen & Sword Military.

Stevenson, D., 2004. *1914-1918: The History of the First World War*. London: Allen Lane.

Strawbridge, The Reverend Dr Jenn, 2019. *Chaplains in the War: Keble's Significant Contribution*. [online] Available at: http://www.keble.ox.ac.uk/about/past/keble-and-the-great-war/chaplains-in-the-war-keble2019s-significant-contribution [Accessed 15 January 2019].

Sunrise Stained Glass Ltd., 2017. *Jude Tarrant: Stained Glass Artist, Designer and Glass Painter*. [online] Available at: http://www.artiststainedglass.co.uk/index.html [Accessed 24 July 2019].

The Gazette, Official Public Record. [online] Available at: www.thegazette.co.uk [Accessed 20 September 2017].

The National Archives (TNA). Series FO 882/27. *Foreign Office Arab Bulletins Nos 75-107*. [online] Available at: https://discovery.nationalarchives.gov.uk/details/r/C1906459 [Accessed 17 November 2018].

The National Archives (TNA). Series FO 371. *Foreign Office: Political Departments: General Correspondence from 1906-1966. Woolley's letter to the Foreign Office, 29 August 1914*. Ref. FO 371/2210. [online] Available at: https://discovery.nationalarchives.gov.uk/details/r/C2759871 [Accessed 20 November 2018].

The National Archives (TNA). Series WO. *Armed Forces Service Records*. [online] Available at: https://discovery.nationalarchives.gov.uk/ [Accessed 10 December 2017].

The National Archives (TNA). Series WO 95, *First World War Unit war diaries 1914-1922*. [online] Available at: https://discovery.nationalarchives.gov.uk/results/r?_q=WO+95&_p=1900 [Accessed 11 October 2017].

The National Archives (TNA). Series WO 95. *Prisoner of War interviews with Company Sergeant Major Alexander Gibb, 2nd Argyle & Sutherland Highlanders*. Reference WO161/100/557. 1914-1918. [online] Available at: https://discovery.nationalarchives.gov.uk/results/r?_q=WO161%2F100%2F557 [Accessed 10 December 2018].

The National Archives (TNA). Series WO 372. War Office: *Service Medal and Award Rolls Index, First World War*. [online] Available at: https://discovery.nationalarchives.gov.uk/details/r/C14576 [Accessed 10 September 2017].

'The Robin Hoods', 1921 (2009 reprint). *1/7th, 2/7th, & 3/7th Battns, Sherwood Foresters 1914-1918 written by officers of the Battalions*. Uckfield: Naval & Military Press Ltd.

The Times, 2019. *The Times Digital Archive 1785 to 1985*. London: Times Newspapers Limited. [online] Available at: https://www.thetimes.co.uk/archive/ [Accessed 28 August 2019].

The War Graves Photographic Project. [online] Available at: www.twgpp.org [Accessed 20 August 2019].

Vardey, E., 1988. *History of Leatherhead, A Town at the Crossroads*. Leatherhead, Leatherhead and District Local History Society.

Walsh, M., 2006. *Brothers in War*. London: Ebury.

War Memorials Trust, 2017. *Dates on war memorials*. [online] Available at: http://www.warmemorials.org/uploads/publications/117.pdf [Accessed 13 October 2019].

Westlake, R., 2009. *Tracing British battalions on the Somme*. Barnsley: Pen & Sword Military.

Williams, E. M. P., 1951. *The Quest Goes On: Being a Short History of the First Hundred Years of St John's School, Leatherhead, 1851-1951*. Leatherhead, St John's School, Leatherhead.

Winstone, H. V. F., 1990. *Woolley of Ur: The Life of Leonard Woolley*. London: Secker and Warburg.

Woolley, L., 1962. *As I Seem to Remember*. London: G Allen & Unwin.

Woolley, L., 1920. *Dead Towns and Living Men*. London: Milford.

Woolley, L., 1921. *From Kastamuni to Kedos. Being a record of experiences of prisoners of war in Turkey, 1916-1918*. Oxford: Blackwell.

Zeepvat, C., 1999. *Prince Leopold: The Untold Story of Queen Victoria's Youngest Son*. Stroud: Sutton.

ACKNOWLEDGEMENTS

It would be impossible to research and write a book on the history of St John's School and the Great War without the assistance, advice and support of others. We would like to thank our editor Martin Collier, Master of Haileybury and headmaster of St John's from 2011 to 2017, for encouraging us to write this book. We are hugely indebted to him for reading and commenting on the many drafts of the text, for his valuable advice and for his contributions to the historical detail of the progress of the war.

The research carried out by Richard Hughes, former Head of History at St John's on the early history of St John's has been a significant resource and we also extend our thanks to Richard for his contribution to the story of Victor Silvester and the Great War.

We are immensely grateful to all those who provided us with information, photographs and documents to illustrate the stories told within these pages. We would like to thank John Millard and his family for sharing their extensive archive collection of photographs, original documents and letters and Michael Godwin, OJ, who gave us access to the papers and photographs of his uncle J C R Godwin. We also thank the Cooke family for allowing us to use extracts and photographs from the Reverend H R Cooke's Great War diary. We are grateful to OJ Anthony Hayward for photographs of his great uncle R P Hoult, to Richard Starr Jukes for background information, and photographs of his grandfather A S Jukes and to Stephen Parfitt who kindly supplied a photograph of his uncle, W R Ekins. Thanks are also due to Christopher Silvester for allowing us to use photographs of his grandfather Victor Silvester, to Michael Walsh, author of *Brothers in War*, for sharing photographs of B R Beechey and F C R Beechey with us and to Alex Yorke for the photographs of his grandfather H E P Yorke. Allan Ledger provided information and help in identifying his relative S C Squire in our unnamed School photographs, while Richard van Emden kindly provided the image of a postcard relating to C S Ireland from his private collection. We are also indebted to Jenny Frith who donated the papers, letters and photographs relating to the Furmston brothers to the School archives in 2018.

Librarians, archivists, local historians and museum curators have also been enormously helpful in our search for photographs and further information about the OJs featured in this book. We would like to thank Jill Geber, Keble College, Oxford; Lt Col Colin Bulleid, The Royal Hampshire Regiment Trust; Amanda Engineer, Barts Health NHS Trust; Paul Russell, Ellesmere College and John Harvey, The Ellesmerian Club; Sarah Fletcher, St Catharine's College, Cambridge; Christopher Gilley, Durham University Library Archives and Special Collections; Andy Fetherston and Max Dutton, The Commonwealth War Graves Commission; Janet Brown and James Pasby, The North East War Memorials Project; John Rowley and Roy Mellick, The Leatherhead & District Local History Society and Steve Rogers, The War Graves Photographic Project, for their assistance.

Neil would like to thank the following who have freely given of their knowledge on all military matters: Chris Baker, Stephen Barker, Taff Gillingham, Jim Grundy, Paul Reed and Jim Smithson. Neil would also like to thank his regular travelling companions on his many visits to the Western Front over the last twenty years, Paul Berry, Nick Bullen, Neil Perriam and Neil Whitmore for their help, encouragement and willingness to travel off the beaten track. Finally, Neil would like to record his grateful thanks to his long-suffering wife, Louise, who so generously tolerates his avid interest in the history of the Great War.

We would like to thank the many members of staff at St John's who have supported and encouraged us on our journey to research and write this book. Special thanks go to Naia Edwards, Alex Kearney, Sarah Naughten, Barbara Rough and Sally Stuart for volunteering to proof-read the text. We thank Alison Wren for interpreting our vision for the layout of the book so well, and for the many hours she spent on the design. We are grateful to our subscribers who have contributed towards the cost of publishing this book and we thank Naia Edwards, Development Officer at St John's, who so expertly managed our fundraising campaign, and whose constant support, encouragement, enthusiasm and wise advice kept us going during the difficult times.

While acknowledging the help we have received with all our research and writing, any errors or omissions are entirely ours.

Sally Todd and Neil Pudney

INDEX

Illustrations shown in **bold**

Advanced Dressing Stations (ADS) 98, 103
Albany, HRH Prince Leopold, Duke of vii, 7, **7**
Albany, HRH Princess Helen, Duchess of vii, 7, **7**, 118, 08
Albany Scholarships 7, 80, 96
Albert, Somme 101
Alderson, Albert Evelyn 13, **92**, 93-94
Allan, Frank Cecil 19-20, 69-70, **70**
Allenby, Field Marshal 109
Ancre, Battle of the 96
Antwerp, defence of 105
Anzacs 33
archaeologists 107, 109
archaeology 107-108
armistice 110
   thanksgiving service 110
Arras, Battle of 45, 65, 72-73, 81, 118
Ashmolean Museum 108
Auchonvillers 101
autograph books 36, **36**

Baden Powell, Thomas 2
Balkan crisis 18
Basilica of Notre Dame de Brebières 101
Beaumont Hamel 58, 60
Bedwell, Victor Leopold Stevens 19-20, 79-80, **79-80**
Beechey, Amy Reeve 96
Beechey, Barnard Reeve **96**, 96-97
Beechey, Frank Collett Reeve 96, **96**, 100
Beechey, Reverend Prince William Thomas 96
Belgian Refugee Committee 40
Belgian refugees 40
Berlin-Baghdad railway 107
billets 69, 101
Blackmore, Edward Charles 5, **5**
Boer War 9, 77, 101
Boldero, Henry Walton 17
Boultbee, Arthur Elsdale **90**, 90-91
Boultbee, Beauchamp St John 90
Bourne, Cyprian 93-94, **94**
boy soldiers 42, 44
Brackley, Ian, Bishop of Dorking 123, **123**
British Army
   Argyll & Sutherland Highlanders 44, 45, 105
   Border Regiment 55, 56, 58, 68
   Cambridgeshire Regiment 69, 88
   Durham Light Infantry 69, 70, 74, 75
   East Yorkshire Regiment 63, 81, 82, 90, 96
   Gloucestershire Regiment 54
   King's African Rifles 112
   King's Own Scottish Borderers 47
   King's Own Yorkshire Light Infantry 61, 93
   King's Royal Rifle Corps 33
   Lincolnshire Regiment 96
   London Regiment 42, 47, 51, 105
   Machine Gun Corps 72-73, 102
   Northamptonshire Regiment 90
   Northumberland Fusiliers 28
   Oxford and Buckinghamshire Regiment 112
   Royal Army Medical Corps (RAMC) 92, 98, 100
   Royal Dublin Fusiliers 58, 60
   Royal Engineers (RE) 33, 61, 67, 86
   Royal Field Artillery (RFA) 30, 101-102, 107, 112
   Royal Fusiliers 33-34, 39, 47, 61, 73
   Royal Garrison Artillery (RGA) 86
   Royal Irish Fusiliers 91
   Royal Irish Regiment 81
   Royal Sussex Regiment 83
   Royal Warwickshire Regiment 65-66
   Sherwood Foresters (Nottinghamshire and Derbyshire Regiment) 58, 62
   South Wales Borderers 64
   Suffolk Regiment 79
   The Queen's (Royal West Surrey Regiment) 60, 93-94
   West Yorkshire Regiment 65, 69
   York & Lancaster Regiment 60, 112
British Expeditionary Force (BEF) 42
British Museum 108, 109
British Red Cross 40, 45, 50, 58, 61, 70, 81-82, 106, 109, 113, 118
Browne, Harold, Bishop of Winchester 6
Browne, James Henry 4-5, **5**
Browne, Richard Maddison 5
Buckler, Arthur Ernest 5, **5**
Burnside, John Harold 11, **117**
   as Bursar 116
   as football coach 117

Canadian Expeditionary Force 83
Carnoy 61
Casualty Clearing Station (CCS) 97-99, 101
Cathcart, Frederick Rolleston 125
cemeteries 118
   Andover Cemetery, Hampshire 87
   Artillery Wood Cemetery, Belgium 64
   Auchonvillers Military Cemetery, France 60
   Canadian Cemetery No 2, Neuville-St Vaast 91
   Carnoy Military Cemetery, France 61
   Foncquevillers Military Cemetery, France 62-63, **63**
   Fricourt New Military Cemetery, France 63, **63**
   Northampton General Cemetery 95
   North Gate Cemetery, Baghdad 72
   Ploegsteert Wood Military Cemetery, Belgium 75, **75**
   Struma Military Cemetery, Greece 94
   St Sever Cemetery, France 70
   Suez War Memorial Cemetery, Egypt 47

INDEX

censorship
  field postcards 49, **49**
  honour envelopes 49, **49**
  letters from the front 40, 45, 101
  press censorship 40
Chaplains (Military)
  Army Chaplains 101-103, 106
  Church of England 101
  Naval Chaplains 101, 104
Clapton House 2, 4
Clarke, Arthur Frederick 60
Chapel 4, 6, 24, 30, **30**, 37, 41, 82, 95, 110, 114-115, **115**, 118, 120-121, 124-125
  stained glass window (2014) 124, **124**
Choir 30, **30**, 82
clubs and societies
  Debating Society 18, 31, 60, 93
  Field Club 27, 31
  Hare and Hounds Club 31
  Literary and Debating Society 27, 31
  Literary and Dramatic Society 31, 68, 91
  Natural History Society 17, 31
  Photographic Society 17, 31
  Protestants Club 93
Coddington, Eustace 25-26, **26**
Committee, the
  after School fire 15
  and Clapton House 2
  and formation of OTC 12
  and move to Leatherhead 2-3
  and wartime economies 21
  appointment of School Bursar 116
  changes to the School constitution 116
  closure of junior boarding house 21
  institution of Old Johnian Day 115
  on death of HRH Prince Leopold, Duke of Albany 7
  on death of V L S Bedwell 80
  responsibilities 1-2
  War Memorial Committee 118, 120, 121
Commonwealth War Graves Commission 91, 118
Congreve *later* Milbourn, Ethel Mary 26, 27, **27**
conscientious objectors 92
conscription 92
Cooke, Henry Robert 101, 102, **102**
Cox, Sir Herbert Vaughan 114
Crofton, Harold Mowatt Maxwell 110-111
Ctesiphon, Battle of 107
Cubitt, Henry, Lord Ashcombe 114
curriculum 6, 25-26
  divinity 6, 29
  English 6, 36
  extra subjects
    drawing 26
    music 6
  French 26
  geography 27

  German 26
  Greek 6, 29, 36
  history 6, 26-27
  Latin 6, 36
  mathematics 6, 25, 96
  science 26

Dardanelles 52, 54-56, 104
Davies, John Timothy 5, **5**
Dawes, Henry 3
death at School 17, 37, 95
Defence of the Realm Act (DORA) 40
Derby scheme 38
Dining Hall 4, 7, **8**, 9, 21, **21**, **22-23**, 31, 113, 115
Downes, Reverend Edmund Audley 11, **11**, 28, 40, 92
Driffield, George Townshend 95
Driffield, Herbert George 95
Driffield, Lancelot Townshend **12**, 12-13, 38-39, 93, 95, **95**
Duckworth, Sir Dyce 37

Egypt 46-47, 107-108
Ekins, Franklin George 81
Ekins, Willingham Richard 81-82, **82**
epidemics, infections and diseases
  dysentery 105
  heart disease 95, 105-106
  influenza 37-38, 110, 112
  measles 6, 13, 17, 37
  mumps 6, 13, 17
  pneumonia 37, 110, 112
  scarlet fever 6, 17
  tonsillitis 6
Evans, Arthur Norman 39
Evans, Neville Vernon 64
examinations 6
  Army 26
  Cambridge University 26
  Civil Service 26
  internal 6
  Naval Clerkship 76-77
  Officer Training Corps 39
  University entrance 7

Field Ambulance 101-102, 106
fire vii, 15, **14-17**, 20, 38, 116
  rebuilding programme 15, 116
first pupils at Leatherhead 4
Fitzgerald, Captain G T 74
Flers-Courcelette, Battle of 36
flying accidents 86-88
flying aces 90
food 98, 105, 109
  in prison camps 105, 109
  price of 21
  rationing 21
  school food vii, 21, 24

Foundation vii, 1
   rules of the Foundation 1
Foundationers 1, 2, 5-7, 9, 24, 116
   Supplementary Foundationers 7, 28, 83
Franz Ferdinand, Archduke of Austria 18, 20
Freeman, Robert Lewis Fitzackerley 37
front line 44-46, 58, 65, 67-71, 73, 75, 81, 83, 92, 96, 98, 100-101
Furmston, Clement Barrington 24, 49, 72, 73, **73**

Gallipoli 42, 54-56, 58, 60, 72, 100, 104
   Achi Baba 55-56
   Cape Helles 54, 104
   Chunuk Bair 54
gas gangrene 70, 100
Gatehouse Divinity Prize 21, **21**, 108
Gedge, Joseph Theodore 42-43, **43**
   Gedge Laboratory 43
   Gedge Medal 43
German Navy
   SMS Blücher 111
Gibb, Alexander 105-106
Gill, Cecil Ernest Gaspar 88
Gill, Eric 88
Gill, Kenneth Carlyle 69, 88-89, **88-89**
Gill, Leslie Macdonald 88
Gill, Louie Gwendolen, nee Cullen 88-89
Godwin, John Charles Raymond 48-49, 82-84, **83, 84**
Gommecourt 58, 62
Gordon Clark, Henry Herbert 121
Governing Body *see* Committee, the
Graves Registration Commission 118
Gray, Edmund Trevennin 13, 18-20, 74-75, **75**
Greenlees, Charles Fouracres 58, 60, **60**
Greville Mount House, Kilburn 1, **1**
Griffin, Basil Walker 66, **66**
Grigson, Lionel Henry Shuckforth 19-20
Grundy, William 2, 7
gymnasium 27, **27**, 38

Haig, Sir Douglas 64
Haldane reforms 12
Harding, Reverend Wilfrid John 66
Hargreaves, William 9, **9**
Hartigan, Kenneth Leslie Stewart 112
Harvey, Robert Leslie 105
Haslewood, Reverend Ashby Blair 1
Hawkins, Anthony Hope 7
Headmasters' Conference (HMC) 7
High Wood 79
'Hill 60' 50-52
Hobson, Reverend Thomas Frederick, Vicar of Leatherhead 114
Hombersley, W St G 32

hospitals
   Blue Sisters' Hospital, Malta 55
   British General Hospital, Kut 107
   German Military Hospital, Trier 105
   Military Hospital, Ras-el-Tin, Alexandria 112
   No 2 Red Cross Hospital, Rouen 50
   Red House Hospital, Leatherhead 40
   Royal Sussex Hospital 100
   Sheffield Children's Hospital 100
   Sheffield Royal Infirmary 100
   Shotley Naval Hospital, Suffolk 110
   St Bartholomew's Hospital, London 37, 100
   St Thomas's Hospital, London 100
   Wilton House Hospital, Wiltshire **98-99**, 100
Hoult, Robert Percy 64-65, **65**
House system vii, 31, 32, 116
   East House 27, 36, 51, 93, 95
   Haslewood House 6
   North House 25, 43, 56, 58, 61-62, 70, 73, 75, 82
   South House 68, 76, 83, 88
   West House 31, **31**, 66, 104
Huck, Richard (photographer) 5, 136

Imperial War Graves Commission 88, 118
Indian Army 42, 45, 71
   22nd Cavalry (Sam Browne's) 71
infirmary 4, 6, **6**, 15, 17, 37, 71
influenza pandemic 110, 112
Ingram, Reverend Clarence White 13, 32, 38, 93
Inns of Court Officers Training Corps 33, 107
Intelligence Service 107-109
Ireland, Cedric Septimus 105-106, **106**

Jackson, Henry Stewart 61, **61**
Johnian, The 15, 40-41, **41**
   extracts from 12, 13, 15, 18-19, 24, 26, 35, 37, 39-41, 45-46, 50, 55, 62, 66-72, 76-78, 80, 86, 90, 94-95, 98-99, 103, 106-112, 114-118, 121-122
Jukes, Arthur Starr 46-47, **46-47**
Jutland, Battle of 77

Keeling, Bertram 108
Keeling, Katharine 108
Kelly, Edward Rowley vii, 45, 67, 68, **68**, 91
King, Frederick 91
Kitchener, Lord 21, 33, 40, 96
   New Army 33
Kut 72, 106-107, 109
   Siege of 72, 106-107, 109

Langemarck, Battle of 64-65
Lawrence, T E (Lawrence of Arabia) 107
Layng, Thomas 7
Leatherhead (Town) 110, 113
legacies 21, 116, 122
Lester, Reverend Gerald James 112, 112

INDEX

letters 87
  from Reverend E A Downes 28-29, **28-29**
  from the front 43, 45, **48**, 48-49, 58, 69-70, **70**, 73, 111
  of condolence 58, 68, 73-74, 80-81, 86-87, 94, 110-111
letter writing 45, 101, 109
Lewis, Reverend Ivor Morgan 104, **104**
Libau, Russian Latvia 105
library **8**, 9, 15, 26, 40-41, 125
Loos, Battle of 75, 93

Mainprice, Bernard Paul 42, **76**, 76-77
Mainprice, Ernest William Loxley 77, **77**
Mametz 58
Marne, Battle of the 42
medals
  1914-15 Star 57, **57**
  British War Medal 57, **57**
  Croix de Guerre 109
  Defence Medal 57, **57**
  Italian Bronze Medal for Military Valour 45
  King's South Africa Medal 77
  Military Cross 72, 81, 88, 90, **90**, 102-103, 106-107
  Queen's South Africa Medal 77
  Victoria Cross **50**, 50-53, **53**
  Victory Medal 57, **57**
Merchant Navy 48
Mercier, Reverend Lewis Page 2
Mesopotamia 42, 71-72
Messines Ridge 64
Middle East 71, 107-108
Military Service Act 92, **92**
Millard, Marjorie Josephine 56-57, **57**
Millard, Patrick Ferguson 56-57, **57**
Millard, Reverend Frederick L H 56-57, **57**, 86
Millard, Richard Frederick 25, 42, **42**, 55-58, **56**, **59**, 86, 99, 100
Millard, Spencer Harold 55-57, **57**, 85, 86-87
Millbourn, Arthur Russell 27, **27**
Millbourn, Ethel Mary (née Congreve) 26-27, **27**
missing persons 79, 81-82, **84-85**
Moloney, Reverend C M 125
Morgan, Reverend S M 74

Newcombe, Captain Stewart 107
Nicholson, Sir Charles (Architect) 120-121
no man's land 67, 81, 97
Northamptonshire County Cricket Club 95

Officer Training Corps (OTC) **iii**, vii, 12-13, **12-13**, 15, 19-20, **38**, 38-39, 45, 93-95, 98, 113-114, 122
Old Johnians
  Old Johnian Club 4, 108
  Old Johnian Day 115
Oppy 81, 91
Oppy Wood 81
Orlebar, Jeffrey Alexander Amherst 100
Ovillers 61, 83

Paris Peace Conference 113
Park, James Wilfrid Haynes **71**, 71-72
Pascoe, Frank Guy Buckingham 91
Pascoe, Reverend Frank 91
Passchendaele, Battle of 64, 66
Payton, Frederick Thomas Croydon 61, **61**
peace celebrations 113-114
  bonfires 110, 113
  festival weekend for Old Johnians 114-115
    concert 115
    memorial service 114-115
  fireworks 113
  Leatherhead Silver Band 113
  lunch for returning servicemen 113
  Peace Day 114
  peace procession 113, **113**
  St John's School Cadet Corps and Band 113
Perkins, Cyril Warton 9-10, **10**
Pilkem 68
playing fields 37, 40
  levelling of 11, **11**, 17
pocket money 24
poetry 40, 41, **41**, **78**, 114, **114**
Polygon Wood 65
Powell, Frederick James 90, 91
Princip, Gabril 18
prisoner of war camps 105, 106
  concerts 109
  conditions 105
  food 105, 109
  Döberitz, Germany 105, **105**
  Latchen, Latvia 105
  plays 109
  Kastamuni, Turkey 106, 109
  prisoners of war 90, 105-106
Puckridge, Cyril Vincent Noel 58-59, **59**

Queen Victoria Jubilee Fund Association 82, **84-85**

RAF/RFC 56-57, 86, 88, 90-91
  10 Squadron 86
  22 Squadron 88
  25 Squadron 91
  41 Squadron 90
  53 Squadron 91
Raggett, Bertram Robert 86, **86**
Ragg, Reverend William Henry Murray 9, **9**
Rasmussen, Miss 26
Reed, Leslie Henry Brett (Doc Reed) 30
refugees 40
Remembrance Day 123
reporting death
  casualty lists 72-73
  telegrams 72-73, 82
Richthofen, Manfred von (AKA the Red Baron) 91
Rivers, Captain W E (Billy Rivers) 24, **24**
Roberts, Cecil Llewellyn Norton 33, **33**, 65-66, **66**
Robinson, Eric Gascoigne 52-53, **53**

Roll of Honour 41, 93, 118
    Roll of Honour boards 93, **120-121**, 124-125
Rose, Alexander Douglas 14, 28-29
Round, William Haldane 13, 58, 62, **62**, 69
route marches 38, 69
Royal Air Force see RAF/RFC
Royal Flying Corps see RAF/RFC
Royal Naval Air Service (RNAS) 86
Royal Naval Division (RND) 105
Royal Naval Volunteer Reserve (RNVR) 48, 105
Royal Navy
    HMS Agamemnon 76
    HMS Amphion 42
    HMS Arethusa 111
    HMS Brilliant 43
    HMS Britannia 52
    HMS Bulwark 76
    HMS Curacoa 111, **111**
    HMS Goliath 104
    HMS Invincible 77
    HMS King George V 76
    HMS Vengeance 52
Russian front 105-106
Rutledge, John Bedell 63, **63**
Rutty, Gilbert Stephen Forder 9, **10**
Rutty, Reverend Arthur Forster 7, **7**, 9, 11, 33

Salonika 56, 93-94, 100-102
School
    architects 3, 122
    changing rooms 30
    classrooms 25, **25-26**,
    concerts 26, 40, 111, 115
    constitution 116
    cups and trophies
        Davy Cup 13, **13**, 15
        Downes Shield 32, **32**
        House Challenge Shield 15, 32, **32**, 35
        Sangar Cup 13, 15
        Victor Ludorum Cup 32
    discipline 27
        corporal punishment 27
        detention 27
    dormitories 30
    finances 116
        cost of the war 116
    food 21, 24
    lessons 25-26
    prizes vii, 18, 19, 21, **21**, 28, 32, 80, 91, 108
    reports 28, **28**
    uniform 25
        cost of 25
        House numbers 25
        School caps 25
        uniform list 24, **24**

schools
    Ardingly 42
    Bedford Modern School 20
    Brighton College 2, 33
    Christ's Hospital School 9, 81, 117
    City of London School 33
    Cranleigh 9, 18, 20, 33, 76, 114
    De Aston School 96
    Dover College 20
    Ellesmere College 61
    Epsom College 9
    Forest School 33, 121
    Guildford Grammar School 20
    Haileybury 20
    Horsham Grammar School 33
    Hurstpierpoint 9
    John Lyon School, Harrow 42
    King's College School, Wimbledon 9
    King's School, Canterbury 20
    King's School, Ely 90
    Lincoln Cathedral Choir School 96
    Wellington College 11
    Whitgift Grammar School 9, 61
secret agents 107
Serre 58, 60, 96
Shannon, Charles Haslewood 5, **5**
Shaw, Edward Domett, Bishop of Buckingham 121
Shenton, Captain Austin Kirk 36
Shenton, Philip Farrer 36
Silvester, Victor Marlborough 42, **42**, 44, **44**
Smith, Bishop John Taylor (Chaplain-General) 101
Smith, Reverend G Vernon 115
Soden, James Newton **45**, 45-46, 59, **59**
Somme, Battle of 36, 42, 49, 55, 58-59, 60-61, 63,
    65, 70, 79, 83, 103, 118
Somme, France 101
South African War see Boer War
Special Reserve 12, 28, 95
Special Reserve of Officers 56
spies 107
Spooner, Reverend Harold Elwyn 106, 107
sport
    association football (soccer) 20, 32-33, 35, 40, 46,
        54, 95, 116-117
    athletics 32, **32**, 37, 71, 83
    cricket 10, 66, 70-71, 75, 77, 114
    fives 4, 32, 35, **35**
    rugby football 4-5, 9, 33, 116-117
spy ships 107
Squire, Stanley Charles 54, **54**
St John's Foundation School vii-viii, 1, **1**,
    see also under School
    locations in London 1-2
    move to Leatherhead 2-3

St Mark's Church, Hamilton Terrace, London vii, 1
Stokes, John Wilfred 100
swagger sticks 20, **20**

Talbot, Edward, Bishop of Winchester 114
tanks, British 36, **36**, 103
Tarrant, Jude 124
Teape, Charles Lewarne 58-59, **59**
teaching staff 9, **9**, 25-27, **93**, 93-95
    temporary teachers 26
    women teachers in wartime 26-27
Territorial Army 42, 50
Thomson, Reverend Anthony viii, 1, 2
Thursby, Sam 37, **37**
Townshend, General Charles Vere Ferrers 106
Treaty of Versailles 113
trench warfare 107
    communication trenches 45, 55, 67, 70
    food 101, 103
    trench digging 67, 101, 105
    trenches, construction of 67
    trenches, naming of 67
    trench letters 70
    trench life 67, 70, 103
    trench system 67
    trench work 69
tuck shop 24
Turton, Richard Dacre 66

Vickers, Geoffrey 62
Victor Ludorum 32, 70-71

Walton, Henry Edward 36, **36**
Wanklyn, Grace 26, 40
Ware, Fabian 118
war effort
    agricultural camp 39
    collecting conkers 39
War Memorials
    Arras Flying Services Memorial, France 91, 118, **118**
    Arras Memorial, France 81
    Community War Memorials 118
    Menin Gate, France 68, 118
    Ploegsteert Memorial, Belgium 96-97
    Portsmouth Naval Memorial, Hampshire 77
    St John's Memorial *see* War Memorials (School)
    St Lukes Church, Spital Tongues, Newcastle 86
    St Peter and St Paul's Church, West Wittering 88-89
    Thiepval Memorial, France 60-61, 79, 83, 118
    Tyne Cot Memorial, Belgium 65-66
    Wisborough Green Memorial, Sussex 77
War Memorials (School)
    appeal fund 118, 122
    commemorative memorials 64, 118, **119**, 120-121
        120-123
    committee 118, 120-121
    cost of memorials 120
    dedication of 121, **121**
    rededication of War Memorial 123, **123**
    restoration of War Memorial 123
    Roll of Honour boards updated 121, 124, 125
    utilitarian memorial 118, 120
        swimming bath 118, 120, 122
War Office 95, 107-108, 114
    Graves Registration Committee 83
War Trophies Committee 114
war trophy 114
    German field gun 114
Western Front vii, 37, 42, 45, 51, 71, 79, 105, 113
Westhoek Ridge 65
Whatley, Hubert Arthur 91
Whitaker, Thomas Stephen 122
Whitefoord, Hugh Penry 24, 27, 37, 38, **38**
Williams, E M P vii, 117
Wilson, John Leonard, Bishop of Birmingham 25, 27
Woodward, Canon Clifford Salisbury 103, **103**
Woolley, Charles Leonard 107-109, **108**
Woolley, Geoffrey Harold 50-51, **51**, 107
Wrigley, Willoughby Thornton 72, **72**

Yorke, Harold Ernest Pierpoint 97, 100, **100**
Young, Eric 35
Young Men's Christian Association 82, **83**
Ypres
    First Battle of 42
    Second Battle of 50, 93
    Third Battle of 64-66
    Ypres Salient, Belgium 64, 66

Zeppelin Raids 102